D1268036

The First Republic of Armenia (1918-1920) on its Centenary: Politics, Gender, and Diplomacy

Armenian Series
Number 10
(Society for Armenian Studies Series 2)

The Armenian Series was established by
the Armenian Studies Program at
California State University, Fresno
and funded by generous support of the
M. Victoria Karagozian Kazan and
Henry S. Khanzadian Kazan Endowment.

Previous Series Titles
Armenians and Kurds in the Late Ottoman Empire, 2020,
Ümit Kurt and Ara Sarafian, editors
Bedros Keljik,
Armenian-American Sketches, 2019,
Christopher Atamian, Lou Ann Matossian, Barlow Der Mugrdechian, editors
Western Armenian in the 21ˢᵗ Century, 2018,
Bedross Der Matossian and Barlow Der Mugrdechian, editors
Krikor Beledian,
Fifty Years of Armenian Literature in France, 2016,
Christopher Atamian, tr.
Vahan Tekeyan: Selected Poems, 2014,
Edmond Azadian and Gerald Papasian, editors
*David of Sassoun: Critical Studies
on the Armenian Epic*, 2013,
Dickran Kouymjian and
Barlow Der Mugrdechian, editors
Diana Der-Hovanessian,
Armenian Poetry of Our Time, 2011
Pete Najarian, *The Artist and His Mother*, 2010
Young Saroyan: Follow *and Other Writings*, 2009
William B. Secrest Jr., editor

Series Editors
Barlow Der Mugrdechian (2008–)
Dickran Kouymjian (1986–2008)

Other Titles
William Saroyan: An Armenian Trilogy, 1986
Dickran Kouymjian, editor
*Warsaw Visitors, Tales from the Vienna Streets:
The Last Two Plays of William Saroyan*, 1991
Dickran Kouymjian, editor

The First Republic of Armenia (1918-1920) on its Centenary: Politics, Gender, and Diplomacy

Edited by

Bedross Der Matossian

The Press
California State University, Fresno

© 2020 by The Press at California State University, Fresno

No part of this book may be reproduced in any form or by any electronic or mechanical means, including photocopy, recording, or any information storage and retrieval system, without permission in writing from the publisher, except by a reviewer, who may quote brief passages in a review.

The Press at California State University, Fresno
2380 E. Keats Ave. MB99
Fresno, CA 93740-8024
press@csufresno.edu

Printed in the United States of America

Cover design: Ruben Malayan

Publisher's Cataloging-In-Publication Data
(Prepared by The Donohue Group, Inc.)

Names: Der Matossian, Bedross, 1978- editor.
Title: The first Republic of Armenia (1918-1920) on its centenary : politics, gender, and diplomacy / edited by Bedross Der Matossian.
Other Titles: Armenian series ; [no. 10].
Description: Fresno, CA : The Press, California State University, Fresno, [2020] | Series: [Society for Armenian Studies series] ; [2] | Includes bibliographical references. | "The origin of this volume was an international conference that was organized by the Society for Armenian Studies for the centennial of the First Republic of Armenia in 2018. Entitled "Innovative Approaches to the History of the First Republic of Armenia, 1918-1920," the conference took place on November 15, 2018 in San Antonio, Texas"-- Provided by publisher.
Identifiers: ISBN 9780912201672 | ISBN 0912201673
Subjects: LCSH: Armenia--History--Revolution, 1917-1920.
Classification: LCC DS195.5 .F57 2020 | DDC 956.62015--dc23

This volume is dedicated to
Richard G. Hovannisian
for his outstanding contribution to the field of
Armenian Studies over the past half century.

Funding for the publication of *The First Republic of Armenia (1918-1920) on its Centenary: Politics, Gender, and Diplomacy* was generously provided by the Armenian Communities Department of the Calouste Gulbenkian Foundation.

CALOUSTE GULBENKIAN
FOUNDATION
ARMENIAN COMMUNITIES

The views expressed in this publication do not necessarily reflect the views of the Calouste Gulbenkian Foundation. The Foundation's support does not constitute endorsement of any specific opinion or perspective.

TABLE OF CONTENTS

LIST OF MAPS AND ILLUSTRATIONS

MAPS

ILLUSTRATIONS

Acknowledgments

This peer-reviewed edited volume is the second in the *Society for Armenian Studies (SAS) Publication Series*, published as part of the Armenian Series of The Press at California State University, Fresno. Subvention for the publication of the book was provided by the Armenian Communities Department of the Calouste Gulbenkian Foundation.

The origin of this volume was an international conference that was organized for the centennial of the First Republic of Armenia in 2018. Entitled "Innovative Approaches to the History of the First Republic of Armenia, 1918-1920," the conference took place on November 15, 2018 in San Antonio, Texas, in conjunction with the Middle East Studies Association Annual Meeting. The conference was co-sponsored by the Society for Armenian Studies (SAS) and the Armenian Communities Department of the Gulbenkian Foundation.

I would especially like to thank the Director of the Armenian Communities Department, Razmik Panossian, for his generous support of the activities of the Society for Armenian Studies. Barlow Der Mugrdechian, general editor of the Armenian Series, played an important role in realizing the publication of this volume. Special thanks to Jesse Arlen for copy editing the volume. I would also like to thank the following scholars for meticulously reviewing the articles: Aram Arkun, Houri Berberian, Jirair Libaridian, Sergio La Porta, Heitor Loureiro, Garabet Moumdjian, Simon Payaslian, Ari Şekeryan, and Vahram Shemmassian. I would like to specifically thank Vartan Matiossian for reviewing multiple articles.

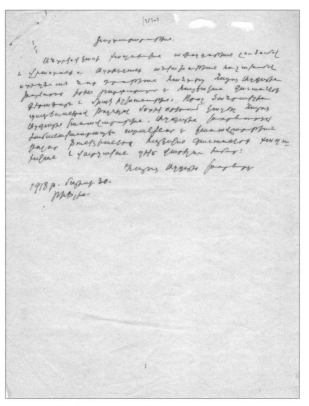

The Declaration of the Armenian National Council, dated May 30, 1918 and effective retroactively to May 28, 1918 (Document: File HH 1/1-1, National Archives of Armenia, Yerevan, Armenia)

"In view of the dissolution of the political unity of Transcaucasia and the new situation created by the proclamation of the independence of Georgia and Azerbaijan, the Armenian National Council declares itself the supreme and only administration for the Armenian provinces. Due to certain grave circumstances, the National Council, deferring until the near future the formation of an Armenian national government, temporarily assumes all governmental functions, in order to pilot the political and administrative helm of the Armenian provinces."[1]

---

[1] Richard G. Hovannisian, *Armenia on the Road to Independence, 1918* (Los Angeles and Berkeley: University of California Press, 1967), 191.

Preface
A Retrospective

Richard G. Hovannisian

As a youngster with a lively interest in politics and diplomacy, I fantasized about serving as Armenia's representative to the United Nations, even though I knew full well that there was no sovereign Armenian state and that there was no space allocated on the UN Plaza for the Armenian tricolor among the flags of the many member countries. Having grown up in central California's San Joaquin Valley in a small farming community that had become home to about a dozen Armenian families, I had passed through the stages of passively marginalizing Armenian ways and striving for acceptance in what was considered to be "American society" to developing into something of a spirited activist. The *Armenian Review* was my English-language window to Armenian history, novels in translation, and other eye-opening literature, as I was then unable to read anything in Armenian. I knew, of course, that there had been an Armenian republic which had not survived and part of which was incorporated into the Union of Soviet Socialist Republics earlier in the century. I had few hard facts to go on but was keenly aware that our small community, like Armenian communities everywhere in the United States, was bitterly torn apart because of deep-felt political differences. One segment virtually canonized the Republic's red, blue, and orange tricolor as a symbol of freedom and independence to be redeemed, while the other regarded it as a symbol of wretchedness and treachery, for which the dominant party of the time was held responsible, and therefore lauded the protection and economic-cultural advancement afforded under Soviet rule.

It was my idealism, on the one hand, and my academic training to be as objective and impartial as possible, on the other, that led me to the decision to undertake the research and writing of a critical history of the Republic of Armenia. A year in Beirut under the watchful eye of Simon Vratsian, the last prime minister of the erstwhile republic, opened the portals of the Armenian language and gave me the essential tool with which to prepare first an MA thesis and then a Ph.D. dissertation on the subject, entirely self-directed as there was not yet a graduate level program in Armenian history anywhere in the United States.

The thirty years that it took me to prepare five volumes on this history hopefully helped to bring the Republic of Armenia out of the shadows and biases to demonstrate the challenges of trying to form an independent state after centuries of foreign dominion – the misery and the progress, the dedication and the inexperience, the great expectations and the overwhelming disappointments. It became inescapably clear that the Republic was born at the worst of times under the most wanting of conditions in 1918. Even with the yeoman efforts of devoted leaders, it was a fragile creation and ultimately failed to achieve fruition through the realization of a united Armenian state combining the Eastern Armenian provinces of the former Russian Empire with a large part of the Western Armenian provinces in the Ottoman Empire. In the end, the Armenian republic and Armenian people were let down by all sides, whose primary bequeathal was a dismal trail of broken pledges and promises.

A small part of the Armenian homeland continued to endure as an entirely dependent Soviet republic situated behind a high invisible wall, whereas the other part of the nation, made up largely of Western Armenian refugees and exiles, scattered over six continents into a difficult diasporan existence.The history of the first Armenian republic became shrouded in rhetoric and polemics, pride and prejudice, partisanship and propaganda. This was the challenge facing me when I undertook the requisite research to discover what actually happened during the short lifespan of the Republic. It was exciting to enter various archives and to rediscover and perhaps help to revive once-important individuals who had become all but forgotten, to touch the musty and dusty packets of documents tucked away in odd repositories, quite possibly never before used, bearing the original signatures of Armenian officials and representatives such as Hovhannes Kachaznuni, Alexander Khatisian, and Avetis Aharonian or of Boghos Nubar, Arshag Chobanian, and Vahan Tekeyan, as well as many other figures who played a significant role in the attempt to forge a viable independent state.

It was personally gratifying that I received both spoken and unspoken encouragement from colleagues in Soviet Armenia, who lauded my work in private or remained silent when logically they would have been expected to write disparaging reviews that reflected the official position of the Soviet authorities. It was at once rewarding and painful, for example, that the sympathetic director of the National Historical Archives of the Armenian SSR was bold enough to take me into a closed section to show the many drawers of documents relating to the first Republic, although we both tacitly understood that they could not be opened for me. Fortunately, by the time I had completed the final volumes of the series after the establishment of the new independent country in 1991, those files were unsealed, with their contents enriching my research.

Armenia on the Road to Independence and the subsequent four volumes of *The Republic of Armenia* have been described by several reviewers as a "definite history." Yet I had long realized that each chapter in the multi-volume study could itself be developed and expanded into a separate monograph. As it happened, that process began during the final years of the Soviet Union and into the period of the new Republic, with studies on the role of the Armenian Apostolic Church and church-state relations, economic and financial issues, administrative and legislative proceedings, structures and activities of the armed forces, intraparty and interparty relationships, and other relevant topics.

Now, in this volume several younger scholars are probing unexplored areas, focusing on specific aspects and drawing their own conclusions. They offer new insights and details or else attempt to evaluate the crucial period in hindsight. Although I may not concur in the postulations and judgments of all the authors and maintain that sound criticism must also factor in the national, regional, and world situations as they were perceived at the time and that it is essential to weigh the options at hand in the goal of achieving Armenia's lasting independence and self-sufficiency, it is a salutary development that the subject is being accorded wider attention. Collectively, the essays in this volume provide significant additional information on particular questions and augur well for a deeper understanding and appreciation of the complexities in the endeavor to create, sustain, and develop the first Republic of Armenia.

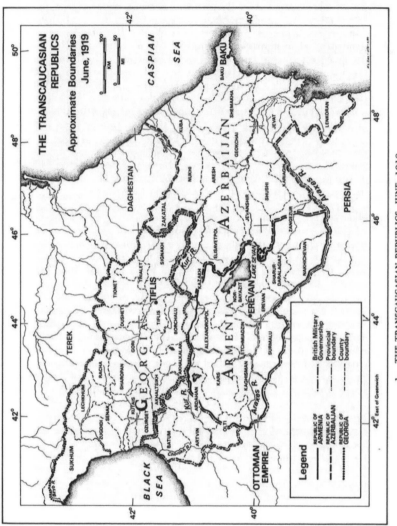

1.   THE TRANSCAUCASIAN REPUBLICS, JUNE, 1919

Introduction

Bedross Der Matossian

World War I had a drastic impact on the course of modern Armenian history. Under the guise of the War, the radical clique within the Committee of Union and Progress, the ruling party of the time in the Ottoman Empire, decided to execute a final solution to the Armenian Question that had been lingering over the Empire since the Treaty of Berlin of 1878. The Armenian Genocide, which commenced in the beginning of the War, led to the annihilation of the majority of the Armenian population of the Empire. The Genocide had an enormous impact on Russian Armenia, also known as Eastern Armenia.

In comparison to their brothers in the Ottoman Empire, the condition of Russian Armenians in the beginning of the twentieth century was not promising either. They had been alienated by Russian imperial policies, endured the Armeno-Tatar conflict, and suffered repression after the Russian Revolution of 1905. Prior to World War I, imperial Russia wanted to gain back the loyalty of the Armenians due to their geo-strategic positioning on the borders of Turkey and Persia. The Caucasus viceroy, Count Illarion I. Vorontsov-Dashkov, demonstrated sympathy to the Armenians by encouraging them to appeal to Tsar Nicholas II to help them with the Armenian Question. With the encouragement of the viceroy, in 1912 Armenians were allowed to establish an Armenian National Bureau in Tiflis with the aim of representing their interests in the Caucasus, Russian Empire, and abroad.

Meanwhile, Nubar Pasha was appointed to lead the diplomatic efforts in Europe on behalf of the Western Armenians. The Balkan Wars of 1912-1913 created an opportunity for the revival of the Armenian Question. The Armenian leadership, aided by the European powers, pressed the Ottoman government to improve the condition of the Armenians in the Eastern provinces. Known as the Armenian Reforms, this international initiative was considered one of the last attempts by Armenians, Europeans, as well as the Ottoman government to find a "solution" to the Armenian Question. The European interest in reforming the provinces should also be seen as part of the competition between the Europeans powers (Italy, Britain, and

France) and Russia on the one hand and Germany on the other. The Armenian Reform project was prepared in Constantinople by André Mandelstam (dragoman of the Russian Embassy) and the representatives of the Armenian National Assembly at a meeting that included the ambassadors of France, Britain, and Italy. However, the reform project signed on February 1914 was abolished by the Ottomans on December 16, 1914, after the Ottoman Empire had already joined the War with the Central Powers (Germany, Austria-Hungary, and initially Italy) against the Entente (Great Britain, France, and Russia).

During this period, Viceroy Vorontsov-Dashkov, through the aid of prominent Armenian figures such as Alexander Khatisian, the mayor of Tiflis, convinced Armenians to create Armenian volunteer battalions within the Russian army to fight against the Ottoman Empire. Eventually, thousands of Armenians from the Eastern provinces of the Ottoman Empire enlisted in the volunteer battalions. The Armenian National Bureau played an important role in organizing these battalions by appointing prominent Armenian revolutionary figures such as Andranik, Dro, Hamazasp, and Keri to lead them. The defeat of the Ottoman forces in the battle of Sarikamish (December 22, 1914, to January 17, 1915) was a major blow to the Ottoman morale, exacerbating the government's attitude towards the Armenians. The Ottomans now blamed Armenians for being the reason for this defeat. While the fear of total annihilation was looming on the Armenians of the eastern provinces, the Russian Armenians were infused with the great hope of saving their brothers across the border. With additional volunteers from Europe and United States, the liberation of Western Armenia seemed to them to be a matter of time. However, the Russian attitude towards Armenians shifted with the appointment of Grand Duke Nicholas (the tsar's uncle) in September 1915 as the viceroy of the Caucasus replacing Vorontsov-Dashkov. His measures against the Armenians coupled with the liquidation of the Armenian volunteer battalions demoralized the Armenians who had held high hopes for Russian support. With its ongoing policies against the Armenians, it seemed in the words of a historian that "the longtime goal of Russian Chauvinists, the acquisition of "Armenia without Armenians" had been achieved."[1]

---

[1] Richard G. Hovannisian, "Armenia's Road to Independence," in Richard Hovannisian (ed.), *The Armenian People from Ancient to Modern Times, vol. II: Foreign Domination to Statehood: The Fifteenth Century to the Twentieth Century* (New York: St. Martin's Press, 1997), 282.

The Russian Revolution of March 1917 was hailed by the Armenians as a new beginning. Along with the Georgian and the Tatars (called Azerbaijanis after 1918), Armenians too believed that the Revolution would provide them some kind of autonomy under the umbrella of Russia. In addition, the positive attitude of the Provisional Government towards Western Armenia, which replaced the authoritarian rule of the tsar, elated the Armenians. With the Russian troops occupying parts of the Eastern provinces of the Ottoman Empire, in the summer of 1917 some 150,000 Armenians returned to their homes. However, the situation changed drastically with the October Revolution. Given the dire situation, prior to the Revolution, on October 13 the Eastern Armenians organized a National Congress in Tiflis with the participation of more than 200 delegates, whose majority were from the Armenian Revolutionary Federation (ARF, Dashnakts'ut'iwn), followed by Armenian Populists (Hay Zhoghovrdakan), Social Revolutionary and Social Democrats. According to Hovannisian, the Congress was "the most comprehensive Eastern Armenian gathering since the Russian conquest of Transcaucasia."[2] The relations between these political parties were not harmonious. Ideological differences, contradictory visions, and disagreements about political systems would carry on to the Republican period. The Armenian National Congress also recommended the demarcation of Armenian lands of Eastern Armenia. These demarcations became identical to the subsequent boundaries of the Republic of Armenia. The National Congress also formed the Armenian National Council (Hay Azgayin Khorhurd), which took over executive function at the creation of the First Republic of Armenia. The ARF, among all the political parties, had the strongest representation in the Armenian National Council.

When the Bolshevik Revolution took place on November 7, 1917 (old calendar, October 25), Armenians, along with the other Transcaucasian nationalities, denounced the Bolsheviks. The willingness of the Bolsheviks to sign the Treaty of Brest-Litovsk with Turkey on March 3, 1918, was a major blow to the Armenian aspirations in Western Armenia. Article 4 of the Treaty read that "Russia will do all in her power to have the provinces of eastern Anatolia promptly evacuated and returned to Turkey."[3] Armenians felt betrayed and declared that the Treaty was null and void. Meanwhile, Enver Pasha issued orders to the Turkish army to occupy

---

[2] Richard G. Hovannisian, *Armenia on the Road to Independence* (Los Angeles and Berkeley: University of California Press, 1967), 87.
[3] See https://avalon.law.yale.edu/20th_century/bl34.asp#art4 (Accessed March 19, 2020).

all of the territories that had been allotted to Ottoman Turkey in the Treaty of Brest-Litovsk. Erzurum and Van fell to the Turkish troops, forcing Armenians to flee towards Yerevan, northern Persia, and Mesopotamia. Furthermore, the Turkish forces captured Batum, angering the Georgians.

In April 1918, Armenians reluctantly agreed to endorse the proclamation of independence by the Transcaucasus, which was brought forth by the Georgian Mensheviks. Thus, the Transcaucasian Federated Republic was established, with prominent Dashnak figures playing an important role. Seeing the weakness of the Transcaucasian Federated Republic, the Ottoman Turks declared that the concessions made in the Treaty of Brest-Litovsk were no longer sufficient. They now presented a larger list of demands whereby the western half of the Yerevan province, along with other important territories should be part of the Ottoman Empire. When the Transcaucasian government protested the move, the Turkish army attacked the Yerevan province. While this was happening, Germany chided the Turkish government for violating the Treaty of Brest-Litovsk, to no avail.

Within this turmoil, the hope for a common Transcaucasian homeland dwindled, leading the Georgian National Council to declare the independence of Georgia on May 26, 1918, with the support of Germany. On May 27, the Muslim National Council followed a similar path and proclaimed the independence of Azerbaijan with Ottoman support.

There was some hesitation on the part of the Armenians to proclaim independence. After long deliberations, the Armenian National Council assumed governmental functions over the Armenian provinces effective May 28, 1918. Due to political uncertainty, the word "independence" did not appear in the proclamation of the Armenian National Council.[4] While this was happening, Armenians in Yerevan were fighting against four invading Turkish divisions. With victories in Sardarabad and Bash-Abaran, and a bravely-fought resistance in Karakilisa, the Armenians compelled the Turkish forces to retreat.

Inspired by these turning points, Armenians were preparing to retake Alexandropol when news arrived from the Armenian National Council to halt the advance because a ceasefire had been agreed with the Turkish side. The negotiations between Armenians and Turks started in Batum on May 29. On June 4, 1918, the Treaty of Peace and Friendship between the Republic of Armenia and the Ottoman Empire was signed. Georgia and

---

[4] Hovannisian, *Armenia on the Road to Independence*, 191.

Azerbaijan also signed similar treaties with the Ottoman Empire, which recognized the independence of the three states.

On July 19, the newly established Armenian government led by Prime Minister Hovhannes Kachaznuni arrived in Yerevan from Tiflis, replacing the military command. Thus, the independent Republic of Armenia was born from the ashes of genocide and destitution with a territory of 4,500 square miles and a population of 700,000 inhabitants. Tatars and Kurds constituted about one seventh of that population. Soon Armenians realized that independence was not the real test, but rather the survival of the newly born Republic. Surrounded by enemies from all sides, the Armenian leadership was faced with both internal and external challenges. While the internal ones ranged from hunger to epidemics, the external challenges dealt with a hostile geographic environment and the difficulties of making a case for Armenia's international recognition. Armenian attempts to represent their demands in the Paris Peace Conference in 1919 proved to be futile. The Great Powers who had used and abused the Armenian Question for their own national and imperial gains were reluctant to support the Armenians.

Despite serious internal political hurdles, Armenians were able to hold elections and convene a parliament. Notwithstanding that the Armenian Revolutionary Federation played a significant role in deciding the fate of the new Republic, other political parties were part and parcel of the political process, such as the People's Party (Populists), the Socialist Revolutionaries, and the Social Democrats. The hopes of the Armenians were elevated with the August 1920 signing of the Treaty of Sèvres, and the decision to have U.S. President Woodrow Wilson draw the boundaries of a future Armenia. However, Wilsonian Armenia, including the provinces of Van, Bitlis, Erzerum, and Trebizond, was never realized. When Mustafa Kemal assumed the leadership of the Turkish National Movement, the rules of the games changed. With one victory after another, the Kemalists became a force to be reckoned with. The European powers, which did not want to risk their interests in the region of the Middle East, abandoned the Armenians. The Republic of Armenia was now between the rock and a hard place. On the one hand they had to face the Turkish armies in the west led by General Kazim Karabekir, and on the other hand they were under Bolshevik pressure from the east. The result was obvious: Armenia became an "independent" Soviet state after the Red Army forces crossed into the country in December 1920. The final blow for the Armenians was when the European powers renegotiated the Treaty of Sèvres, which was replaced by the Treaty of Lausanne signed in July 24,

1923, between the newly formed Ankara government of Mustafa Kemal and the Europeans. The Treaty of Lausanne proved to be the ultimate nail in the coffin of the Armenian Question.

The historiography of the First Republic of Armenia in the West has been mostly shaped by Richard G. Hovannisian, who has made a significant contribution to the understanding of this crucial phase of modern Armenian history.[5] Hovannisian's decades of meticulous research on the subject has provided us with a sophisticated understanding of the period. His scholarship covered a plethora of topics ranging from agrarian reforms to political parties and from diplomatic history to economic considerations. Despite the fact that academic articles were published in the *Armenian Review* and *Hairenik'* monthly (in Armenian) by historical figures and historians who partook in the decision-making process during the first republic, the fact remains that there is not a single edited book on the period in English, demonstrating how research on the Republic in the west has lagged in relation to the study of the Armenian Genocide.[6]

The current volume provides a multifaceted and interdisciplinary approach to the history of the First Republic. Topics range from diplomacy, intra-Armenian politics, to gender, church politics, and historiographic debates. The first chapter by Richard G. Hovannisian provides a detailed contextual overview of the Republic. Based on more than half a century of research, Hovannisian provides a sophisticated

---

[5] Richard G. Hovannisian, "The Republic of Armenia," vol. I: *The First Year, 1918-1919*: vol. II: *From Versailles to London, 1919-1920*; vol. III: *From London to Sevres, February-August, 1920*; vol. IV: *Between Crescent and Sickle: Partition and Sovietization* (Berkeley: University of California Press, 1971, 1982, 1994, 1996, respectively). For other studies in European languages see, for instance, Serge Afanasyan, *L'Arménie, l'Azerbaidjan et la Géorgie: de l'independence a l'instauration du pouvoir soviétique* (Paris: L'Harmattan, 1981), Anahide Ter Minassian, *La République d'Arménie: 1918-1920* (Bruxelles: Éditions Complexe, 1989), and Ronald Grigor Suny, *Looking Toward Ararat: Armenia in Modern History* (Bloomington; Indianapolis: Indiana University Press, 1993), 119-132.

[6] See the special issue in the *Armenian Review* edited by Richard G. Hovannisian, "The Republic of Armenia, 1918-1920: A Seventy-Five Year Perspective," *Armenian Review*, 1-4, Spring-Winter 1993, 1-215. On the Soviet and post-Soviet historiography on the First Republic see Aram Simonyan and Ashot Nersisyan, "Hayastani aṛajin Hanrapetut'yan patmagrut'yan gnahatman hayetsakargayin himk'erĕ" [The Conceptual Grounds for the Evaluation of the Historiography of the First Republic of Armenia], *Hayagitut'yan harts'er,* Yerevan, No. 3, 2014, 11-19.

analysis of the history of the Republic by situating it in the local, regional, as well as global contexts. He analyzes the internal political tribulations during the first year of the Republic, the relations of the Republic with the surrounding republics, the Armenian efforts in the Paris Peace Conference, and ends with the with the sovietization of the Republic.

The second chapter by Houri Berberian provides the first detailed study of the Armenian Revolutionary Federation (ARF) leader Abraham Giulkhandanian (1875-1946), who served as a parliamentarian, Minister of Internal Affairs, and Minister of Justice during the First Republic. Berberian traces the political path of Giulkhandanian and his fluctuating radical political as well as ideological allegiances, from a leftist politician to national socialist cooperating with Nazi Germany against the Soviet Union. Berberian dissects the post-war Armenian nationalist narrative of Armenian collaboration with Nazi Germany, through the life and work of Giulkhandanian. She demonstrates how Giulkhandanian was the by-product of the constant shift of political context in the first five decades of the 20th century.

In chapter three, Ari Şekeryan discusses the reactions of the Ottoman Turkish and Armenian intellectuals and the press towards the establish-ment of the Republic of Armenia within the context of World War I until the establishment of the Republic of Turkey. His study demonstrates how the Armenian press called the newly established Republic to cooperate with the Ottoman Empire in the first months of its existence. Şekeryan sees this as an act of self-preservation of the remaining Armenian community of the Empire. He demonstrates how, after the Armistice of Mudros of October 1918, the attitude of the Armenians of Istanbul changed.

In chapter four, Seda Ohanian discusses a marginalized topic in the historiography of the Republic: the role of women in social and political life. She examines in detail the participation of important figures such as Dr. Katarine Zalian-Manukian, Berjouhi Barseghian, and Varvare Sahakian, among others, in the development of the parliamentary activities and the intellectual life of the Republic.

In chapter five, Rubina Peroomian deals with the subversive activities of Armenian Bolsheviks during the period of the Republic with a specific concentration on the Yerevan-Moscow Negotiations (1918-1920). Her article validates how the Armenian Bolsheviks played a dominant role in the Sovietization of Armenia. With their total dedication to the ideology of communism and internationalism, they strove to bring Armenia under the realm of the Soviet Union. Another factor, which facilitated the sovietization of Armenia, was the threat from Mustafa Kemal and his advancing forces.

Vartan Matiossian, in chapter six, deals with the recognition of the First Republic of Armenia in South America. In this extensive study, Matiossian demonstrates the role of Etienne Brasil in seeking recognition and establishment of diplomatic relations with several countries in Latin America. He positions the efforts of Brasil within the larger context of both North and South American political transformations of the period.

In chapter seven, Jakub Osiecki dwells upon the relations of the Vatican with the Republic of Armenia. By analyzing the visit of Rev. Antoine Delpuch to the South Caucasus in 1919, Osiecki establishes how the Vatican went beyond supporting the newly founded Republic to suggesting the union of the Holy See with the Armenian Church. He concludes that the sovietization of Armenia halted the process of gradual rapprochement between the Roman Catholic and the Armenian Apostolic Church.

Garabet Moumdjian, in chapter eight, concentrates on the domestic politics in the Republic. After identifying the background of the major political parties of the period, he provides an in-depth discussion of the internal divisions. He argues that the core disagreements between the different political forces defined the nature of the future democratic state.

In his concluding chapter, George Bournoutian gives a theoretical argument on the territorial expectations of Armenian and non-Armenian leaders during the short-lived period of the Republic. Bournoutian examines some of the political decisions taken by the leadership which led to the final outcome.

It is my hope that the articles within this volume will open the doors for more research on the period. Going beyond partisan inclinations and historiographic biases, scholars should approach this period from different interdisciplinary perspectives. As this volume demonstrates, there is ample room for more research on the political, socio-economic, religious and cultural dimensions of this crucial period within modern Armenian history.

The Republic of Armenia:
A Contextual Overview[*]

Richard G. Hovannisian

May 28 has become the symbol of resurrected Armenian statehood after centuries of foreign dominion. As it happened, Armenian independence in the prevailing conditions of mid-1918 may actually be seen as a virtue born out of sheer necessity. The road to independence was marked by repeated disheartening retreats and abandonments. And, even when the very small, landlocked Republic of Armenia in the Caucasus became a de facto reality during the final months of World War I, the challenges facing the desperate Armenian leadership were seemingly insurmountable. Somehow, the fledgling state managed to survive until the Allied Powers defeated the German and Ottoman empires a few months later. Thus, from mid-1918 through the end of 1920, the Armenian people strove to emerge from the tragedy of war and revolution, genocide, and absolute devastation into a viable, democratic republic. The obstacles to creating the first Armenian sovereign state in centuries were enormous, yet world leaders had made grand manifestations of sympathy and were publicly pledged both to the restoration, rehabilitation, and emancipation of the surviving Armenians and to the punishment of the Young Turk perpetrators of mass atrocities that constituted genocide. It seemed that a new dawn might indeed break for the enervated Armenian nation.

The course to independence had been completely uncharted. The Armenian reform and revolutionary movements had been directed toward the historic Armenian territories in the Ottoman Empire, in what was known as Turkish Armenia or Western Armenia, not toward Yerevan province and other traditional Armenian areas in the Caucasus region of the Russian Empire. It was the Ottoman Armenian provinces that had been the focal point of international diplomacy relating to the "Armenian Question." Several reform plans imposed on the Ottoman sultans in the nineteenth century and on the Young Turk government in the early twentieth century had come and gone without effective implementation.

---

[*] This overview is based largely on my previous books and essays.

Thus, the outbreak of World War I in 1914 was seen by some Armenian political leaders as an opportunity to achieve national autonomy under the aegis of the Russian Empire, whose armies invaded and occupied a large part of the Turkish Armenian provinces in 1915-17.

But history once again played tricks on the Armenians. The Russian revolutions of 1917 led to the withdrawal of the Russian armed forces from the occupied territories and caused a new wave of flight for those Armenians who had survived the genocidal operations of the Young Turk government. The Turkish armies of Minister of War Enver Pasha gained renewed momentum and did not stop at the previous Ottoman-Russian international boundaries but now proceeded into the South Caucasus (Transcaucasia) itself. The attempts of the Armenians to collaborate with the other peoples of the region – mainly Georgians and Muslim elements – to defend the area through a regional executive body known as the Transcaucasian *Commissariat* and a provisional legislative body known as the *Seim* proved unsuccessful, especially after Soviet Russia under Lenin had exited the World War by ceding large swaths of territory to Germany and its allies, including Turkey, in the Treaty of Brest-Litovsk in March 1918. By that treaty Soviet Russia recognized the right of the Turkish armies to reoccupy all of Turkish Armenia and also ceded to Turkey the three districts of Kars, Ardahan, and Batum from the Russian side of the border. The protests of political leaders in the Caucasus that the treaty was null and void because Soviet Russia was not recognized as a legitimate entity were of no avail, as Turkish armies pressed forward to claim these territories.

In April of 1918, the Seim was compelled to agree to the Turkish ultimatum to accept the Brest-Litovsk boundaries and relinquish all claims to Turkish Armenia and to Kars, Ardahan, and Batum. The Turkish armies did not stop there, however, and continued to advance into the Russian Caucasian provinces of Yerevan and Tiflis (Tbilisi) themselves. It was at that juncture that the Georgians sought salvation through secret negotiations with German representatives, withdrawing from the new Transcaucasian federative state and declaring independence on May 26, 1918. As prearranged, they then immediately placed their country under German administrative and military protection. Then the Muslim National Council of the Caucasus followed suit by declaring the independence of the Republic of Azerbaijan encompassing "eastern and southern" Transcaucasia. Turkish sponsorship of the new state was natural in view of the close racial, linguistic, religious associations.

The Armenians had been fully abandoned to face the invading armies alone. The last-ditch efforts of Armenian defenders in places such as Sardarabad and Bash-Abaran may have helped to spare at least a small part of the province of Yerevan, which the Armenian National Council (located in Tiflis) indirectly declared as an Armenian state as of May 28, 1918. Shortly thereafter, the Ottoman Empire recognized this miniscule and entirely vulnerable Armenian entity in a crushing treaty signed in Batum on June 4, 1918. The city of Yerevan and its immediate surroundings of a few thousand square kilometers now constituted the entirety of the Republic of Armenia.

The brief history of the Republic of Armenia, 1918-1920/21, passed through several phases. The first period, from May to November 1918, was the most trying, as the Armenians labored to organize the rudiments of government at a time when all of Western (Turkish) Armenia and most of Eastern (Russian) Armenia lay under Turkish occupation. Even Yerevan itself was within range of Turkish artillery. The Armenian National Council, representing the Armenians of the Russian Empire, was then located in Tiflis and had to make the difficult decision of giving up this Armenian cultural and economic stronghold, which had now become the capital of the Republic of Georgia, and transferring to the squalor and misery of backward Yerevan. It was a nightmare. Somehow, the Armenian government survived the excruciating months of the summer and autumn of 1918 until the end of the World War.

The conclusion of World War I ushered in the period of a coalition government, November 1918 to June 1919, during which the boundaries of the Republic expanded and Armenian spokesmen at the Paris Peace Conference advanced their case for a free and united Armenian state. The year from mid-1919 to mid-1920 was characterized by serious efforts to establish the parameters of a parliamentary democracy, to define the mutual relations between the ruling party and government, and to find a way to settle the embroiled territorial disputes with neighboring Georgia and Azerbaijan. On the external front, Armenia continued to seek political, military, and economic support from the West, but showed concern that the Allied Powers had already begun to redefine their obligations toward the Armenians.

A new phase began with an abortive Bolshevik rising in May 1920 in the immediate aftermath of the sovietization of Azerbaijan and continued defiance of the Muslim-populated districts of the Republic. Now the highest organ of the dominant party Hay Heghapokhakan Dashnakts'ut'iwn (Armenian Revolutionary Federation) took the reins of government to crush both Bolshevik and Muslim insurgencies. At the same time envoys were sent to Soviet Russia to seek a modus vivendi with the communist regime. But the Dashnakts'akan leaders were never able to abandon their Western orientation, on which the hopes of a future united Armenia rested. As it turned out, the West would make a paper award of a moderately sized united Armenian state but would do nothing to implement that decision. By the autumn of 1920, the Armenian government had to face a new Turkish invasion and intense Soviet pressure to submit to its control. In the end, there was no Western orientation left to choose, and the hard-pressed Armenian leaders had to pick between engulfment by Nationalist Turkey or an attempt to save whatever possible by accepting Soviet rule. It was in fact no choice at all.

The First Months

Having traveled the treacherous road to independence, the Republic of Armenia in mid-1918 was beset with the urgent need to organize a workable system of administration while also maintaining the precarious peace with the Ottoman Empire. Under these circumstances, the Dashnakts'ut'iwn sought but failed to organize a coalition government. The Socialist Revolutionary and Social Democrat left-wing parties refused to enter a government that included the bourgeois Zhoghovrdakan-Constitutional Democratic party, while the Zhoghovrdakans insisted that the Dashnakts'ut'iwn, having been discredited by the collapse of Western Armenia and the Turkish occupation of most of Eastern Armenia, should withdraw from the political arena. It was not until the end of June 1918 that the Armenian National Council in Tiflis confirmed an abbreviated cabinet slate in which all except the non-partisan military minister were Dashnakts'akans:

Position	Name
Prime Minister (Minister-President)	Hovhannes Kachaznuni
Foreign Affairs	Alexander Khatisian
Internal Affairs	Aram Manukian
Financial Affairs	Khachatur Karjikian
Military Affairs	General Hovhannes Hakhverdian

With great difficulty the Armenian leaders transferred from Tiflis, with its many advantages and conveniences, to Yerevan, the unimposing, overgrown town that was to serve as the provisional capital of the Republic. Taking over on July 19, 2018 from popular dictator Aram

Manukian who had been in charge in Yerevan until then, Prime Minister Kachaznuni tried to lay the foundations of government without having the benefit of a preexisting national administrative apparatus. The central chancelleries, arsenals, printing presses, railway garages, and financial and commercial institutions all lay behind in Tiflis, becoming a part of the rich inheritance of the Republic of Georgia.

Establishment of the parliamentary system of government required the existence of a legislature, but because elections were then out of the question, the Armenian National Council agreed to triple its membership and serve as an interim legislative body, the *Khorhurd* (Soviet). Thus, when the Khorhurd convened on August 1, 1918, it was composed of eighteen Dashnakts'akans, six Socialist Revolutionaries, six Social Democrats, six Zhoghovrdakan Democrats, two non-partisans, and, representing the minorities, six Muslims, one Russian, and one Yezidi. In calling the legislature to order, Avetik Sahakian reviewed the tragic events leading to the formation of the Republic but, in the presence of German and Turkish envoys, declared optimistically: "I believe that our borders will expand with the iron force of life, with the defense of our just and indisputable right to the occupied lands." Two days later, Kachaznuni delivered his inaugural address, in which he described the existing state of affairs as "boundless chaos" (*andzev kaos*). His cabinet would not present grandiose plans but rather labor to employ practical methods to bring the chaos within bounds, reopen the avenues of communication and transportation, and assist the refugee population. In foreign affairs, the Armenian government would honor all treaty obligations and seek Turkish withdrawal from at least the occupied parts of Yerevan province and the return of the thousands of wretched refugees to their native district.

Even though a coalition cabinet had not materialized, Armenia nonetheless was guided along coalitional lines through the multi-party legislative standing committees for finance, administration, education, provisions, refugees, land, labor, local government, and medical-sanitary affairs. Even in these extraordinary conditions, the Khorhurd tried to exercise a degree of parliamentary democracy, the debates on the floor often reaching a high pitch and the opposition parties using this legal forum to call the cabinet to account. The six-member Social Democrat faction even included one Bolshevik, Arshavir Melikian, whose stinging criticisms were nonetheless often tempered by his clear understanding of the stark realities facing the Armenian people.

As the government grappled with the chaos caused by the breakdown of law and order, the plight of more than a quarter million refugees, and the complete hostile encirclement of the landlocked state, its envoys in the capitals of Germany and the other Central Powers strove to win diplomatic and economic support. For five months, from June until the end of the World War in November 1918, they toiled under extremely difficult, often humiliating, conditions, with petitions, statistics, and logic as their only weapons. In Berlin, Dashnakts'akan Hamazasp Ohanjanian and Social Democrat Arshak Zohrabian tried to persuade the German government to restrain its Turkish allies and force them to honor the boundaries of the Treaty of Brest-Litovsk, thereby returning the strategic Araxes River Valley to Armenia. German encouragement inspired hope, but as the weeks turned into months the sense of optimism faded. Germany would not or could not bring about a Turkish withdrawal from Yerevan province or even the repatriation of Armenian refugees to the occupied districts.

Another Armenian delegation composed of Dashnakts'akans Avetis Aharonian and Alexander Khatisian and Zhoghovrdakan Mikayel Papajanian traveled to Constantinople, the capital of the Ottoman Empire. Initially, based on assurances of German military representatives in the Caucasus, the Armenians were given to believe that a general conference of the Central Powers led by Germany and of the Caucasian states would redraft the terms of the onerous Treaty of Batum, which Germany found unacceptable. When it became apparent that no such conference would take place, the Armenian delegation sought to deal directly with the Turkish government. The reports of Aharonian and his colleagues lay bare the depth of their emotions as they even had to express gratitude to Grand Vizier Talaat and Enver for allowing the existence of any Armenian state at all. During these discussions Talaat cast the blame for Armenian misfortunes on the Kurds, the military authorities, irresponsible local officials, and the Armenians themselves. Enver, the most candid of the Young Turk leaders, offered no sympathy and categorically rejected all entreaties for Turkish withdrawal. The Young Turk Committee of Union and Progress, he noted, had after considerable deliberation consented to a small Armenian state on former Russian territory provided that it could never have the means to interfere with the interests of the Turkish Empire. The borders as laid down in the Treaty of Batum would remain firm.

Only in September, when the Turkish armies were being driven back in the Balkans and in Palestine, did Turkish leaders intimate that the Armenian republic might soon be allowed to expand to the Brest-Litovsk boundary. Then, at the end of the month, Talaat Pasha announced that his government was prepared to make several major concessions to the Armenians. But time had run out for the Young Turk dictatorship. Their cabinet fell in early October, allowing General Ahmed Izzet Pasha to prepare for surrender to the Allied Powers.

The Ottoman Empire capitulated by terms of the Mudros Armistice on October 30, 1918 and Germany surrendered a few days later on November 11, 1918. World War I was at an end. Armenians everywhere rejoiced. The time of reckoning was at hand. The Allies were pledged to punish the Turks and to reward the Armenians. Yet a careful reading of the terms of the Mudros Armistice indicated that there was serious cause for misgivings. While the British negotiators were firm in demands relating to Allied control of the strategic waterways, the disarmament of the Straits, the immediate release of prisoners of war, and Turkish withdrawal from northern Persia and the occupied sector of the Caucasus, they consented to alter the term requiring evacuation also of the six eastern Ottoman provinces known as Turkish Armenia. Instead, Article 24 of the Armistice simply reserved the right of the Allied Powers to occupy any part or all of the region "in case of disorder." Turkish military and civil authorities, therefore, would continue to control the area until its fate had been determined by the world peace conference that soon was to gather in Paris. Even though the Turkish resistance movement against Allied, Greek, and Armenian encroachments was to take form in this very region and a great deal of "disorder" would occur, the Allied Powers never chose to implement Article 24 of the Armistice.

In their evacuation of Yerevan province, the Turkish armies stripped everything clean, taking food supplies, livestock, implements, clothing, furniture, and even doors and windows and railway ties. When the Armenian army reoccupied Alexandropol on December 6, 1918, not a single operative locomotive or freight car remained on the entire railway line. Nonetheless, about 15,000 square kilometers of fertile territory had been returned to the Armenians, who were further heartened by the landing of British armed forces at the ports of Batum on the Black Sea and Baku on the Caspian Sea. The Allies were now present in the Caucasus and, it was believed, would surely help to protect the Armenians while the Allied political leaders found a way to guarantee the Armenians a secure national future.

The Coalition Government

The momentous changes on the international scene had a wholesome effect on the political situation in Armenia. Many who had previously used the terms "independence" and "republic" with skepticism and even disparagement now began to feel that perhaps an independent republic could be something more than self-delusive fantasy. The Armenian professionals and businessmen who made up the Zhoghovrdakan party in particular indicated a willingness to participate in the affairs of government. Banking executive Minas Berberian and Central Committee Chairman Samson Harutiunian traveled from Tiflis to Yerevan to explore the possibility of a coalition cabinet. They found the Dashnakts'akans to be receptive, not only because of the important skills and experience the Zhoghovrdakan Democrat members could bring to Armenia but also because the socialist Dashnakts'ut'iwn wanted to send a clear signal to the Allied Powers that Armenia would be a politically moderate state worthy of Western support and open to foreign investment. In the resulting coalition cabinet, the Dashnakts'akans contented themselves with less than half the portfolios, but they held firmly to the premiership and the strategic ministries of foreign affairs and internal affairs:

Position	Name	Party
Prime Minister	Hovhannes Kachaznuni	Dashnakts'ut'iwn
Foreign Affairs	Sirakan Tigranian	Dashnakts'ut'iwn
Internal Affairs	Aram Manukian	Dashnakts'ut'iwn
Welfare	Khatchatur Karjikian	Dashnakts'ut'iwn
Financial Affairs	Artashes Enfiajian	Zhoghovrdakan
Judicial Affairs	Samson Harutiunian	Zhoghovrdakan
Education and Culture	Mikayel Atabekian	Zhoghovrdakan
Provisions	Levon Ghulian	Zhoghovrdakan
Military Affairs	Hovhannes Hakhverdian	non-partisan
State Controller (non-voting)	Minas Berberian	Zhoghovrdakan

The coalition cabinet was optimistic that the Allied Powers would soon create a securable, united Armenia and provide for its defense and development. But even in the best of circumstances, the winter of 1918-19 would have claimed an extremely heavy toll. The homeless refugee masses, lacking food, clothing, and medicine, suffered excruciating months under freezing winds and blizzards. The starving people some-times rioted for food, but these sporadic outbursts were of no avail; the state granaries were empty. Interior Minister Aram Manukian at times used high-handed methods to requisition food from the districts least impacted by the Turkish occupation, drawing bitter protests from the affected peasantry and critics in the legislature. Aram "Pasha" also took harsh measures against the lawless bands, identified by the Mauser revolvers that many carried. Guerrillas and freedom fighters in the years of struggle against Turkish oppression, the Mauserist bands now robbed and looted in broad daylight, a government unto themselves. It took all the determination and prestige that Aram commanded to deal with freedom fighters turned outlaws.

By the beginning of the winter season, Armenia was already starving. American and Allied officials who came to Yerevan brought hope that relief supplies would arrive before long. Until then the nation had to endure. But soon even this hope vanished. From all over the country reports of famine and epidemic inundated the government. The conditions were so acute that daily bread rations were steadily reduced until they reached four ounces a day, and this only for those who were fortunate enough to qualify. The pitiful multitude lay in the snow, in partially destroyed buildings, on doorsteps of churches, eventually too weak to protest or even to beg any longer. They lived in the "Land of Stalking Death," waiting with sunken face and swollen belly for release. And death came, delivering from anguish thousands upon thousands of refugees and native inhabitants alike. Many who withstood the exposure and famine were swept away by ravaging epidemics. Typhus was the main killer, striking in every district and at every age group, taking its largest toll from among the children. During the winter of 1918-19, nearly 200,000 Armenians – 20 percent of the population of the Armenian republic – succumbed to the triple-headed hydra – famine, exposure, pestilence. For each 1,000 persons there were 8.7 births and 204.2 deaths in 1919. The genocide was still in progress.

It was American relief that saved the Armenian remnants. The defeat of the Central Powers at the end of 1918 enabled the sympathetic American public to renew and intensify its earlier relief operations. The American Committee for Relief in the Near East (ACRNE) raised nearly $20 million in private donations in 1919. In January, the president of ACRNE, James L. Barton, led a commission to study firsthand the needs of the region. The field party that visited the Caucasus brought back appalling reports. It was not until March that the first ACRNE medical teams reached Armenia where, by agreement with the government, ACRNE took charge of eleven hospitals and ninety orphanages with 13,000 children. Many others among the 30,000 orphans in the country were eventually taken in by ACRNE.

By summer's end, ACRNE incorporated in August as the Near East Relief (NER), had dispatched more than 30,000 metric tons of food and clothing, with more than half the supplies being distributed to the destitute in Constantinople and the western provinces of Anatolia. But even if all private American charity in the Near East had been directed to the Republic of Armenia, it could not have met the basic needs of the utterly dependent population. It was the United States government and its American Relief Administration (ARA) that were to come to the rescue. In a year when much of the world lay in ruins, gripped by famine, the United States responded with more than $1 billion in worldwide relief. In this great American crusade, the trickle of supplies that reached Armenia was enough to shore up the Republic for its second, hopefully brighter, year of existence.

Congress created the ARA in February 1919 to administer a $100 million appropriation to assist non-enemy countries as well as "Armenians, Syrians, Greeks, and other Christian and Jewish populations of Asia Minor, now or formerly subjects of Turkey." Herbert Hoover headed the ARA and served simultaneously in Europe as the Allied director general of relief. The first shipment of supplies destined for Armenia reached Batum in April, followed by two more steamers in May and three in June 1919. These deliveries totaled more than 20,000 metric tons of flour, grain, condensed milk, and other foodstuffs. The final four shipments of ARA supplies arrived in August, bringing the total to some 50,000 metric tons. For each ARA shipment, the Armenian government issued promissory notes to be deposited in the United States Treasury, whereas the ACRNE contributions were the direct gift of the American people to the Armenian people. The total deliveries of both ACRNE and ARA goods amounted to almost 84,000 metric tons in 1919. While this figure represents only 2 percent of America's worldwide distribution, it was sufficient to give the Armenian people a new grasp on life.

Workings of the Coalition Government

Such were the conditions under which Hovhannes Kachaznuni's coalition cabinet functioned. Most of the country lay beyond the firm control of the government and contributed nothing to the state revenue, whereas the inhabitants of the government-controlled districts did their utmost to evade the onerous obligations imposed on them. Many peasants, reluctant to leave their families amid starvation and insecurity, attempted to avoid military service. A government did exist in Yerevan, but it was hardly the embodiment of the self-administration so long coveted by politically engaged Armenians. Moreover, the Western Armenian refugees did not consider this their country. The Yerevan republic, bearing the strong imprint of Russia, was alien to them, especially as their national consciousness had developed more rapidly and firmly than that of the Eastern Armenian masses.

The burden of several hundred thousand unsheltered and unemployed people was enough in itself to cause economic calamity. Even in normal times, the land under the government's jurisdiction could not have supported so needy a population. Industry had never been developed in Eastern Armenia during the century of Russian rule. Yerevan province retained its agrarian character, with the Shustov cognac and wine works being the only significant source of industrial income. Home manufacture of furniture, textiles, implements, and handicrafts accounted for nearly all other non-agricultural revenue, but in 1919 this was extremely limited because of the scarcity of raw materials and the widespread devastation of the country. Industrial income had never been high, but in that year, it totaled only 8 percent of the prewar level.

The outcome of the dislocation was that, compared with the more than 300,000 hectares (748,000 acres) of land cultivated in 1914, less than 83,000 hectares (slightly more than 200,000 acres) was sown in 1919. Tremendous losses were registered in grain, fruits and vegetables, and cotton. The overall agricultural decline exceeded 80 percent. The sharp decrease in livestock and farm implements paralleled the ruin in industry and agriculture. Thousands of animals had been slaughtered for food by the Turkish armies of occupation and thousands more were driven toward Kars when those same armies withdrew at the end of 1918. Most of the remaining animals were eaten by refugees or else succumbed to the same diseases that ravaged the population. Thousands of farmers were left without a single draft animal. The slump in livestock when compared with 1914 exceeded 65 percent. A soaring inflation resulted from these heavy losses. The unsecured paper money became nearly worthless as the price of food and essential items doubled and multiplied time and again. The government was faced with a catastrophe that it had not created but for which it was held accountable.

Compounding its difficulties, the coalition government lost several key figures during the winter of 1918-19. In November, Welfare Minister Khachatur Karjikian was assassinated by a deranged political comrade who blamed him for collaborating with the Georgian Mensheviks and contributing to the fall of Kars to the Turks and the subsequent disaster. The typhus epidemic took two other members of the cabinet in January. First to succumb was State Controller Minas Berberian, a wealthy patriot who had been instrumental in bringing about Zhoghovrdakan participation in the coalition government and who had foregone his position and life of ease in Tiflis to serve Armenia. The heaviest blow fell on January 26 when the steadfast Aram Manukian lost his battle against the raging epidemic. Aram "Pasha," as he was known to friend and foe alike, had been a veritable founder of the Armenian republic. While the feeble Caucasian administrative bodies harangued in Tiflis in 1918, Aram had established a dictatorship in Yerevan and took an active role in the successful defense against the Turkish offensive in May of that year. Following the declaration of Armenian independence, Aram and Dro (Drastamat Kanayan), as the de facto administration in Armenia, continued in power until Kachaznuni's government finally transferred to Yerevan in July. And even after the cabinet had begun to function, there were many who believed that Aram Manukian operated as a virtual dictator. His impatience with the slow pace of parliamentary procedures was evident, and under the existing conditions it was not difficult for the minister of internal affairs to find ample justification for strong, swift, centralized measures. Aram's death deepened the gloom in Yerevan. The ministry of interior devolved upon Alexander Khatisian, but it would never again command the power, prestige, and awe that characterized the critical era of Aram Manukian.

The fundamental, vexing issues notwithstanding, Kachaznuni's cabinet labored assiduously to bring order out of chaos. The Zhoghovrdakan ministers, having been given the opportunity to put their ideals into practice, were especially enthusiastic. Samson Harutiunian, a seasoned jurist and civic leader, undertook to reorganize Armenia's judicial system to include branches for civil, criminal, and administrative law, appellate courts, a supreme court, and the jury system. Finance Minister Artashes Enfiajian laid plans for the introduction of a national currency, a sound budgetary system, and a progressive income tax. Mikayel Atabekian initiated studies for the eventual adoption of a general curriculum based on universal, secular, compulsory elementary education, with emphasis on technical training and the trades. He hoped to transfer the Gevorgian Academy (Jemaran) of Etchmiadzin to the capital as the first step toward founding a state university. The idealistic fervor of the Zhoghovrdakan ministers may have escaped reality, but it inspired hope at a time when pessimism was the prevailing sentiment among many circles in Armenia.

The coalition cabinet also took some immediate practical measures. The Shustov cognac and wine complex, one of the few immediate sources of state revenue, was nationalized. Several textile mills were renovated, providing employment for a few hundred refugee women. Hospitals were opened even though basic equipment and medications were lacking, and thousands of orphans were made wards of the state. In February 1919 teams of civil and mining engineers and technicians from other parts of the Caucasus and from southern Russia were employed to study the soil, survey mineral deposits, assess the industrial potential, and formulate plans for the reconstruction of Armenia. The government also took concrete steps to improve the routes of transportation and communication. When the winter snows thawed, crews of laborers repaired the railways and the depots that had been badly damaged during the Turkish invasion, and they restored and expanded the telegraph network.

The decision to substitute the Armenian language for Russian in the performance of all official functions was perhaps the most difficult administrative measure to implement. To discard a system developed during a hundred years of Russian dominion was no easy task. Few of the more experienced bureau chiefs could read or write Armenian. They had passed through Russian schools, had entered the Romanov civil and military hierarchy, and had served in various parts of the empire. The Armenian government could conceivably dismiss those who did not know Armenian, or it could teach them to read, to write, and in many cases to speak the language. Either alternative held in store a host of troubles. Still, if Armenia was to rise as an independent republic and gain the loyalty of all its people, the agonizing process of transition had to begin. By April 1919 a few ministries had initiated the awkward and cumbersome move toward Armenianization of the administrative hierarchy.

The structure of the military establishment posed another formidable obstacle. The army command, adept in the tsarist school of traditional warfare, found it extremely difficult to adjust to the needs of a small, emerging state. The military cadre knew little Armenian, used Russian in administrative work and training programs, and even included many Russian officers. The top-heavy structure decreased the combat potential of the army as did the lack of weapons, ammunition, and spare parts. The men under arms were continuously involved with Muslim insurgency and never enjoyed a calm long enough for advanced military training or effective reorganization. In dealing with the problem, the government reshuffled the military hierarchy in March 1919, elevating Colonel Kristapor Araratian to the rank of major general and naming him minister of military affairs. Dro, the experienced partisan leader, was picked as assistant military minister. It was hoped that the pair would be able to create a tight, disciplined, yet flexible army command.

When the various ministerial vacancies were filled and the realignments completed in the spring of 1919, the political balance of the coalition government remained unchanged. The Dashnaktsʻutʻiwn, in control of the strategic ministries, still held fewer than half the posts.

Caucasian Relations

Foreign affairs during the coalition government focused on attempts to regulate relations with the neighboring states of the South Caucasus (Transcaucasia) and on advancing the Armenian case at the Paris Peace Conference and in Allied countries. The breakup of the South Caucasus into three separate states created enormous problems that would take years to sort out and resolve. Relations were always strained. The Armeno-Georgian territorial dispute focused on the southern districts of Tiflis province. The Armenians staked historic, ethnographic, and geographic claims to Lori and Akhalkalak (Javakhk/Javakheti). These districts along the northern perimeter of Yerevan province were a part of the Armenian highland and were populated overwhelmingly by Armenians. In fact, an Armenian plurality existed right up into the city of Tiflis, now the capital of the Georgian republic. When the Turks evacuated the province of Kars in early 1919, the dispute was to spill over into its two northern counties, Olti and Ardahan. Georgian kingdoms had extended into all these areas at one time or another, and if the Armenians were now a majority in certain districts, this, said the Georgians, was owing to the hospitality of the Georgian people, who for decades had made room for the Armenians fleeing from the Ottoman Empire.

The dispute led to a brief armed conflict in Lori in December 1918, deeply embarrassing the two peoples who had lived in peace down through the centuries. The British military authorities in Tiflis finally arranged a truce, whereby the southern portion of Lori remained occupied by the Armenians, while the northern sector was made into a neutral zone. Armenian leaders were not allowed to forget that the Republic's rail lifeline from the port of Batum passed through Georgia and that the half-million Armenians living in Georgia were vulnerable. Fortunately, the scope of Armenian-Georgian disagreements could be defined and localized. Both governments realized that the survival of one republic was essential for the well-being of the other. By mid-1919 the two sides were putting forward compromise proposals to settle the remaining disputes. Subsequently, in 1921, the Lori neutral zone became a part of Soviet

Armenia. Georgia held on to Akhalkalak. In the long run, neither side was to have Ardahan and Olti.

Hostility between Armenians and Azerbaijanis was deep-seated and widespread. Racial, religious, and cultural differences were only the backdrop to the bitter territorial feuds. Azerbaijan claimed all of the provinces of Baku and Elisavetpol (Ganja/Gandzak), a part of Tiflis province, most of Yerevan province, and all of Kars and Batum. According to Azerbaijani maps, the Republic of Azerbaijan would extend from the Caspian to the Black Sea, entirely encircling a small Armenian state at Yerevan. Armenia, on the other hand, advanced historic, economic, cultural, and strategic claims to the whole of Yerevan province and the western, highland sector of Elisavetpol province, from Kazakh to Mountainous Karabagh and Zangezur.

Armenian-Azerbaijani relations in 1919 were characterized by repeated clashes along the still-undefined borders and even deep within the two republics. The Muslim-populated districts to the south of the city of Yerevan refused to acknowledge the authority and officials of the Armenian republic and, with arms and money furnished by Turkey and Azerbaijan, maintained a semiautonomous existence. The Armenians of Karabagh and Zangezur, on the other hand, rejected Azerbaijani claims and declared themselves integral parts of the Armenian republic. When World War I ended, Western Armenian partisan commander Andranik struck out from Zangezur toward Shushi, the main city of Karabagh, but his force was stopped short of its objective when Allied officers intercepted him and insisted that he return to Zangezur and await the just decision of the Paris Peace Conference. A redoubtable warrior, Andranik could not bring himself to defy the Great Allies of the West and therefore withdrew his force to Goris (Gerusy) in Zangezur. That action was to have a decisive effect on the fate of Karabagh.

The British command at Baku, which had become the capital of Azerbaijan, came to accept the Azerbaijani rationale for provisional jurisdiction in Karabagh and Zangezur and assented to the appointment of Dr. Khosrov Bek Sultanov as governor general of the region. The Zangezur Armenians effectively defied this arrangement and threw back every Azerbaijani attempt to seize the district. Karabagh, too, through its local national assembly and national council, refused to hear of even temporary Azerbaijani jurisdiction. But the acts of Armenian defiance led to the massacre and razing of four local Armenian villages in June 1919. Caught up in its desperate struggle for survival, the Yerevan government could offer little assistance to the isolated Karabagh Armenians. Finally, in August 1919, the Karabagh National Assembly yielded to provisional and conditional Azerbaijani jurisdiction. The twenty-six conditions strictly limited the Azerbaijani administrative and military presence in the region and underscored the internal autonomy of Mountainous Karabagh. Still, this was a momentous Azerbaijani victory.

Immediate violations of the agreement by Azerbaijan culminated in an abortive rebellion in March 1920. In retribution, the Azerbaijani forces burned the beautiful city of Shushi, hanged the prelate Bishop Vahan, and massacred much of the population. It was the death of Armenian Shushi. After Armenia was sovietized at the end of 1920, Soviet Azerbaijan ceded Karabagh and the other disputed districts to Armenia, but the decision was soon rescinded. Then, in 1923, a part but not all of Mountainous Karabagh was formed into an autonomous region (*oblast'*) within Soviet Azerbaijan. Armenian resentment smoldered down through the decades until in 1988 it erupted into mass demonstrations for Karabagh's reunification with Armenia.

While Armenians and Azerbaijanis were at loggerheads over the disputed territories, the Turkish armies finally complied with terms of Mudros Armistice and evacuated the province of Kars in February 1919. Arms, supplies, and demobilized Turkish officers were left behind to assist the local Muslim population organize an autonomous administration and prevent Armenian expansion into the area. The Armenian army, with the support of the British command, nonetheless succeeded in occupying Kars in April, allowing thousands of Russian Armenian refugees from the province to return as far as Kaghzvan (Kaghisman), Sarikamish, and the surrounding villages. Thousands of Turkish Armenians also pressed into Kars to be closer to their native provinces, now just beyond the prewar frontier.

In May 1919, "General" Dro headed an expeditionary force, again with British cooperation, southward into the Muslim-populated districts of Yerevan province. An Armenian administration was installed at Nakhichevan, and Armenian representatives traveled all the way to Julfa, where they relayed greetings to the Persian government. If the railway from Yerevan to Nakhichevan and Julfa resumed operations under Armenian jurisdiction, Armenia could take advantage of trade and communications with and beyond Persia. Hence by mid-1919, the Republic of Armenia had filled out into most of the region formerly known as Russian Armenia, expanding from its approximately 10,000 square kilometers (barely 4,000 square miles) to nearly 45,000 square kilometers (17,000 square miles).

This was no little achievement, and, if the Paris Peace Conference acted favorably, the new Armenia would become more than double that size.

The Paris Peace Conference

The heads of state of many countries gathered in Paris in January 1919 to conclude peace with Germany and the other defeated Central Powers and to establish the mechanism of a world organization to maintain peace – the League of Nations. The participants included President Woodrow Wilson and Prime Ministers David Lloyd George of Great Britain, Georges Clemenceau of France, Vittorio Orlando of Italy, and scores of petitioners from large and small states and from internationally recognized and non-recognized delegations. It was here that the Armenians were to present their case and to call on the Allied and Associated Powers to fulfill the solemn pledges regarding the future of Armenia and the Armenian people. Lloyd George had captured the essence of public indignation when he condemned the perpetrators of the Armenian genocide and promised that Armenia, "the land soaked with the blood of innocents," would never again be restored to the "blasting tyranny of the Turk."

In November 1918, shortly after the end of the war, the Armenian legislature named Avetis Aharonian to head an Armenian delegation to Paris, along with Hamazasp Ohanjanian (Dashnakts'akan), who was already in Europe, and Mikayel Papajanian (Zhoghovrdakan). After heated debate, the legislature instructed the delegation to advance claims to the six Turkish Armenian provinces and an outlet on the Black Sea. Some deputies insisted unsuccessfully that Cilicia and a Mediterranean outlet should be included in these claims.

It took Aharonian many weeks to travel to Paris, and when he arrived in February 1919, he found that other Armenians headed by Boghos Nubar Pasha and the Armenian National Delegation were already hard at work. A world congress of Western Armenian representatives then taking place in Paris was emphatic that Cilicia must be included in the new united Armenian state. Aharonian's Western Armenian Dashnakts'akan political comrades were no less adamant and persuaded Aharonian, for the sake of presenting a united front, to adopt the claim to Cilicia. Hence, when Boghos Nubar and Aharonian appeared before the Allied Supreme Council on February 26 as the Delegation of Integral Armenia, they made their case for an Armenian state extending from Transcaucasia and the Black Sea to Cilicia and the Mediterranean Sea. Subsequently ridiculed as being unrealistic and perhaps even imperialistic, the Armenian claims nonetheless closely paralleled those already secretly sketched in the British Foreign Office and in the United States Department of State. The French had their own plans for Cilicia and were not pleased with the Armenian claim there, but Clemenceau ultimately assented to Cilicia's inclusion in Armenia if the United States would assume a protective mandate for the country.

The Paris Peace Conference, among its first acts, had already declared that "because of the historical misgovernment of the Turks of subject peoples and the terrible massacres of Armenians and others in recent years, the Allied and Associated Powers are agreed that Armenia, Syria, Mesopotamia, Palestine and Arabia must be completely severed from the Turkish Empire." Armenia and the other states could be recognized provisionally as independent nations "subject to the rendering of administrative advice and assistance by a mandatory power." On the heels of great expectations sometimes follow greater disappointments. Despite the sympathy of the Allied Powers, Armenia was not given a seat at the peace conference, official recognition, or the financial and military support that it sought. Western Armenia stayed under Turkish military control, and the refugee population remained homeless. Allied spokesmen advised patience, as many of these issues would be resolved once a peace settlement had been imposed on Turkey and the boundaries of Armenia had been determined. The extent of those boundaries depended on whether a mandatory or protective power was found for Armenia. President Woodrow Wilson favored an American mandate for Armenia, which was the unanimous choice of the Armenian people as well, yet he decided to hold the issue in abeyance until he could get the Senate to ratify the peace treaty with Germany, which incorporated the Covenant of the League of Nations (including mandate regulations).

In discussions of the mandate question, many Americans with experience in the Near East called for a joint United States mandate over Armenia, Anatolia, and the Constantinople-Straits area. Only in this way could there be uniform progress, and could the Armenians be protected. But Armenians and their influential supporters of the American Committee for the Independence of Armenia (ACIA) categorically rejected and denounced that proposal. Armenia should be completely severed from Turkey, they insisted. Experience had shown that every past reform measure had resulted in bloodshed, and the Armenians now demanded absolute and unconditional separation. It would be better to have no mandate at all than a joint mandate, cried Armenian spokesmen. Instead, the United States could recognize the Armenian republic and extend to it financial, administrative, and military aid and advisors, but no joint mandate.

When the Treaty of Versailles between the Allied Powers and Germany was signed on June 28, 1919, President Wilson still had not put the mandate question to the Senate. And now the Allied heads of state dispersed without having resolved either the Armenian or the larger Near Eastern question. The European powers were not entirely unhappy about the delay, as it gave them time to maneuver for the greatest possible gains in Anatolia and the Arab provinces. But the postponement was a major setback for the Armenians and provided impetus to the emergence of the Turkish resistance movement led by Mustafa Kemal Pasha. Still, nothing was very clear in mid-1919, and the Armenians were encouraged by the sharp rebuke that the Allies gave Turkish Grand Vizier Damad Ferid Pasha when he pled the Turkish case during the closing days of the peace conference. Admitting that the Young Turks had committed such crimes as "to make the conscience of mankind shudder with horror forever," Damad Ferid asked that the Turkish people not be punished for this aberration and that the territorial integrity of Anatolia be maintained, with the possibility of a border rectification in favor of the new Armenian state in the east. In their reply, the Allied leaders condemned Turkey as the subservient tool of Germany and the perpetrator of massacres "whose calculated atrocity equals or exceeds anything in recorded history." As for leaving alien races under Turkish rule, "the experiment has been tried too long and too often for there to be the least doubt of its results." A spirit of unbending resolve pervaded the Allied response, giving the Armenians fresh hopes that a favorable settlement was in the wind.

The Act of United Armenia

While Avetis Aharonian and Boghos Nubar tried to put aside their sharp personal differences and the mutual suspicions of Eastern Armenians and Western Armenians to act as the Delegation of Integral Armenia, the coalition government in Yerevan became increasingly polarized. The initial enthusiasm of the Zhoghovrdakan ministers soon began to fade into distress and disillusion. The conditions in Yerevan made life unbearable. The Armenian bourgeoisie, accustomed to the comforts and luxuries of Tiflis, found adjusting to the situation especially difficult. But the magnetism of Tiflis and the misery of Yerevan were not all that disenchanted the Zhoghovrdakan Democrats. As members of a liberal constitutional party, they were bitterly disappointed that there was little possibility for the early establishment of true parliamentary democracy. They felt intimidated by the brashness of Dashnakts'akan militants and frustrated by the disorganization that still prevailed. More than one Zhoghovrdakan minister found occasion to depart for Tiflis on "urgent business." Their absence from Yerevan was sometimes prolonged and for two ministers, Mikayel Atabekian and Levon Ghulian, it was permanent. Still, as late as April of 1919, a show of unity was maintained as Dashnakts'akan Prime Minister Kachaznuni and Zhoghovrdakan Finance Minister Enfiajian embarked on a joint mission to Europe and America to secure financial loans and assistance for the Republic.

It was the Declaration of United Armenia, proclaimed during the celebration of the Republic's first anniversary on May 28, 1919, that provided the immediate cause for the collapse of the coalition cabinet. In preparing for the anniversary, the cabinet, with the concurrence of the Zhoghovrdakan ministers, decided to declare the symbolic union of Eastern and Western Armenia, even though no part of Western Armenia was yet under Armenian rule. May 28 was organized as a day of rejoicing, as Armenia had pulled through the terrible winter, American flour had arrived, and the organs of government had begun to function. Townspeople and orphans lined the streets decorated with the Armenian red, blue, and orange tricolor flag and applauded as the military band struck up with the strains of the national anthem, *"Mer Hayrenik"* (Our Fatherland). Two floats, one depicting the tragedy of Western Armenia and the other, in white, holding forth the promise of a bright future, passed along the parade route to the legislature. There Acting Prime Minister Alexander Khatisian proclaimed the Act of United Armenia, which read in part:

> To restore the integrality of Armenia and to secure the complete freedom and prosperity of its people, the Government of Armenia, abiding by the solid will and desire of the entire Armenian people, declares that from this day forward the separated parts of Armenia are everlastingly combined as an independent political entity....
>
> Now in promulgating this act of unification and independence of the ancestral Armenian lands located in Transcaucasia and the Ottoman Empire, the Government of Armenia declares that the political system of United Armenia is a democratic republic and that it has become the Government of the United Republic of Armenia.
>
> Thus, the people of Armenia are henceforth the supreme lord and master of their consolidated fatherland, and the

Parliament and Government of Armenia stand as the supreme
legislative and executive authority conjoining the free people of
United Armenia.

Twelve Western Armenian deputies were then seated in the legislative
Khorhurd to give symbolic meaning to the symbolic act.

A few days later, in a startling reversal, the central committee of the
Zhoghovrdakan party in Tiflis declared that the proclamation had been an
act of usurpation. Boghos Nubar and his Armenian National Delegation
spoke for the Western Armenians, yet they had not been consulted
regarding the Act, and the Yerevan government had illegally arrogated to
itself legislative and executive authority over "United Armenia." The Act
was therefore null and void, and the Zhoghovrdakan ministers, as a sign
of protest, were withdrawing from the coalition cabinet. Not mentioning
the fact that four Zhoghovrdakan ministers had affixed their signatures to
the Act, the central committee's announcement veiled deeper underlying
dissatisfaction with the policies and practices of the dominant
Dashnakts'ut'iwn. The Zhoghovrdakan Democrats hoped that once a
united state had actually been formed a coalition with the Western
Armenian Constitutional Democrats (Sahmanadir Ṛamkavar) and other
non-socialist elements aligned with Boghos Nubar might successfully
challenge the Dashnakts'ut'iwn for political ascendancy.

Parliamentary Elections

The crisis surrounding the Act of United Armenia evolved amid a
brisk campaign for the first popularly elected parliament of Armenia. In
keeping with progressive, democratic principles, the election regulations
enfranchised all adults regardless of sex, race, religion, and provided that
the elections be conducted on the basis of general, direct, equal voting and
proportional representation. That the Armenian Revolutionary Federation
would gain an absolute majority in a popular election was a foregone
conclusion, as the Dashnakts'ut'iwn had struck root throughout the
Caucasus and had directed collective Armenian action there since the turn
of the century. Even if it had been possible to conduct the electoral
campaign under ideal conditions, the opposition parties would be
overshadowed. The Armenian affiliate of the Socialist Revolutionary
party, other than emphasizing the need for integral bonds with Russia and
interracial harmony, offered little that was not already contained in the
platform of the Dashnakts'ut'iwn. The small Marxist Social Democrat
groups were split into at least five rival factions, composed mainly of

students and intellectuals, and handicapped by the absence of a significant proletariat in the Armenian provinces. The liberal Armenian Zhoghovrdakan party, like the socialist opposition parties, functioned under the anomaly of having more followers in Tiflis and Baku than in Yerevan and of directing organizational affairs through a central body situated outside the Armenian republic. But unlike the Socialist Revolutionaries and Social Democrats, the Zhoghovrdakan Democrats had shared responsibility in the coalition cabinet from December 1918 to June 1919, and the rank-and-file members identified increasingly with the concept of national independence. The party had the potential of becoming the catalyst for the various non-socialist elements. Hence, even though the Zhoghovrdakans could not have won many seats in 1919, their decision to withdraw their slate of candidates and declare a boycott on the eve of the elections was a serious setback for the democratic experiment in Armenia.

Disappointments and shortcomings aside, Armenia's first national election was conducted as scheduled, June 21-23, 1919. The totals posted by the central election bureau showed that the Dashnakts'ut'iwn had received nearly 90 percent of the popular vote, as compared with 5 percent for the second second-place Socialist Revolutionary party. Some observers believed that the Dashnakts'ut'iwn had used the ruse of a democratic mechanism to tighten its control over the government rather than to place the state on more popular foundations. The Armenian Revolutionary Federation, on the other hand, was not a monolithic organization, since it had provided a broad umbrella in the decades-long emancipatory struggle. The Dashnakts'akan deputies could be expected to stand unanimously on the principle of free, independent, united Armenia, but their divergent social and economic views could easily give rise to internal cleavages and expose the rivalry between the generally conservative and traditionalist Western Armenian leaders and the more radical, internationalist Eastern Armenian intellectuals.

The Parliament (*Khorhrdaran*) of Armenia convened on August 1, 1919 in an air of excitement enhanced by the arrival from Rostov-on-Don, Baku, Tiflis, and Constantinople of several of the recently elected eighty deputies, three of whom were women. Alexander Khatisian was called upon to form the cabinet or council of ministers, which the Parliament confirmed on August 10. As it was hoped that a coalition government of integral Armenia would result from negotiations with the National Delegation's representatives, who were then en route from Paris, four of the Dashnakts'akan ministers each temporarily assumed two portfolios:

Positions	Name
Prime Minister and Foreign Affairs	Alexander Khatisian
Internal Affairs and Judicial Affairs	Abraham Giulkhandanian
Provisions and Finance	Sargis Araratian
Welfare-Labor and Agriculture	Avetik Sahakian
Education and Culture	Nikol Aghbalian
Military Affairs	General Kristapor Araratian

At forty-five years of age, Alexander Khatisian was by disposition and experience a man of government. Laying aside a degree in medicine early in his career, he had entered the public arena, rising rapidly to become mayor of Tiflis and president of the Union of Caucasian Cities. Following the Russian revolutions in 1917, he served as a member of the Armenian National Council, and as a minister in the short-lived Transcaucasian federative government in April-May 1918, then as minister of internal affairs in Kachaznuni's coalition cabinet, and, since April of 1919, as acting prime minister. Although his cabinet was Dashnakts'akan, Khatisian believed that his party should uphold the government without interfering in its day-to-day operations and that the principal criteria for civil service should be training and competence. Hence, every state ministry included non-partisans, Zhoghovrdakans, Socialist Revolution-aries, and Social Democrats, several of whom were division and bureau chiefs. Khatisian's critics complained that it was unreasonable to stand on cumbersome democratic procedures or expect the peasantry to remain patient amid worldwide social ferment and an apparent reluctance to sweep away the tsarist class structure. Not sterile legalisms, but swift, revolutionary action held the key to Armenian survival. Moreover, the enlistment of so many comrades in governmental work hindered the task of rebuilding the party and raised the specter of tainting it with the inevitable shortcomings of a deficient administration. By and large, however, Khatisian's views prevailed until mid-1920, and under his direction the departments of government gained increasing independence from the party.

The question of party-state relations was debated heatedly during the ninth world congress of the Hay Heghapokhakan Dashnakts'ut'iwn, which took place in Yerevan from late September to early November 1919. Arguing that direct party control of the government was essential in steering the country through great peril, veteran revolutionary Ruben Ter Minasian stood at the fore of those delegates demanding unqualified submission of the Dashnakts'akan ministers to the dictates of the supreme party Bureau. At the other extreme, Khatisian's adherents emphasized the party's history of unrelenting opposition to centralized authoritarian regimes and its wholesome tradition of democratic decentralization. If Armenia was to avoid the Bolshevik malady of party-government synonymy and self-perpetuating elitism, the independence of the state machinery had to be maintained and the Bureau's influence channeled through the Dashnakts'akan faction of the legislature. The exchanges gave way to bitter taunts before it was decided that the party's parliamentary faction, in consultation with the Bureau, would select the candidate for prime minister, who in turn would then secure the faction's approval of his proposed ministerial slate before submitting it to the full Parliament for confirmation. Comrades in the cabinet were to hold no party post, and members of the Bureau who might enter the government were required to withdraw from active participation in the supreme party organ during that tenure. The Dashnakts'akan parliamentary faction would discharge its organic duties without undue external interference, although it would admit the Bureau's right to enforce the decisions of the world congresses. While Ter Minasian criticized the cumbersome features of the scheme and protested that the parliamentary faction had essentially been given the power to neutralize the Bureau in the affairs of state, Khatisian and other champions of the distinction between party and government were gratified by the prospect of mutual cooperation rather than unilateral dictation.

Khatisian's Government

Under Alexander Khatisian's administration, Armenia remained beset by many serious problems. A disgruntled and impatient refugee population caused an enormous strain on the resources of the state. The bitter territorial disputes with Azerbaijan continued unabated, and, to make matters worse, a Muslim uprising within Armenia drove Armenian administrators and thousands of peasants out of Sharur and Nakhichevan and sealed the route to Persia. Under these circumstances, financial solvency was not possible. Expenditures exceeded income many times over. More than 70 percent of the outlay was allocated to the ministries of welfare, provisions, and military affairs – the agencies involved in sustaining the population rather than rebuilding the country. As unsecured paper money rolled off the press, inflation became rampant, and corruption was commonplace.

Since the peasantry of Armenia made up nearly 90 percent of the population, land reform and agrarian revival were of pressing importance.

The Dashnakts'ut'iwn had always advocated the right of the tillers to enjoy the benefit of their toil. Yet the legislation setting maximum limits to individual land ownership and requiring the breakup of the small number of large estates remained, with few exceptions, unimplemented. The peasantry fell deeper into debt and often prey to shrewd speculators. Khatisian's cabinet tried to deal with this situation by annulling the forced sales and establishing boards of conciliation to compensate the buyers, but significant progress in land reform was never achieved.

A slight revival of industrial output was registered by the end of 1919. Some 5,000 workers were employed in 300 small factories and 400 distilleries. Although the government's labor plank included guarantees against exploitation, harsh working conditions prevailed. The ministry of welfare and labor called attention to the violation of fair employment practices and ordered government inspectors to enforce the eight-hour workday, the prohibition of child labor, the set procedures for dismissal, and other laws designed to protect the workers. Owners and managers were to be warned that failure to comply with these regulations would result in fines and prison terms of up to six months. There is no evidence, however, that sentences of that type were ever imposed. Until 1920 labor unrest was limited to economic demands, which were usually couched in expression of patriotism and loyalty. The Dashnakts'ut'iwn tried to keep abreast of the movement by patronizing the professional unions, but it soon became apparent that some of the workers in the railway center at Alexandropol and in the post-telegraph union had been radicalized beyond the control of their union leaders.

The unremitting struggle for survival obscured most of the small, positive achievements in the Republic. Yet conditions had improved significantly. A thousand miles or about 1,500 kilometers of roads were in operation, several segments being upgraded for automobile traffic between Yerevan and the district towns, and hundreds of kilometers of telegraph lines were repaired and extended. The first intercity telephone link was opened with service between Yerevan and Etchmiadzin. The Armenian Railway Administration, which had begun to function in 1918 with 2 locomotives, 20 freight cars, and less than 10 kilometers of railroad track, had expanded to some 650 kilometers (400 miles), with 2 complete passenger trains, 32 locomotives, and some 500 freight cars and cisterns. Daily service was introduced on the Alexandropol-Kars and the Yerevan-Tiflis runs, and the volume of freight increased tenfold.

Unable to satisfy the land hunger, the agricultural administration was nonetheless one of the best staffed and organized departments of government. Functioning with divisions for agriculture, veterinary medicine, water resources, mountain resources, forestry, and state properties, the administration introduced a number of projects that would bring many long-range benefits if the Republic endured. Programs of horticultural instruction were developed; five field research stations and a school of agriculture were opened; a nationwide campaign of animal inoculation was launched and five of sixteen projected ambulatory stations were set up; breeding farms and model dairies were organized in Kars and Lori; workshops to manufacture simple farm implements were equipped; and a comprehensive study was commissioned with the goals of harnessing the Zangu (Hrazdan), Arpa, Kazakh, Garni, and Abaran rivers for hydroelectric energy and bringing an additional 200,000 hectares (500,000 acres) of land under cultivation. A state campaign to plant every field in 1920 resulted in the purchase and distribution of 65,000 tons of seed grain, which was sufficient to produce the largest wheat crop since the early years of the Great World War.

Small but significant gains were also registered in the other state ministries. Under the direction of the ministry of internal affairs, the municipal charters were liberalized and broad prerogatives were granted the city administrations in public works, enlightenment, local economy, and provisions. Rural self-administration through the medium of local and country assemblies (*zemstvo*) had long been an objective of nearly all liberal and revolutionary societies in the Caucasus, and after months of preparation the first elections for county assemblies were held in January 1920 in Yerevan, Etchmiadzin, and Alexandropol. In legal affairs, the ministry of justice had to begin the long process of reversing the deep-rooted popular aversion to the courts. Litigation in the Russian language, terrifying preliminary investigations, and the bleak prospect of gaining favorable decisions without influential intermediaries had kept most Armenians away from the courts. It was now necessary to nationalize the legal system and create a judicial hierarchy with courts of cassation and a supreme court. These had been organized by 1920, and in March, after weeks of preparation, Armenia's first trial by jury took place. The case was simple and the jury's verdict was swift in coming, but there was much ado about the event. The newspapers hailed it as a milestone in justice, and Prime Minister Khatisian spoke in the courtroom of its significance in the evolution of a democratic republic. The actual legal proceedings were awkward and even amusing, as the prosecutor, public defender, and judges of the tribunal groped for the proper Armenian legal terminology, but there was above all a sense of exhilaration. After centuries of submission to the courts and discriminatory regulations of alien governments, the Armenians had succeeded in introducing the jury system in their national language.

The ministry of education and culture was headed by Nikol Aghbalian, a man of boundless optimism who planned to replace the old-style parochial school system with compulsory five-year elementary education based on a progressive curriculum. While the existing harsh realities did not permit the enrollment of all school-age children in 1919-20, the 420 elementary schools had 38,000 pupils, and with the opening of new gymnasia at Yerevan, Alexandropol, Dilijan, and Karakilisa the number of secondary schools increased to twenty-two, with more than 5,000 students. Although these figures do not take into account the erratic operation or closure of some schools because of lack of heating fuel or because of requisitions for hospitals and orphanages, they nonetheless stand in sharp contrast with the previous year's statistics of 135 elementary and 10 secondary schools, with a combined enrollment of 14,000. Adult literacy classes and people's universities were opened in several cities, and in January 1920 the State University was inaugurated with much fanfare at Alexandropol, giving cause for new hope and celebration.

During the spring of 1920, Prime Minister Khatisian hoped to advance from the emergency measures needed to sustain a dependent population toward a program of national reconstruction. Negotiations with Boghos Nubar's envoys for a united Armenian government had not succeeded, so the various ministries were reorganized or expanded to prepare for the reconstruction campaign. Pending further negotiations and the formation of a new coalition government, all except the minister of military affairs and the state controller were Dashnakts'akan. Yet whatever the composition of the cabinet, Armenia could not achieve lasting independence without the help of a major power. The Armenian gaze remained fixed on the United States and the European Allied Powers.

Retreat of the West

Armenia's Western orientation was founded on the firm conviction that there was no other way to achieve a stable united state. But by the beginning of 1920, the West was in retreat. Despite its long record of humanitarian and religious involvement with the Armenians, the United States, after months of vacillation, finally rejected President Wilson's request to assume the Armenian mandate. The president had been tactless in dealing with the Republican majority in the Senate, which refused to ratify the German peace treaty, including the League of Nations Covenant and its regulations regarding the assumption of mandates. Instead, the United States extended diplomatic recognition to the Armenian republic in April 1920 and received Garegin Pasdermadjian (Armen Garo) as minister plenipotentiary.

Because of the Senate's rejection of the Versailles treaty and because the United States had not actually declared war on the Ottoman Empire, the Department of State gave notice to the Allied Powers that the United States would no longer participate in the Turkish peace settlement. Meanwhile, Turkophile sentiment began to resurface among European colonial and mercantile circles, which warned of the dire economic consequence of a drastic partition of the Ottoman Empire and of the unrest that such a measure would arouse in the Muslim-populated colonies of Great Britain and France. Jealous and suspicious of one another, the Allied governments were also individually torn by sharp internal division and dissension. In January 1920, for example, the Allied Supreme Council granted recognition to the three Transcaucasian republics as a reaction to the defeat of the Russian White Armies and the southward thrust of the Red Army. In that context, British Foreign Secretary Lord (George Nathaniel) Curzon won a decision to provide the Armenian army with surplus uniforms, equipment, and weapons, but the British War Office, headed by Winston Churchill, delayed delivery for more than six months in the belief that any matériel given the Armenians and Georgians would end up in Bolshevik or Turkish hands. Ironically, the War Office's calculated delays contributed in no small measure to the fulfillment of its own prophecy.

The European Allies worked on the Turkish settlement in London and at San Remo, Italy, from February through April 1920. The beginning of these meetings coincided with the receipt of alarming reports that the Armenians of Cilicia were again being massacred. Following the war, more than 150,000 Armenians had returned to the cities and villages of Cilicia, which was placed under French supervision. By the beginning of 1920, however, the Turkish Nationalist resistance movement had chosen this region for its first test of strength. The battle for the city of Marash culminated on February 10, 1920 with the withdrawal of the French garrison, the crazed Armenian flight into a raging blizzard that claimed thousands of lives, and the massacre or captivity of those unable to escape. The struggle for Cilicia would continue until 1922, when the Armenians were forced to abandon the Taurus and Amanus mountains and the great alluvial plain of Adana and pass into permanent exile.

The problems in Cilicia reinforced the view of the Allied leaders, that the new Armenian state should, in the interest of the Armenians themselves, be awarded territories that could be readily defended and where the Armenians could attain a majority within a few years. Hence, Armenian pretensions to Cilicia and the western half of Turkish Armenia could not be accepted. Rather, the new united Armenian state should extend only into the three easternmost Ottoman provinces of Van, Bitlis, and Erzerum, with an outlet on the Black Sea. The Allies took no action on the many petitions by Armenians and their supporters to include at least the region of Kharpert (Harput) and even expressed grave misgivings about awarding the city and fortress of Erzerum to Armenia.

In their halfhearted attempts to draw an Armenian boundary without having to commit armed forces to implement their decision, the Allied leaders struck upon a clever way out of the dilemma. At Prime Minister Lloyd George's suggestion, they invited President Wilson to draw the final boundaries within the limits of the provinces of Van, Bitlis, Erzerum, and Trebizond. The strategy was intended to coax the United States back into the perplexing Armenian settlement and to shift some of the responsibility for future developments on to the shoulders of the American president. Wilson took the bait and agreed to appoint a commission to draw Armenia's boundaries within the specified limits. Thus, the European Allies were able to announce to the world that they had fulfilled their solemn pledges to the Armenian people.

When the Treaty of Peace with the Ottoman Empire was finally signed at Sèvres on August 10, 1920, the Turkish government committed itself to accept the boundary that President Wilson would lay down within the four provinces. Turkey also recognized Armenia as an independent, sovereign state and accepted the obligation to assist in the repatriation and restoration of the Armenian survivors, the rescue of Armenian women and children still held in Muslim households, and the prosecution of the perpetrators of the Armenian atrocities. Avetis Aharonian, as the delegate of the Republic of Armenia, was a signatory to the treaty, and both he and Boghos Nubar signed an additional protocol guaranteeing religious, cultural, and other freedoms to Armenia's minorities.

As a signatory to the Treaty of Sèvres, Armenia received formal diplomatic recognition of all other signatory states. Moreover, in the Western Hemisphere, Argentina, Brazil, and Chile joined the United States in granting recognition. Armenian legations or diplomatic personnel operated in London, Paris, Rome, Brussels, Berlin, Belgrade, Bucharest, Sofia, Athens, and Constantinople; in Tehran, Tabriz, Baghdad, Djibouti, and Addis Ababa; in Tiflis, Baku, Batum, Sukhum, Vladikavkaz, Rostov-on-Don, and other parts of the former Russian Empire; and in Harbin and Yokohama. The assimilated communities of Central and Eastern Europe stirred with renewed consciousness and sent representatives to Yerevan to explore the possibility of returning to the homeland after centuries in the dispersion. If Armenia could endure as an independent state, a reversal of the unceasing tides of exodus could bring back hundreds of thousands of partially assimilated Armenians living on five continents.

It was not until November 1920 that President Wilson finally submitted his commission's decision on the Armenian boundaries. "Wilsonian Armenia" was to encompass most of Van, Bitlis, and Erzerum, with exclusion of the southernmost and westernmost sectors for ethnographic, economic, and geographic reasons. The city and port of Trebizond were added to Armenia along with much of the coast of Lazistan to the east to give the Republic a broad outlet to the sea. A viable, united Armenian state had been created – at least on paper. For the Armenians, it was sad and bitterly ironic that Wilson's decision was relayed to the Allied governments in Europe at a time that the Republic of Armenia was waging a losing struggle to preserve its very existence.

Soviet-Turkish Relations and Armenia

While the Allied Powers proceeded with plans to partition the Ottoman Empire without facing up to the fact that military enforcement of the terms would be required, Mustafa Kemal (Atatürk) and other Turkish resistance leaders sought Soviet support in the struggle against the common adversaries. Soviet leaders, in their turn, recognized the potential role that Turkish influence could play in stirring the Muslim colonial world against the Western powers and thereby saving the Bolshevik revolution and Soviet state. Preliminary contact had already been made through the deposed Young Turk fugitives who had found haven in Germany, Russia, and the Caucasus. Although Mustafa Kemal regarded the Young Turk clique headed by Enver and Talaat as political rivals, he did not hesitate to use their good offices in efforts to draw Soviet Russia into the Turkish struggle for political survival. Mustafa Kemal and General Kiazim Karabekir, the commander of the XV Army Corps at Erzerum, also dispatched their own agents to contact the Bolshevik underground in Baku with the goal of forming a land bridge between Russia and Turkey. This was to be achieved by placing Azerbaijan in the Soviet sphere, neutralizing Georgia, and crushing Armenia. In Azerbaijan, the dominant Musavat party aspired to national independence but was not immune to Turkish pressure and prestige. Several thousand Turkish officers and civilians served in that republic as military cadre, administrators, and police officials. Moreover, Young Turk fugitives such as Khalil (Halil) Pasha and Nuri Pasha (Enver's uncle and half-brother respectively) were treated as honored guests. They were to play a significant role in the sovietization of Azerbaijan.

In April 1920, immediately after the Turkish Nationalists had organized in Ankara (Angora) a counter-government to that of the sultan in Constantinople, Mustafa Kemal acknowledged Soviet Russia as the champion of colonial peoples and gave assurances of Turkish support against the imperialist powers. He wrote Foreign Affairs Commissar Grigorii Chicherin that once Russia had gained sway over Georgia and brought about the expulsion of the last remaining British garrison at Batum, the Turkish Nationalists would begin military operations against "the imperialist Armenian government" and exert pressure on Azerbaijan to enter the Soviet state brotherhood. To hasten effective collaboration, Soviet Russia should supply arms, food, technical assistance, and financial aid, including an initial shipment of 5 million gold liras.

Events were already unfolding swiftly in Transcaucasia. Soviet Russia, having overpowered General A. I. Denikin and his Volunteer Army in the Russian civil war, had reached the flanks of the Caucasus Mountains and now gave orders to capture the rich oil fields of Baku and to sovietize Azerbaijan. The Red Army advanced across the frontier on the night of April 27, 1920, and by dawn the first echelons had entered Baku in a near-bloodless coup. Armenian reaction to Azerbaijan's sovietization was not all unfavorable. In fact, many Armenians welcomed the change, reasoning that the Christian minority in the southeastern Caucasus area would be safer under any form of Russian rule than under the Turkic Musavat regime. Some Armenian officials even believed that the Soviet leaders could be persuaded that a united, independent Armenia would be in the best interest of Russia itself. An Armenian mission departed for Moscow on April 30 to propose a treaty of friendship based on Soviet recognition of the independence of the Armenian republic, inclusive of Karabagh, Zangezur, and Nakhichevan; acceptance in principle of the goal of a united Armenian state; and permission for thousands of Armenian refugees in Russia to emigrate with all their movable belongings to the Caucasus.

The three-member delegation of Levon Shant, Hambardzum Terterian, and Levon Zarafian arrived in Moscow on May 20 and soon began discussions with Foreign Affairs Commissar Chicherin and Assistant Commissar Lev Karakhan (an Armenian). The two officials gave assurances that Soviet Russia had no desire to subvert the Armenian government and would assent to the transfer of the refugees to Armenia. The Armenian republic, they agreed, should include the disputed territories of Zangezur and Nakhichevan, while the fate of Karabagh could be decided through arbitration or plebiscite. Armenia, on the other hand, should recognize the need of Soviet Russia and Nationalist Turkey to collaborate against the Western imperialists and should desist from any measure that might hinder communication and cooperation between the two revolutionary movements. Chicherin implied that at least a part of Western Armenia should be included in the Armenian republic and offered Soviet mediation in bringing about an equitable settlement with the Turkish Nationalists. Encouraged by the cordial reception and swift pace of the discussions, the Shant delegation wired the Yerevan government on June 10 that agreement in principle had been reached on the major issues and all that remained was the need to work out the details and give substance to the treaty.

The anticipated treaty, however, did not materialize. The delay of a positive response from Yerevan may have been attributable to difficulties in communication but possibly also to the Armenian government's concern that the premature announcement of a friendship treaty with Soviet Russia might adversely affect the disposition of the Allied Powers, which had recently determined that the Armenian republic should be awarded much of the Ottoman eastern provinces. But there was more to the Soviet decision to interrupt the negotiations and insist upon their continuation in Yerevan. A Turkish Nationalist delegation was en route from Ankara with proposals for a Soviet-Turkish alliance, the new Soviet Azerbaijani government bitterly opposed any modus vivendi that would give Nakhichevan, Zangezur, and possibly even Mountainous Karabagh to Armenia, and Armenian Bolsheviks such as Anastas Mikoyan and Avis Nurijanian had intensified their denunciations of the Yerevan government before the party leaders in Moscow. A bloody Dashnakts'akan reign of terror, the Caucasian comrades claimed, had been unleashed against Bolsheviks and their sympathizers who had supported an abortive coup d'état known as the May rebellion. The subject of extensive literature, intense controversy, and significant historical re-evaluation, the May uprising turned the Armenian government toward dictatorial power.

The May Uprising and Bureau Government

The splintering of the South Caucasus into three independent states in 1918 weakened and undermined the Bolshevik organizations in the region. The nationality question added to the dissension within the ranks, but finally the Baku comrades took the lead in concluding that the best way to break the grip of the dominant anti-Bolshevik parties was to accommodate national sentiment by calling for the creation of Soviet republics federated with Russia. Most veteran Bolsheviks in Georgia and Armenia, having denounced Musavat, Menshevik, and hated Dashnak separatism, rejected the proposal as an unorthodox ideological deviation. But in the end even Lenin concurred that revolutionary work in the de facto border states would be facilitated through advocacy of separate Soviet republics and even separate national party organizations joined at the regional level as affiliates of the Russian Communist party.

In contrast with Azerbaijan, Armenia had no significant proletariat or any of the objective conditions considered prerequisites for a Marxist revolution. The country was overwhelmingly agrarian and had been so terribly devastated that even veteran Bolsheviks such Arshavir Melikian argued that, instead of militant revolutionary activity, there should be a long period of peaceful agitation and education of the masses. While the younger Communists repudiated their teachers and demanded the immediate overthrow of the "Dashnak lackeys of imperialism," Bolshevism did not gain a significant following in Armenia before 1920. In fact, when the Georgian Mensheviks cracked down on their Marxist Bolshevik competitors, the Armenian government granted haven to many Armenian Communists and provided them employment as teachers and civil servants. This influx in 1919, together with the efforts of professional cadre sent by the party's regional committee, produced a loose organizational network, with the auto and rail garages in Alexandropol becoming the most active links. Still, at the end of the year, there were according to Soviet statistics fewer than 500 Bolsheviks in all Armenia. During the first party conference at Yerevan in January 1920, the twenty-two participants restructured the Armenia Committee (*Armenkom*) of the Russian Communist party and charged it with the responsibility of coordinating preparatory measure for the eventual seizure of power. Resolutions and exhortations aside, most local Bolsheviks continued to believe that success could be achieved only with the supportive active intervention of the Red Army. The Armenkom's own behavior between January and May reflected this attitude, in deed if not in word.

The sovietization of Azerbaijan in late April and the approach of the Red Army toward the Armenian frontiers excited and emboldened the Bolsheviks. By that time some elements of the army and citizenry had been radicalized because of the Allied failure to extend measurable political and military support, the inability of the government to meet the basic needs of the populace, the repressive actions of partisan bands, and the general fatigue of many Eastern Armenians and their yearning for a return to normalcy under the accustomed wing of Russia. During the May Day celebrations in Yerevan in 1920, the Dashnakts'akan-organized rallies were countered by Bolshevik orators and marchers, while in Alexandropol a public gathering turned into an angry manifestation of anti-Dashnakts'akan and anti-government sentiment. Securing the neutrality or tacit sympathy of the local army garrison, the Alexandropol Bolsheviks seized the railway station on May 2 and organized the Revolutionary Committee of Armenia (*Revkom*) there five days later. Then, on May 10, the Revkom declared Armenia a Soviet republic and the "Dashnak government of mauserist and imperialist speculators" liquidated.

Disturbances of lesser proportions and shorter durations also occurred at Sarikamish, Kars, Dilijan, Nor-Bayazit (Gavar), and several other towns and villages. Yet the conspirators did not act with the requisite resolve and aggressiveness. The Armenkom in Yerevan was caught off guard by the Alexandropol rising and failed to respond decisively to the unexpected situation. Even the more militant Revkom assumed a basically defensive stance, not venturing out of its armored-train headquarters or taking advantage of the friendly disposition of the Russian Molokan and Muslim villages around Alexandropol. The inability of either the Armenkom or the Revkom to provide clear direction and to capitalize on the temporary confusion of the government made suppression of the movement inevitable. On the night of May 13/14, loyal troops and Western Armenian partisan units moved into Alexandropol, dispersing the Revkom. Several rebel leaders were killed, and many more fled to Baku. But the Armenian Bolsheviks had received their baptism of fire and offered up a small pantheon of martyrs, memorialized in Soviet literature and monuments.

The May rebellion resulted in widespread demoralization within the country and the loss of trust and prestige abroad. The gradualist, evolutionary policies of Alexander Khatisian had been discredited, and on May 5 his cabinet was replaced by the entire Bureau of the party Dashnakts'ut'iwn:

Positions	Name
Prime Minister and Foreign Affairs	Hamazasp Ohanjanian
Internal Affairs and Military Affairs	Ruben Ter Minasian
Financial Affairs and Judicial Affairs	Abraham Giulkhandanian
Communications	Arshak Jamalian
Agriculture-State Properties and Labor	Simon Vratsian
Education and Culture	Gevorg Ghazarian
Welfare and Reconstruction	Sargis Araratian

The Bureau justified its violation of the restrictions imposed upon it by the party's world congress on grounds that the very existence of the Republic was at stake. The loyalty of all non-Bolshevik parties during the uprising and the spirit of unity during the celebrations marking the Republic's second anniversary on May 28 strengthened the Bureau's position. During the summer of 1920, Ohanjanian's Bureau-Government drove the Bolsheviks underground or out of the country and turned the regular army and Western Armenian detachments against the constantly defiant Muslim-populated districts from Zangibasar and Vedibasar in the vicinity of Yerevan to Sharur and the lower Araxes River Valley. The triumphant sweep to the south, after two years of a policy of containment, vindicated Ruben Ter Minasian's position in the eyes of many previous skeptics. But if patriotic dictatorship was the answer to Armenia's crises, there was not to be enough time to prove the point.

The strain in Armenian-Soviet relations after the May rebellion contributed to the interruption of the negotiations in Moscow. At the beginning of July, Chicherin informed Levon Shant that Boris V. Legran, an official of the foreign affairs commissariat, was assigned to resume the parleys in Yerevan and to do whatever possible to resolve the disputes between Armenia and its neighbors. Legran soon entrained for Baku, accompanied by Khalil Pasha, who had been pleading the Turkish Nationalist cause in Moscow and was returning with a large Soviet consignment of gold to be delivered for Mustafa Kemal in Anatolia. It was not until early August 1920 that Shant's delegation was able to procure transportation to the south and not until mid-September that the Armenian envoys returned at last to Yerevan. Meanwhile, critical Soviet-Turkish negotiations were being conducted in Moscow.

A Draft Soviet-Turkish Treaty

Mustafa Kemal and other Nationalist leaders were gratified by the Soviet disposition to extend military and financial assistance but were wary of the political ramifications. While Chicherin's messages praised the heroic Turkish struggle for independence and welcomed cooperation against the imperialist powers, they also implied that the fate of areas of mixed Armenian, Kurdish, Laz, and Turkish habitation in the eastern Ottoman provinces should be regulated on the basis of the prewar population and the principle of self-determination, taking into account all those people who had been forced to flee. The Soviet government was prepared to serve as a mediator in attaining a just and equitable boundary settlement between Turkey, Armenia, and Persia. In May, a Turkish Nationalist delegation headed by Foreign Affairs Commissar Bekir Sami Bey departed for Moscow to deal with such complications and, more important, to formalize relations and hasten the shipment of desperately needed arms and currency.

During the negotiations, which began shortly after Bekir Sami's arrival on July 19, 1920, Chicherin and Karakhan readily offered Soviet military and financial aid and concurred that a land bridge between Russia and Turkey should be created quickly. Karakhan revealed that the Eleventh Red Army was already under orders to occupy the Karabagh-Nakhichevan corridor. The Soviet officials nonetheless urged the Ankara government to resolve the Armenian Question, which had roused worldwide concern, by assenting to a frontier rectification that would give the Armenians the districts of Van, Bitlis, and Mush and, on the other hand, would allow Turkey to occupy the strategic mountain passes near Sarikamish on the former Russian side of the frontier. A mixed commission could determine the exact boundaries and facilitate the work of repatriation and any exchanges of population. Adamantly refusing to make territorial concessions for promises of material assistance, Bekir Sami agreed only to apprize his government of Chicherin's suggestions. He maintained that Soviet aid should be dispatched immediately as a sign of good faith and that a preliminary treaty on non-territorial issues should be concluded. This position was supported both by Soviet leaders Stalin, who was unsympathetic toward the Armenian case, and by Lenin, whose main concerns at that time were the difficulties on the Crimean and Polish fronts and the broader question of relations with the West.

Hence, on August 24, 1920, just two weeks after the sultan's plenipotentiaries in Paris had signed the Treaty of Sèvres, which required Turkey to recognize the independence of Armenia and to cede to it most of the eastern border provinces, a draft Soviet-Turkish Nationalist accord was initialed in Moscow. All previous treaties between Russia and Turkey were declared null and void, Russia would decline to recognize any international act not ratified by the Ankara government, and both sides were to make every effort to open an unobstructed avenue between the two countries for the flow of men and matériel. Other provisions related to trade and transit, the status of nationals of one country living in the other, and future diplomatic relations. Separate protocols on Soviet military and economic aid were also drafted. Yusuf Kemal (Tengirşenk), a member of the Turkish delegation, carried the treaty, together with the initial consignment of a promised 5 million gold rubles, to Trebizond. From that Black Sea port, he wired the terms to Ankara on September 18. In their reports to Mustafa Kemal, Bekir Sami, and Yusuf Kemal drew attention to the reserved attitude of Chicherin and Karakhan but added that Lenin was sympathetic and had given the impression that Russia would soon assume a more aggressive role in the Caucasus. Two days after receiving the terms of the draft treaty, Mustafa Kemal authorized XV Army Corps commander General Kiazim Karabekir to begin the offensive against Armenia. This was the theater chosen by the Nationalist leaders to impress upon the world their adamant rejection of the Treaty of Sèvres.

The Armeno-Turkish War

The Turkish armies captured the strategic border posts and Sarikamish by the end of September and then advanced in the direction of Kars. According to military specialists, the mighty fortress city could withstand a lengthy siege but in one of the worst military fiascos in Armenian history, Kars fell amid uncontrollable panic and desertion on October 30, 1920. The Armenian will to resist had been broken, and by November 6 the Turks had advanced into Alexandropol, forcing Ohanjanian's government to accept a truce based on the Brest-Litovsk boundaries and permitting temporary Turkish occupation of Alexandropol and its environs. Additional Turkish demands on November 8 for the surrender of large quantities of arms and matériel and for control of the entire railway from Alexandropol to Julfa elicited a final desperate defense effort, but within a week Armenia was compelled to submit. Alexander Khatisian departed for Alexandropol on November 23 to begin negotiations with Karabekir Pasha for what no one doubted would be a crushing Armeno-Turkish treaty of peace.

Despite the need for a Russo-Turkish alliance, the Soviet government viewed the Turkish offensive with apprehension and tried unsuccessfully to halt the fighting through its good offices. The resulting friction did not obscure the desirability for cooperation with Turkey, however, and preparations to dispatch additional arms and money to Anatolia were not interrupted. Meanwhile, two weeks after the Turkish offensive had begun, Boris Legran and his Soviet mission were finally received in Yerevan on October 11.

Conditions had changed so drastically that Legran now called upon the Armenian government to renounce the Sèvres treaty, permit the free movement of men and supplies between Turkey and Soviet Russia and Azerbaijan, and seek Russian mediation in the conflict with Turkey. The Red Army, Legran urged, should be invited to protect the country. Unwilling to turn away from the long-sought European solution to the Armenian question or to condone foreign military occupation, Ohanjanian's cabinet nonetheless did accept the offer of friendly intercession. Moreover, according to terms of a draft treaty concluded by Legran and Shant on October 28, Soviet Russia was to relinquish all sovereign rights over the former Russian Armenian provinces and influence Turkey to bring about the union of a part of Western Armenia with the Armenian republic. The status of Mountainous Karabagh, Zangezur, and Nakhichevan was to be settled by mutual concessions or plebiscite. Russia was to have free transit privileges through Armenia and, if Zangezur and Nakhichevan were awarded to Armenia, was to be granted telegraph, radio, and other facilities to maintain communication with friendly or allied governments. When Legran put the draft treaty before the Communist party's Caucasian Bureau (*Kavburo*) in Baku in early November, serious objections and reservations were expressed. Since Kars had now fallen to the Turkish army and there was no time for consultations in Moscow, Boris Legran returned to Yerevan to demand Armenia's sovietization. Georgian comrade Budu Mdivani accompanied him to serve as the Soviet mediator in the Armenian-Turkish conflict, but General Karabekir summarily rejected any such attempted intercession.

Sovietization and Peace

Defeated and discredited, Armenia's Bureau-Government gave way on November 23, 1920 to a cabinet headed by party stalwart and former cabinet member Simon Vratsian, who was thought to be more acceptable to the Soviet leadership. To that last cabinet fell the heavy obligation to conclude peace and preserve the physical existence of the Armenian people at almost any price. Only the Socialist Revolutionary party agreed to enter a coalition government at that grave moment:

Positions	Name
Prime Minister, Foreign Affairs and interim Internal Affairs	Simon Vratsian
Military Affairs	Dro (Drastamat Kanayan)
Agriculture and State Properties	Arshak Hovhannisian
Financial Affairs and interim Welfare	Hambardzum Terterian
Judicial Affairs and interim Commercial Affairs	Arsham Khondkarian
Education and Culture	Vahan Minakhorian

For a few days, Vratsian tried to persuade Legran that sovietization would invite greater tragedy, since Armenia would be blockaded by still-independent Georgia and deprived of external economic aid at a time when Russia itself was gripped by famine. Renunciation of the Sèvres treaty, moreover, would be tantamount to a sentence of death on the Armenian question, bringing to naught the untold sacrifices in the national movement for emancipation. On November 30, 1920, Legran announced that the decision to sovietize Armenia was irreversible. He demanded that Armenia break all bonds with the Western imperialist powers and unite with the Russian workers and peasants. A few Armenian Bolsheviks had already crossed the frontier on November 29 from Azerbaijan into Karvansarai (Ijevan), where they proclaimed Armenia a Soviet republic and appealed for the intervention of the Red Army.

In these circumstances, Vratsian's government bowed to the inevitable and appointed Dro and Hambardzum Terterian to arrange for the transfer of power. The treaty signed by Legran and the Armenian representatives on December 2, 1920 gave some ground for hope. Armenia became an independent Socialist Soviet Republic, and Soviet Russia acknowledged as indisputable parts of that state all territories that had been under the jurisdiction of the Armenian government prior to the Turkish invasion, Zangezur included. Russia was to take immediate steps to furnish the requisite military force to consolidate and defend the Republic. Neither the army command nor members of the Dashnakts'ut'iwn and other socialist parties were to be persecuted for their previous anti-Soviet activities. Power would pass temporarily to a military revolutionary committee composed of five members appointed by the Communist party and two left-wing Dashnakts'akan members, selected with the approval of the Communist party. Until that body was organized, the government would be entrusted to Dro, the military commander, and to Otto A. Silin, the plenipotentiary of Soviet Russia. For the government of independent Armenia, all that remained was to issue its final decree:

> In view of the general situation in the land created by
> external circumstances, the Government of the Republic of
> Armenia, in its session of December 2, 1920, decided to resign
> from office and to relinquish all military and political authority
> to Dro, the commander in chief, now appointed as minister of
> war.

The announcement of Armenia's sovietization did not remove the Turkish menace, since General Karabekir threatened to resume the offensive unless his government's peace terms were accepted forthwith. Those terms obliged Armenia to renounce the Treaty of Sèvres and all claims to Turkish Armenia and the province of Kars, to accept temporary Turkish jurisdiction in Sharur-Nakhichevan, to recall all representatives from Europe until the Ankara government had settled its differences with those adversary states, and to reduce the size of the Armenian army to 1,500 men. In case of need, Turkey would extend military assistance to the remaining small Armenian state. Only after all these terms had been fulfilled would the Turkish army withdraw from the Alexandropol region and establish the Arpachai (Akhurian) River as the new international boundary. Even though the Armenian government had officially relinquished power, Khatisian signed the Treaty of Alexandropol (Gümrü) shortly after midnight on December 2-3, 1920. Denounced and branded a traitor by Soviet and other non-Dashnakts'akan authors, Khatisian justified his action as an exigency measure taken with the knowledge of the new Yerevan Soviet caretaker administration and intended to give time for the Red Army to enter Armenia in sufficient numbers to block a further Turkish advance. Realizing that he had no legal jurisdiction, Khatisian hoped that the new Soviet government, with the support of Russia, would repudiate his action and force the Turks to withdraw at least to the prewar boundaries. As it turned out, these calculations proved ill-founded. The efforts of the Soviet Armenian government to recover a part of the lost territories were supported only with mild diplomatic notes by Soviet Russia, which proceeded toward normalization of relations with the Ankara government by reneging on most of its pledges regarding Armenia.

The Aftermath

The Military Revolutionary Committee of Armenia arrived in Yerevan on December 4, 1920, followed two days later by the first echelons of the Red Army. The Revkom, dominated by young, vindictive Bolsheviks, immediately repudiated the treaty negotiated between Legran and the former Armenian government on December 2 and initiated an aggressive course of War Communism. Hundreds of former government officials and non-Bolshevik political leaders were imprisoned, the army officer corps was exiled, and a harsh regime of retribution and requisition was imposed. These oppressive policies, coupled with the trenchant anti-Russian and anti-Bolshevik sentiment of the Western Armenian refugee population and the collusion of some Dashnakts'akan partisan leaders, produced a surge of rebellion in February 1921. The Revkom was driven out of Yerevan and a Salvation Committee was swiftly organized under Simon Vratsian's presidency to coordinate the movement sweeping the countryside.

Not until the Republic of Georgia had been sovietized in March 1921 were sufficient Red Army reinforcements brought in to suppress the Armenian revolt. In April the Salvation Committee and thousands of insurgents and civilians withdrew into Zangezur, where the battle was continued under the command of Colonel Garegin Nzhdeh until a reorganized Soviet Armenian government issued an amnesty and gave assurances that Zangezur would become a permanent part of Soviet Armenia. Lenin had already chided his Caucasian comrades for their overzealousness and advised that conditions in the local republics necessitated a "slower, more careful, and more systematic transition to socialism." Alexander Miasnikian, a trusted veteran party professional, was transferred from the European theater to head the Armenian government. In July 1921, as Miasnikian began to implement the more cautious measures of the New Economic Policy (NEP), thousands of anti-Bolshevik rebels and bewildered civilians crossed the Araxes River into Persia to begin the bitter life reserved for expatriates and exiles.

On the international front, Soviet Russia sacrificed the Armenian question to cement the Turkish alliance. Having rejected all attempts at mediation, Mustafa Kemal even made a ploy to occupy Batum and the border districts of Akhaltsikh (Akhaltskha) and Akhalkalak in Georgia. The maneuver, apparently intended to win additional concessions regarding Armenia, bore results. By the Treaty of Moscow (March 1921), which established normal relations and friendship between Soviet Russia and the Ankara government, Turkey dropped its claims to Batum and the other districts in return for Russian abandonment of efforts to redeem for Soviet Armenia the Surmalu district of Yerevan. In that sector, the new Turkish boundary was extended to the Araxes River, thus incorporating the fertile Igdir plain and emblematic Mount Ararat. What was more, the treaty provided that Sharur-Nakhichevan would not be attached to Soviet

Armenia but would instead be constituted as an autonomous region under Soviet Azerbaijan, even though it was separated from the eastern Caucasus by intervening Armenian territory. Whatever qualms Chicherin and Karakhan might still have had were sublimated to the decisive support the Turkish delegation received from Stalin. As stipulated in the Treaty of Moscow, almost identical terms were included in the Treaty of Kars (October 1921) between Turkey and the three Transcaucasian Soviet republics – Armenia, Azerbaijan, Georgia. Described by a Soviet historian later purged by Stalin as one of the most oppressive and ignominious treaties in the annals of history, that document clamped the lid on the Armenian question and locked Soviet Armenia within its limited, landlocked territory. The European Powers put their own seal on the Armenian question two years later by renegotiating the Treaty of Sèvres. The Turkish victory in the resultant Lausanne treaties was so thorough that neither the word "Armenia" nor "Armenian" was allowed to appear anywhere in the texts. It was bitterly ironic for the Armenians that, of the several defeated Central Powers in World War I, Turkey alone expanded beyond its prewar boundaries and this, only on the Armenian front.

The interlude of Armenian independence had ended. Born of desperation and hopelessness, the Armenian republic lacked the resources to solve its awesome domestic and international problems. Yet within a few months it had become the fulcrum of national aspirations for revival, unification, and perpetuity. Limitations and shortcomings aside, the rudiments of government were created and organic development did occur. The failure to achieve permanent independence left a worldwide Armenian dispersion with unrequited grief, frustration, and resentment. Nonetheless, the legacy of the Armenian republic was not lost. Armenian governance and statehood had been recovered for the first time in centuries. The staggering Armenian sacrifices had not been entirely in vain, for the core of the Republic of Armenia continued as the Armenian Soviet Socialist Republic and then since 1991 as the new independent Armenian republic, where a part of the nation would strive to etch its place in the sun.

The following select sources were used for this survey:

Aftandilian, Gregory. *Armenia. Vision of a Republic: The Independence Lobby in America, 1918-1927.* Boston, 1981.

Avalashvili [Avalov], Zourab. *The Independence of Georgia in International Politics, 1918-1921.* London, 1940.

Baldwin, Oliver. *Six Prisons and Two Revolutions.* London, 1926.

Barton, James L. *Story of Near East Relief (1915-1930).* New York, 1930.

Bedoukian, Kerop. *Some of Us Survived: The Story of an Armenian Boy.* New York, 1978.

Borian, B.A. *Armeniia, mezhdunarodnaia diplomatiia i SSSR,* 2 vols. Moscow-Leningrad, 1928-1929.

Çebesoy, Ali Fuat. *Moskova hâtıraları (21/11/1920-2/6/1922).* Istanbul, 1955.

Elliot, Mabel E. *Beginning Again at Ararat.* New York, 1924.

Eudin, Xenia Joukoff and Robert C. North. *Soviet Russia and the East, 1920-1927: A Documentary Survey.* Stanford, 1957.

Gidney, James B. *A Mandate for Armenia.* Kent, Ohio, 1967.

Great Britain. Foreign Office. *Documents on British Foreign Policy, 1919-1939,* 1st series, eds. W.L. Woodward, Rohan Butler, J.P.T. Bury et al., 27 vols. London, 1947-1970.

Helmreich, Paul C. *From Paris to Sèvres: The Partition of the Ottoman Empire at the Peace Conference of 1919-1920.* Columbus, Ohio, 1974.

Hovannisian, Richard G. *Armenia on the Road to Independence, 1918.* Berkeley, Los Angeles, London, 1967.

_____. *The Republic of Armenia,* 4 vols. Berkeley, Los Angeles, London, 1971-1996.

Karabekir, Kâzim. *İstiklâl Harbimiz.* Istanbul, 1960.

Kazemzadeh, Firuz. *The Struggle for Transcaucasia (1917-1921).* New York and Oxford, 1951.

Kerr, Stanley E. *The Lions of Marash.* Albany, New York, 1973.

Khatisian, Al. *Hayastani Hanrapetut'ean dzagumn u zargatsume.* Athens, 1930.

Nassibian, Akaby. *Britain and the Armenian Question, 1915-1923.* London and New York, 1984.

Parti Ouvrier Social-Démocrate de Géorgie: *La Géorgie Indépendante.* Geneva, 1919.

Pipes, Richard. *The Formation of the Soviet Union: Communism and Nationalism, 1917-1923,* rev. ed. Cambridge, Massachusetts, 1964.

Ross, Frank A., Luther C. Fry, and Elbridge Sibley. *The Near East and American Philanthropy: A Survey Conducted under the Guidance of the General Committee of the Near East Survey.* New York, 1929.

Surface, Frank M. and Raymond L. Bland. *American Food in the World War and Reconstruction Period.* Stanford, 1931.

Swietochowski, Tadeusz. *Russian Azerbaijan, 1905-1920: The Shaping of National Identity in a Muslim Community.* Cambridge, London, New York, 1985.

Tengirşenk, Yusuf Kemal. *Vatan hizmetinde.* Istanbul, 1967.

United States, Department of State. *Papers Relating to the Foreign Relations of the United States: The Paris Peace Conference,* 13 vols. Washington, D.C., 1942-1947.

Vratsian, S. *Hayastani Hanrapetut'iwn.* Paris, 1928 (2nd ed., Beirut, 1958).

Walker, Christopher. *Armenia: Survival of a Nation.* New York, 1980.

From Nationalist-Socialist to National Socialist? The Shifting Politics of Abraham Giulkhandanian

Houri Berberian

In 1905, at his trial for anti-militarist activities, French socialist August Hervé uttered these biting words: "For you, the country is a mother; for us, it is a cruel stepmother, a shrew whom we detest."[1] His staunchly anti-nationalist creed made no allowance for a motherland (or fatherland). By 1912, however, Hervé had made an about-face and had embraced the nation, an "authoritarian domestic programme," as well as traditional Catholicism.[2] Addressing charges of betrayal by former comrades, he exclaimed, "I am persuaded that it is not I who has changed, but the circumstances." Hervé's account of his transformation to a nationalist – perhaps even fascist – after serving years in prison was an attempt to explain what his contemporaries and ardently socialist and antimilitarist former peers considered cruel duplicity. Paul Miller asks, "How had the circumstances changed, and for whom? The nationalist revival; the realization that the Germans would not follow an insurrectional movement initiated by France; and the CGT's [Confédération Générale du Travail, France's national trade union] declining strength certainly had an impact. Yet many hardened revolutionaries forged ahead with their antimilitarist doctrines and resented Hervé's 'betrayal.'"[3]

---

* My sincere gratitude to Sebouh Aslanian and Talinn Grigor for their close reading and feedback.

[1] For an English translation of Hervé's speech, see "Anti-patriotism," 1906, https://www.marxists.org/archive/herve/1905/anti-patriotism.htm. (Accessed May 1, 2019).

[2] Michael B. Loughlin, "Gustave Hervé's Transition from Socialism to National Socialism: Another Example of French Fascism?" *Journal of Contemporary History* 36, no. 1 (Jan. 2001): 12, 25. See also idem, *From Revolutionary Theater to Reactionary Litanies: Gustave Hervé (1871-1944) at the Extremes of the French Third Republic* (New York: Peter Lang, 2016).

[3] Paul B. Miller, *From Revolutionaries to Citizens: Antimilitarism in France, 1870–1914* (Durham: Duke University Press, 2004), 192. According to Loughlin,

At first glance, it would seem that the Armenian revolutionary Abraham Giulkhandanian (1875-1946) had a similar reversal.[4] (Fig. 1) While he had strong nationalist-socialist and revolutionary credentials in the early twentieth century as a leftist member and leader of the Armenian Revolutionary Federation (ARF), the revolutionary became a statesman in the First Republic (1918-1920), serving as parliamentarian, Minister of Internal Affairs, and Minister of Justice. In 1920, moreover, Giulkhandanian was part of the delegation that – under duress – signed the agreement that ended the experiment of the first independent Republic and ushered in the next seventy years of Soviet rule. Arriving in Paris before WWII as an émigré, the revolutionary turned statesman went through yet another transformation as vice-president of the Armenisches Nationales Gremium (ANG/Armenian National Committee),[5] which collaborated with Germany's national socialist Nazi authorities against the Soviet Union.

Given these shifting, radical political allegiances within the broader context of a polarized world, crucial questions arise. What do fluctuating ideologies or political allegiances signify? How are we to make sense of such variations? What historical and structural reasons propel historical actors to shift alliances? More specifically, why does Giulkhandanian seem to change, especially from nationalist-socialist revolutionary to national socialist collaborator? Could it be because of personal advancement and opportunism? Could it be ideological? Or like Hervé, could it have been a matter of a change in circumstances? Much of the rather small literature on the subject whether scholarly or popular has been concerned with either casting blame or exonerating Giulkhandanian and other members of the ARF who formed the ANG and cooperated with the Nazis.[6] This essay is interested in neither simplistic approach. Instead, by exploring the complex and ostensibly contradictory figure of Abraham Giulkhandanian – revolutionary, statesman, and collaborator – the essay

---

after WWI, Hervé "explain[ed] his transition" by emphasizing "how the war had destroyed his naivete." Loughlin, "Gustave Hervé's Transition," 17.

[4] Giulkhandanian had a number of pseudonyms, including Abro, Abramovich, Ruben (also his son's name), and Sevian. His name in English appears in a variety of spellings as well; for example, Gulkhandanian and Kiulkhandanian.

[5] Armenisches Nationales Gremium has also been translated as Armenian National Council.

[6] Vahe Sahakyan is an exception. See his "Institutions, Politics and Identities in the Post-Genocide Armenian Diaspora (1920s to 1980s)," Ph.D. dissertation (University of Michigan, 2015).

contends that his many faces and roles, the factors behind his multiple transmutations, and his refashioning of identities and undertakings are indicative of the more extensive Armenian experience, itself a part of the broader global context of the first half of the twentieth century. In particular, this study argues that three elements operating together account for or influence Giulkhandanian's transfigurations: first, an eclectic mélange of socialist, nationalist, and pragmatist outlooks;[7] second, a genuine concern for the safety and survival of Armenians in Europe informed by the recent trauma of genocide (1915-1918) and loss of independence (1920) – a concern that ultimately involved ignoble attempts to sever any perceived connections between Jews and Armenians by "Aryanizing" the Armenians and betrayed underlying anti-Jewish sentiments; and third, a continued reliance on a European, in this case German, savior – what Rafael Ishkhanian calls the "law of the third force" – which would help defeat the Bolshevik enemy and restore independence to Armenia.

This essay begins with a discussion of Giulkhandanian's early years as a revolutionary and socialist and then moves to his short-term position as a member of the first Armenian Republic's government. An exploration of Giulkhandanian's leadership role in Armenian-German collaboration during the World War II and confidence in German support follows. This section draws particular attention to his close relationship with his comrade and fellow leader of the pro-German Armenian National Committee, Artashes Abeghian, as a way to help explain Giulkhandanian's commitment to a problematic pro-German stance and action.

Revolutionary and Socialist

Giulkhandanian, born in 1875 in Echmiadzin into a fairly well-to-do family, attended Etchmiadzin's Gevorgian Seminary. At the age of nineteen, he joined the ARF and traveled to Baku, a bustling urban environment and magnet for local and foreign investors, oil refiners as well as migrant workers and revolutionaries. Giulkhandanian's revolutionary fervor and socialist convictions developed particularly after his arrival in Baku, in the mid-1890s, as a newly minted member of the revolutionary party. His own account, written in the 1930s, of turn-of-the-century Baku speaks to his own activities as well as the milieu of the city,

---

[7] In a similar vein, Miller refers to Hervé's pragmatism but as a "tendency to subjugate ideas and doctrines to base instincts and political understandings." Miller, *From Revolutionaries to Citizens*, 194.

especially the oil fields where he and his comrades organized and propagated revolution and socialism among workers through various means, including under the guise of evening "parties" to avoid the watchful eye of Russian authorities.[8]

In his memoir, Giulkhandanian underscores the growing interest starting in 1901 among workers in labor activity. He refers to that year as a "rebirth" (*veratsnund*) for workers which culminated in 1903 in Baku's first strike, attracting "thousands of workers," including the participation of those affiliated with the ARF – which he labels a "defender of workers' interests."[9] Giulkhandanian's account speaks to the vital role that oil fields played in radicalizing workers. He writes that Armenian workers obtained periodicals and books and set up reading rooms in the oil fields. In some instances, they formed groups and read revolutionary literature, including Marx's *Das Kapital* in Russian and contributed 1 to 10 percent of their salaries to the purchase of newspapers and books, thus creating a sizeable library. Giulkhandanian, furthermore, emphasizes the activist environment of the oil fields and attests to Baku's extensive role in transferring arms, ammunition, and explosive material for bombs.[10]

His writings also portrayed Giulkhandanian as a strong supporter of the Caucasian platform in 1905 whereby for the first time in its history, the ARF officially endorsed involvement in socialist and revolutionary activity in the Caucasus.[11] As a participant in the Caucasian Regional

---

[8] A[braham] Giulkhandanian, *Bagui derĕ mer azatagrakan sharzhman mēj* [Baku's role in our liberation movement] (Tehran: Alik, 1981), 84-85. For details about his life, see Gabriel Lazian, *Dēmk'er Hay heghap'okhakan sharzhumēn* [Figures from the Armenian revolutionary movement] (Montebello: A.R.F. Dro Committee, 1993), 301-310.

[9] Giulkhandanian, *Bagui derĕ,* 49, 59, 166, 191.

[10] Giulkhandanian, *Bagui derĕ,* 23, 25, 27, 98; Houri Berberian, *Roving Revolutionaries: Armenians and the Connected Revolutions of the Russian, Iranian, and Ottoman Worlds* (Oakland: University of California Press, 2019), 93.

[11] See his treatment of these factors in Abraham Giulkhandanian, *Kovkas: erkirĕ, zhoghovurdĕ, patmut'iwnĕ – K'artez ew bazmat'iw vichakagrakan twealner* [Caucasus: the country, the people, the history – Map and numerous statistical figures] (Paris: Librairie Universitaire J. Gamber, 1943), 193-202. See *Niwt'er H.H. Dashnakts'ut'ean patmut'ean hamar* [Materials for the history of the A.R. Federation], ed. Hrach Dasnabedian (Beirut: Hamazgayin Vahē Sēt'ean Tparan, 1973 and 1985), 2:236-37; also, in Eastern Bodies Regional Meeting in Tiflis in March-April, 1906. Giulkhandanian presided over the Caucasian Regional Meeting, December 28, 1907 – January 8, 1908. See *Niwt'er*, 2:258 (Original in ARF Archives, 1587-15).

Meeting in November 1905 and other such direct involvements, he thus offers his assessment of the larger political environment of those years, which mirrors his own ardent beliefs and ideological sympathies: "our near two-year activity carried out in the oil region [navt'ashrjan] and the multiple written and oral declarations as well as the mood of the oil region's Dashnakts'akan [Federalist/ARF] masses demonstrate that the Dashnakts'ut'iwn [Federation/ARF] is progressing without retreat toward socialism; thus, to change that path is without purpose and useless."[12] Giulkhandanian went on to take increasingly central leadership roles in the movement, starting in 1903, to regain church properties confiscated that same year by Russian authorities as well as in the Armeno-Azeri clashes (1905-1906) in Baku, simultaneously organizing ARF defensive and offensive fighting units and negotiating with Azeri leaders in an effort to prevent "bloody skirmishes."[13] Later, he recorded the details of this conflict in a series of articles published by Boston's *Hayrenik Amsagir* (Fatherland Monthly) from 1932 to 1935. His narrative of the first stage of skirmishes appeared as a volume in 1933.[14]

By 1906, Giulkhandanian was appointed as the editor of the Baku-based ARF newspaper, *Groh* (Mob), and two years later as, what the foremost historian of the Armenian Republic, Richard Hovannisian calls, one of the "philosophically socialist and functionally nationalist" members of the Bureau – the highest-ranking ARF body.[15] Tsarist Russia's intelligence service, Okhrana, placed him under surveillance due to his revolutionary activities and made him "subject to immediate arrest" by

---

[12] Giulkhandanian, *Bagui derě*, 204-205.

[13] Lazian, *Děmk'er,* 302, 303. Lazian completely ignores Giulkhandanian's WWII collaboration but provides ample detail for other parts of his life. Like Lazian, the *Hushamatean Hay Heghap'okhakan Dashnakts'ut'ean albom-atlas*, too, skips this part of Giulkhandanian's life. See *Hushamatean Hay Heghap'okhakan Dashnakts'ut'ean albom-atlas,* vol. 1, *Diwts'aznamart* [Commemorative album-atlas of the Armenian Revolutionary Federation, vol. 1, Heroic combat] (Glendale, CA: ARF Central Committee, 1992), 97.

[14] A. Giulkhandanian, *Hay-T'at'arakan ěndharumnerě: Hator A. Bagui arajin ěndharumnerě* [Armenian-Tatar clashes: Vol. I, Baku's first clashes] (Paris: Impr. franco-caucasienne, 1933).

[15] Richard G. Hovannisian, *The Republic of Armenia, Vol. I: The First Year, 1918-1919* (Berkeley and Los Angeles: University of California Press, 1971), 266. The others were Arshak Jamalian, Simon Vratsian, Sargis Araratian, and Hamazasp Ohanjanian.

Russian authorities.[16] Shortly after, in 1910, he was arrested along with other revolutionaries and released two years later.[17] His comrades considered him as one who was "Not turned into but born *revolutionary* in the term's classical sense... His essence was the *revolution*... whether as intrigue [*davadrakan gortz*] or as a mass [*zangowatsayin*] movement.[18] Hamo (Hamazasp) Ohanjanian, the prime minister of the First Republic from May to November 1920, characterized Giulkhandanian's main role in the workings of Armenian political life as to "prepare, inspire, ... push" and "direct" youth.[19]

---

[16] Document 16 I "A report regarding the ARF Bureau's leadership and the Fifth General Congress." October 7, 1909 - Indexed 26585 - Chief of the Tiflis Provincial Gendarmerie Directorate - September 28/29, 1909 – 12484 – Tiflis - To: Odessa Provincial Gendarmerie Directorate, Signed: Colonel in Vartkes Yeghiayan, ed., *The Armenians and the Okhrana, 1907-1915: Documents from the Russian Department of Police Archives* (Los Angeles: The Center for Armenian Remembrance, 2016), 65. See also Document 17 I "Further information regarding the leadership of the ARF bureaus" - To the head of the Odessa Provincial Gendarmerie Directorate Ministry of Internal Affairs - Department of Police - Special Section - October 8, 1909 – 131038 - Signed: In the Place of the Deputy Director (Signature). In the Place of the Section Chief (signature) in *Okhrana*, 66-67.

[17] Lazian, *Dēmk'er,* 304; Simon Vratsian, *Hushapatum H.H. Dashnakts'ut'ean, 1890-1950* [Memorial to the A. R. Federation, 1890-1950] (Boston: Hratarakut'iwn H.H.D. Biwroyi, 1950), 482. For the trials, see Onur Önol, *Tsar's Armenians: A Minority in Late Imperial Russia* (London: I.B. Tauris, 2017), chapter 2. For a contemporary account, see E. Aknouni [Khachatur Malumian], *Political Persecution: Armenian Prisoners of the Caucasus (A Page of the Tzar's Persecution),* trans. A.M. and H.W. (New York: [n.p.] 1911); E. Aknuni [Khachatur Malumian], *Boghok'i dzayn: kovkasahay k'aghak'akan bantarkialnerĕ (ts'arakan halatsank'i mi ēj)* [The voice of protest: Caucasian Armenian political prisoners (A page from tsarist persecution)] (Beirut: Ghukas Karapetean, 1978).

[18] V[ahan] Navasardian [member of parliament in the first republic], in *Husaber* (Hope bearer), January 26, 1946, cited in Lazian, *Dēmker*, 303-304.

[19] Ohanjanian cited from *Husaber*, January 26, 1946 in Lazian, *Dēmk'er,* 303. Lazian provides a glowing account of Giulkhandanian's revolutionary days, especially his role in the Armeno-Azeri clashes in Baku. Minas Makarian stops at 1918. See his "Abraham Giulkhandanian," *Hayrenik Amsagir* 25, no. 1 (Jan-Feb 1947): 93-96. Beno, on the other hand, takes the account to his death in 1946 but skips over the period between 1929 and 1946. Beno, "Husher Abr. Giulkhandaniani masin," *Hayrenik Amsagir* 24, no. 5 (Sept-Oct 1947): 83-92. See also Avo [Avetis Tumayian] "Abraham Giulkhandanian," *Heghap'okhakan*

Just as Hervé's accusers judged him and others like him as "closet fascists" and "never true socialists, much less Marxist," one may challenge or question Giulkhandanian's socialism.[20] How do we define or understand his socialism? In many ways, both his and the ARF's socialism was similar to that of Hervé who privileged practical matters and circumstances on the ground over theoretical considerations. According to Loughlin, for Hervé – and one could argue for Giulkhandanian – "The moment, the event and the results outweighed theory."[21]

ARF socialist members like Giulkhandanian adopted an eclectic brand of socialism, strongly peppered with pragmatism and straddling between orthodoxy and reformism most closely reflected by French socialist Jean Jaurès, who according to ARF leader and party historian Mikayel Varandian never gave up class conflict but also had a more favorable view of the national question. What appealed most to the ARF about Jaurès were four interrelated aspects of his approach: first, his view of the close relationship between democracy and socialism; second, his nondeterminist conception of history; third, his advocacy of cross-class cooperation with the nonsocialist, liberal bourgeoisie; and fourth, his melding of the ideal and the real.[22] As Geoffrey Kurtz explains, Jaurès rejected the historical determinism of orthodox Marxists. While accepting the very basics of Marxian analysis of economic development, he "insisted that Marx's 'materialist conception of history' be understood in a flexible and nuanced way." Thus, Jaurès reasoned that economic conflict was not the only driving force of history, thus relegating a more important role to ideas and politics. By inserting ideas and politics into a Marxist conception of history, then, Kurtz contends that Jaurès helped explain the significance of

---

Albom 5, 4 (52) (1964), issue devoted largely to Giulkhandanian. Avo refers to Giulkhandanian's time during WWII in the following way: "he worked to soften the war's terrors relating to the Armenian people." See ibid., 110. For similar language, see also Vratsian, *Hushapatum*, 485.

[20] Loughlin, "Gustave Hervé's Transition," 30. Loughlin argues that also Hervé's ideology had "atavistic strains" and his socialism was "highly unorthodox and eclectic," and that he "remained deeply suspicious of German power." See Loughlin, "Gustave Hervé's Transition," 5-6, 10.

[21] Loughlin, "Gustave Hervé's Transition," 37.

[22] Irving Howe, cited in Geoffrey Kurtz, "A Socialist State of Grace: The Radical Reformism of Jean Jaurès," *New Political Science* 28, no. 3 (2006): 402. See also Geoffrey Kurtz, *Jean Jaurès: The Inner Life of Social Democracy* (University Park: Pennsylvania State University Press, 2014). For a brief discussion of Jaurès and Armenians, see Madeleine Rebérioux, "Jean Jaurès and the Armenians," *Armenian Review* 44, no. 2/174 (1991): 1–11.

reforms as well as participation in democratic government through cross-class alliances with liberal bourgeoisie in the service of the interests of the working class. Thus, he brought "the socialist ideal into contact with political reality."[23] These aspects of Jaurès' thinking closely aligned with the ARF's own merger of the ideal and the real, its criticism of economic determinism at the expense of other elements, its openness to working with liberal nonsocialist forces, a general commitment to democratic liberal principles along with socialist goals, and a concern and engagement with the national question.

In the first decade of the early twentieth century, this engagement and privileging of the national question was reflected in the Armenian revolutionary press's discussion of belonging to a fatherland – Ottoman and Iranian. It was imperative for Armenian activists and intellectuals to reconcile socialism, on the one hand, and cultural and political autonomy for nationalities, on the other, and to demonstrate that not only were the two not incompatible but that they were, in actuality, supported by many European socialists. By appealing to their European co-ideologues, Armenian activists both joined the more considerable debate taking place among socialists on the national question and, at once, tried to silence their own critics, especially but not exclusively those further on the left who accused them of only bearing a "socialist mask" (*sōts'ialisti dimak*), of operating in "the claws of nationalism" (*nats'iōnalizmi chanker*), of "decorat[ing] themselves with socialism's feathers" (*sōts'ializmi p'eturnerov en zardarvum*) and of spreading their "chauvinist venom" (*shovinizmi t'oyn*).[24]

For ARF thinkers and propagandists, arguments on socialism and the national question revolved around three key points: first, that the local, regional, and global reality dictated their position on the national question; second, that every socialist party in any given country was national; and third, that the national question had not only not disappeared but in actuality had become even more poignantly relevant to the new century of revolutions. This approach, which explains Giulkhandanian's early revolutionary years as well, did not allow focusing exclusively on class

---

[23] Kurtz, "Socialist State of Grace," 404, 405.

[24] See, for example, *Hnch'ak* [Bell] August 1904, no. 8, 84**; *Dzayn* [Voice] (Tiflis), October 8, 1906, no. 2, 18; *Hosank'* [Current] (Tiflis), January 17, 1907, no. 39, 1; *Hosank'*, January 24, 1907), no. 44, 1. See also, *Hosank'*, February 8, 1907, no. 57, 2–3. For a full discussion of ARF's socialism, see Berberian, *Roving Revolutionaries*, especially chapter 4.

struggle and drove the national cause to center stage. It was a stage he had trouble exiting.

Statesman

Giulkhandanian's pragmatism coupled with his patriotism and focus on the national question carried through into the next phases of his life. After his release from prison in 1912, Giulkhandanian studied law, graduating and marrying two years later before the beginning of WWI. As a veteran activist, he headed the Armenian National Council in Baku and along with Sargis Araratian and ARF co-founder Rostom (Stepan Zorian) "spearheaded the Armenian effort to stave off the Turkish offensive at Baku in 1918."[25]

With the creation of the first Armenian Republic in May 1918 on territory a fraction of the size of ancestral lands that had not seen an Armenian state since the eleventh century, Giulkhandanian became a member of an ARF-led parliament and government along with seventy-two ARF comrades and seven others. Among his parliament and cabinet colleagues were several individuals who played an essential role during Giulkhandanian's WWII days. Key were Artashes Abeghian and Drastamat Kanayan (Dro).[26] Giulkhandanian's experience as an organizer and leader in Baku as well as his studies in law may have prepared him for his post as Minister of Internal Affairs with the additional post of Minister of Justice from August 1919 to January 1920. These experiences may have also primed him well for the assault from opposite corners for holding two

---

[25] Richard Hovannisian, *The Republic of Armenia, vol. II: From Versailles to London, 1919-1920* (Berkeley and Los Angeles: UC Press, 1982), 18, 286; Lazian, *Dēmk'er,* 305; Simon Vratsian to American C.C. [Central Committee] Comrades, February 20, 1915, in Yervant Pambukian, comp. and ed., *Niwt'er H.H. Dashnakts'ut'ean patmut'ean hamar* [Materials for the history of the A.R. Federation (Beirut: Hamazgayin Vahē Sēt'ean Tparan, 2015), 11:195. (Original document in ARF Archives, SV. 144-19).

[26] Artashes Abeghian was the son of linguist and philologist Manuk Abeghyan (1865-1944), who was behind the orthographic reform of Eastern Armenian in 1920s Soviet Armenia. Other comrades were Arshag Jamalian (Minister of Communications), Alexander Khatisian (Prime Minister and Minister of Internal and Foreign Affairs), Vahan Papazian (Parliament member), Sargis Araratian, Rupen Ter Minassian, and Hamazasp Ohanjanian (Prime Minister). The latter two, Ter Minassian and Ohanjanian stood against collaboration. See Levon Thomassian, *A Study of German-Armenian Relations during the Second World War* (Atglen, PA: Schiffer Military History, 2012), 34.

cabinet portfolios. While those on the right expressed concern that both portfolios held by the same person would mean that the ARF would be "dispens[ing] their own 'justice' and influential party members could wangle releases or pardons for guilty comrades," those on the left opposed instead the "perpetuation of the tsarist legal system" pointing to the lack of faith people had in the courts, thus shunning them "as symbols of oppression and discrimination."[27] As Minister of Internal Affairs, Giulkhandanian – following the lead of the ARF's strong advocacy of autonomy – enacted measures to increase rural self-administration through local elected councils (*zemstvos*) with the intention of encouraging democratic participation.[28] During Giulkhandanian's tenure, the Ministry also put forward a proposal to parliament to increase the wages of government employees to ensure sufficient income.[29]

Giulkhandanian's work, however, almost came to an end in April 1920, about a month before the beginning of celebrations of the second year of the Armenian Republic, when the British recriminated the Armenian government, in particular Kanayan, Ohanjanian, and especially Giulkhandanian, for carrying out the "most acts of aggression" in Kars.[30] The reference was to the escalating violence in northeastern Kars province where Armenian Republic forces came to blows with Muslim rebels and were accused of excessive violence toward the Muslim population.[31] In a meeting with Avetis Aharonian and Boghos Nubar, British Foreign Secretary George Curzon advised the two delegate leaders to the Paris

---

[27] Hovannisian, *Republic of Armenia*, 2:293. Much has been written on Kanayan and Nzhdeh but mainly from a nationalist and even apologetic perspective. A critical, scholarly contribution regarding both men would be a welcome intervention that could inform and enhance our understanding of the full context of World War II.

[28] Hovannisian, *Republic of Armenia*, 2:287-89.

[29] See *Hayastan Parlament. Gorts petakan tsaṛayoghneri ṛochikneri havelman gortsi,* No. 14, *Hayastani Hanrapetut'iwn: Ōrēnkneri havak'atsu* [Armenian parliament: Case of Public Servants' Replenishment Case, No. 14, Armenian Republic: Collection of laws (Vagharshapat: Elektrasharzh, 1920). For changes and waivers in conscription, see *Hayastan Parlament. Ōrinagits nets'uknerin zōrakoch'its' azatelu masin* [Armenian parliament: The draft law on deportation], No. 26, Armenian Republic: collection of laws], No. 26 *Hayastani Hanrapetut'iwn: Ōrēnkneri havak'atsu* (Vagharshapat: Elektrasharzh, 1920).

[30] Hovannisian, *Republic of Armenia, The Republic of Armenia, Vol. III: From London to Sèvres, February–August 1920* (Berkeley: University of California Press, 1996), 128.

[31] Ibid., 121-22, 126.

Peace conference that all three be removed from their posts. Prime Minister Aleksander Khatisian denied the charges and Aharonian, representing the Republic's delegation, advised Khatisian against such a foolhardy move, pointing out the "heavy price" of heeding English demands.[32] Despite the tensions in the joint Delegation of Integral Armenia to the post-WWI peace conferences, it was Boghos Nubar's intervention on June 7 that halted the Foreign Office pursuit of the dismissal of Giulkhandanian and his colleagues.[33]

Before he had found out that the Foreign Office would not pursue his dismissal, on May 28, 1920, at the festivities of the Republic's second anniversary, Giulkhandanian reflecting on the country's independence, having in mind perhaps the violence in Kars, British meddling, and ancestral lands under Turkish rule, noted that "the freedom and independence we celebrate are still not whole."[34] Weighing in briefly on the development of Armenian collective identity from religious to national, he paused to comment on the nature of the "Armenian patriot," seemingly coming to his defense and explaining his relationship to the homeland. During the last months of the independent republic, he declared that "the Armenian patriot was not chauvinist; he loved the Armenian wherever he was to be found. He recognized the Armenians' shortcomings [*pakasut'iwn*] and aspired to elevate him," adding, "He was a patriot because he had no idea about the fatherland; he was born and nourished not in Armenia but outside Armenia. He dreamed about Armenia...."[35] The

---

[32] Ibid., 129-30.

[33] Ibid., 131. The Delegation of Integral Armenia was a compromise between the two delegation at the peace conferences: the official one led by Aharonian represented the first Republic's interests and Armenians of the Russian Empire while the Armenian National Delegation with Boghos Nubar as its president represented the interest of surviving Armenians in and from the Ottoman Empire. For a full discussion of the debates and internal workings of the Integral Delegation, see Houri Berberian, "The Delegation of Integral Armenia: From Greater Armenia to Lesser Armenia," *Armenian Review* 44, no. 3/175 (Autumn 1991): 39-64.

[34] *Haraj* [Forward] 110 (May 28, 1920): 2.

[35] Ibid. Despite the fact that Armenian is gender-neutral, I have chosen to use the masculine pronoun because – although Giulkhandanian published an article on Armenian revolutionary women in 1939 – he would have most likely had Armenian men in mind when referring to the "Armenian patriot," as he saw women to have important but ancillary and supporting roles. For example, he wrote the following about Armenian women's contribution to revolution: "*Na t'ev u t'ikunk' dardzav hay tghamardun; nra het miasin payk'arets', zohets' ew*

Armenia that occupied the imaginings of Giulkhandanian and others was a "United, Independent Armenia" that encompassed the Eastern Asia Minor provinces as well as the new Republic. As Hovannisian points out, Giulkhandanian had – months before –

> liken[ed] Armenia to a giant with his heart in Erevan, his hands in Alexandropol, his head in Karabagh, and his feet in Diarbekir and the Black Sea. The giant had slept through the centuries, and some wondered if he was still alive: "But we know that his heart never ceased beating and his hands never stopped working. Today, the Allies have realized that fact, and we are confident that soon the titan will move his head, stretch his feet, and stand erect. And at that time, we shall again gather to celebrate the recognition of United, Independent Armenia."[36]

Giulkhandanian's use of organic imagery and the trope of waking from a deep slumber and becoming conscious of one's national identity is typical of nationalist discourse, not only in the Armenian case but more generally. For Giulkhandanian, a "United, Independent Armenia" was an unfulfilled vision; yet, it remained one that he never abandoned. In May 1920, he took up the cabinet portfolios of Finance and of Justice, relinquishing the latter in August of the same year.[37] At the end of that year, faced with mounting pressures and the advancement of Turkish and Soviet troops, he along with Foreign Minister Khatisian and Governor-General of Kars Stepan Ghorghonian/Korganian signed the Treaty of Alexandropol with Turkey. Because the signing came a day after the Armenian government had already resigned and surrendered the Republic to Soviet control, the treaty with Turkey – which renounced the Treaty of Sèvres and ceded Kars and other parts of the Armenian Republic – was technically invalid at signing. It was, however, ratified as the Treaty of

---

zohvets'; kamavor kerpov krets' bolor zrkank'ner, tanjank'ner ew darnut'iwnner." In the English translation of his article, "*kamavor kerpov*" (willingly) is transformed: "She stood by her man, fought alongside with him, sacrificed and was sacrificed herself, *cheerfully* [emphasis added] bore all sort of privation, torture and bitter experiences." See *Heghap'okhakan Hayuhiner* [Revolutionary Armenian women], vol. 1 (Paris 1939), 3; A. Kiulkhandanian, "Heroines of the Armenian Revolution," Part 1, *Armenian Review* (Spring 1959): 52-59 (52); A. Giulkhandanian, "Heroines of the Armenian Revolution," Part 2, *Armenian Review* (Summer 1959): 126-131.

[36] Hovannisian, *Republic of Armenia,* 2:513.

[37] Hovannisian, *Republic of Armenia,* 3: 265, no. 17.

Kars between Turkey and the three Soviet South Caucasian republics almost a full year later in October 1921.[38]

In his memoirs, Ghorghonian describes Giulkhandanian during negotiations as an agitated man – pacing, smoking nonstop, talking to himself, protesting forcefully, and sighing.[39] According to the former, the latter seemed unable to give up the idea of Wilsonian Armenia "from sea to sea" and was unwilling to let go of the promises of the Sèvres Treaty. Yet neither he nor the embryonic Republic seemed to have another option for the time being. During World War II, they explored other options. The route Giulkhandanian and some of his comrades chose, however, was a thorny and morally unprincipled one.[40] To some degree, their decision to ally with Nazi Germany during WWII reveals the unique post-genocide and post-loss-of-independence context of Armenian émigrés and refugees who landed on European shores. It also, however, exposes their Nazi sympathies – sympathies shared even in such dissimilar places as the Middle East and the United States, from Reza Shah to the Fords.

Collaborator

Fears of "Judaization" and Attempts at "Aryanization"

In 1924, only a few years after the crushing defeat of the First Armenian Republic and the signing of the Treaty of Alexandropol and in an attempt to explain the necessity of keeping the Armenian question alive through struggle, Giulkhandanian betrayed both his fears and his prejudice. In April of that year, he mused in the *Hayrenik* monthly, "It is combat that will keep our question alive... It is that combat which will save the Armenian people from the *judaizing danger* [*hrēanalu vtangits'*]; finally, it is that combat which will save the day-to-day subjugated

---

[38] Hovannisian, *Republic of Armenia, vol. iv: Between Crescent and Sickle: Partition and Sovietization* (Berkeley: University of California, 1996), 391, 394.

[39] I have translated Ghorghonyan's "*brunts'k'alits' boghok'um ēr*" as "protesting forcefully" because of his reference to a "fisted" protest.

[40] "Gylkhandanyan, Sevr, Aleksandrapol: nahangapet Ghorghonyani husherits' mijots'ov" [Giulkhandanian, Sèvres, Alexandropol: Through Governor Ghorghonyan's memoirs], December 29, 2016, Armenian Research Center (https://www.aniarc.am/2016/12/29/abraham-gulkhandanian-in-stepan-korganyan-memories-alexandrapol-1920/).

Turkish-Armenian people..."[41] Giulkhandanian's dread is clear. His anxiety in 1924 that Armenians will be "Judaized," which he understood to mean becoming cowardly and weak – a common anti-Semitic trope – betrays his views on Jews and may explain at least in part his decision less than two decades later to collaborate with Nazi Germany.

Our knowledge of Giulkhandanian's bigotry against Jews rests primarily on three things. First is his language above, which is undeniably anti-Semitic. Second is his close affiliation with two ARF comrades, Garegin Nzhdeh (1886-1955) and Dr. Artashes Abeghian (1878-1955); the latter was also a family friend. (Figs. 2-3) According to Christopher Walker, Nzhdeh, an ARF leading member until his expulsion in the late 1930s, was a fascist.[42] The estimated date of his expulsion from the ARF

---

[41] Abraham Giulkhandanian, "Bagui derĕ mer azatagrakan sharzhman mēj" [Baku's role in our liberation movement], part 5, in *Hayrenik Amsagir* 2, 6 (April 1924): 103. Emphasis mine. The series of articles were republished in book form under the same title Giulkhandanian, *Bagui derĕ*, 50.

[42] Walker claims that "Except for Nzhdeh, no Armenian has ever been a theoretical Fascist." See Christopher Walker, *Armenia: The Survival of a Nation* (London: Routledge, Revised Second Edition, 1990), 357. According to Sahakyan (and based on Vache Ovsepian, *Garegin Nzhde i KGB: Vospominaniia razvedchika* [Garegin Nzhdeh and the KGB: Memoirs of an Agent] (Yerevan, 2007): "Noravank," 3-4; 10), Garegin Nzhdeh [Ter Harutiwnian] had a long career in the ARF and was a key military figure in the first republic. He was born in Nakhijevan, received his early education at a Russian school in the city of Nakhijevan, and pursued studies in law at the St. Petersburg University. His interests, however, were primarily in military matters. He attended ARF's military school in Sofia, Bulgaria and after graduating in 1907, joined the Iranian Constitutional Revolution in 1908. His arrest in 1909 by Russian authorities resulted in three years in prison before he escaped. He was Kanayan's second-in-command of the Armenian Regiment of the Russian Army during WWI. He continued to serve in a military capacity during the short-lived independent Armenian Republic. During WWII, he helped lead the Armenian Legion under Nazi Germany with the goal of regaining Armenian independence after the defeat of the Bolsheviks. He was ousted from the ARF at the end of the 1930s, arrested in 1944 by the Soviets, sentenced to twenty-five years in prison in 1948, and died in prison in 1955. For his expulsion, see Sahakyan, "Institutions, Politics and Identities," 253-56. For discussions of Nzhdeh's creation of a nationalist youth organization – Ts'eghakron which became the Armenian Youth Federation, see Sahakyan, "Institutions, Politics and Identities," 301 no. 104; R. Panossian, "The Past as Nation: Three Dimensions of Armenian Identity," *Geopolitics* 7, no. 2 (Autumn 2002): 130–6, Sarkis Atamian, *The Armenian Community. The Historical Development of a Social and Ideological Conflict* (New York:

indicates that his collaboration with the Nazis and his role in the ANG came after his parting of the ways with the ARF.[43] The fact that he was expelled by a party that sanctioned and encouraged decentralization and varying points of view in its ranks may indicate that Nzhdeh's views were deemed more dangerous than those of his ANG colleagues – such as Giulkhandanian and Abeghian –although Abeghian's expressed views and actions may have placed him close behind. Abeghian, an ARF member and also parliamentarian in the First Republic, held a post as professor in Armenian Studies from 1926-1945 at Berlin university.[44] This is telling given that German universities were hotbeds for Nazi sympathies and activism even before 1933. Abeghian wrote prolifically in German and Armenian on Armenians and Armenology.[45] Third is Giulkhandanian's leadership role in the ANG, which collaborated with the Nazis and his editorship of the short-lived *Azat Hayastan* (*Freies Armenien*), of which only two issues appeared in August and September/October of 1943. As its organ, the newspaper represented ANG's official views, much shaped not only by Giulkhandanian but also by both Abeghian as its director and

Philosophical Library, 1955), 392; cf. 388–96. John Roy Carlson (pseudonym of Avetis / Arthur Derounian) likened Ts'eghakron to "race worshipping" nationalists "similar to the Hitler Youth" and the ARF as pro-fascist. See his *Under Cover: My Four Years in the Nazi Underworld of America – The Amazing Revelation of How Axis Agents and Our Enemies Within Are Now Plotting to Destroy the United States* (New York: E. P. Dutton & Co., Inc., 1943); see also Sahakyan, "Institutions, Politics and Identities," 271, 292.

[43] Sahakyan writes, "Many scholars [for example, Ovsepian (2007) and Panossian (2006)] believe that the expulsion of Nzhdeh from the Dashnaktsutyun was because of his 'extreme and racist views'" Sahakyan, "Institutions, Politics and Identities," 271, 301. See also Thomassian, *Summer of '42*, 151. Thomassian tries to exonerate Nzhdeh by privileging his anti-Communist views: "Nzhdeh has also been labeled as either pro-Nazi or fascist. Although it is true that he admired the National Socialists, Nzhdeh's admiration appeared to lay with the party's anti-Communist views, and not with the party itself." Thomassian, *Summer of '42*, 99, 101.

[44] Thomassian, *Summer of '42*, 151.

[45] See, for example, Artashes Abeghian's contributions in *Hayrenik' Amsagir* throughout the 1930s about German contributions to Armenology or on Armenians. On the latter, see for example, several issues in 1936. See also "Mer ashkhatakits'neru namaknerě" [Our coworkers' letters], *Hayrenik' Amsagir* 42, no. 3 (March 1964). I am thankful to my colleague Matthias Lehmann for a conversation that helped contextualize 1920s-1930s German universities.

Nzhdeh as its deputy editor.[46] It ceased publication with the dissolution of the ANG.[47]

After Sovietization of the First Republic, Giulkhandanian first moved to Tiflis, then Istanbul, and settled a bit in Bucharest, Romania, finally moving to Paris in 1933. (Fig. 4) Here he began to classify the ARF Archives (*Divan*), with close to 100,000 documents, until his arrest after the liberation of France in August 1944 from Nazi occupation.[48] (Fig. 5) During his time in Nazi-occupied Paris, Giulkhandanian became the primary editor of the unambiguously pro-German Armenian National Committee organ *Azat Hayastan* in 1943. According to ARF sources, after the liberation of France, Giulkhandanian having been falsely accused by Armenian Bolsheviks served eleven months from October 1944 to September 1945 in prison and was released once French authorities became aware that he was a victim of defamation.[49] It is more likely, however, that French authorities imprisoned him due to his collaboration during the war with Nazi Germany and released him because of his deteriorating health, which sent him to the hospital twice during imprisonment. Only a few months later – on the first day of 1946 – Giulkhandanian died of heart failure.

The years of Giulkhandanian's stay in Paris were critical in shaping the turn that he took to active collaboration, of which his views on Jews were part and parcel.[50] Either on his own or through his camaraderie, friendship, and close working relationship with Abeghian, Giulkhan-

---

[46] Walker, *Armenia*, 357. The ARF Archives may shed more light on this issue, but only the years up to 1926 have been catalogued and thus documents after 1926 are not available for researchers.

[47] For details regarding the disbanding of the ANG and the aftermath, see Thomassian, *Summer of '42*, 43-44.

[48] Lazian, *Dēmk'er*, 309-10; *Hushamatean Hay Heghap'okhakan Dashnakts'ut'ean albom-atlas*, 1:97.

[49] *Heghap'okhakan albom*, 110.

[50] According to Walker, neither "theoretical" Fascism, except perhaps in the case of Nzhdeh, nor "a purely vengeful desire to retake Armenia from the Bolsheviks" was the reason for Armenian collaboration. He points to other factors, including the possibility that the Nazis might lump the Armenians with the Jews. Thus, they attempted to seek to establish the "Aryan" credentials of Armenians, so as not to face the same fate as WWII Jews or WWI Armenians. Another factor was that Soviet Russia as Romanov Russia before it, could fall apart; therefore, it was necessary to prepare for the eventuality of a strong force to follow the fall of Bolshevism and as a bulwark against possible Turkish aggression. Walker, *Armenia*, 357, 358.

danian must have been aware of the appearance of Armenians in racialist discussions in Germany. According to Stefan Ihrig, Armenians had become a part of the discourse in particular on the "Aryan race. . . and on the Jews" and by the 1930s, at least in passing "had made an appearance in many of the central texts of German anti-Semitism and racialist worldviews."[51] Through a discussion of racialist and populist anti-Semitic texts, Nazi propaganda, and "many texts on the New Turkey," Ihrig demonstrates that, on the one hand, Armenians and Jews were conflated and, on the other hand, Armenians were often portrayed as "even 'worse'" than Jews, taking "on qualities of 'über-Jews' or the 'original Jews.'" "For top Nazis such as Hitler and Alfred Rosenberg," Ihrig notes, "the Armenians were equal to or even worse than the Jews" in perceived avarice and shrewdness. Hans F.R. Günther, the "most prolific and popular German writer of 'race handbooks,'" underscored the "'enterprising mercantile initiative' of the 'cunning' Armenians," "their inclination for fraud," and "the cold cruelty [with which] they often exploit their victims."[52] For Hitler especially, Armenians were an inferior race equal to the Jews. At one of "his famous table talks [1941-44], the Nazi leader clarified that 'In the education of the German people about its race laws it has to be emphasized time and again that these race laws are also meant to protect against the contamination of German blood by Armenian or otherwise un-Aryan blood.'"[53] Moreover, Ihrig draws attention to a certain Nazi appreciation and awareness of the Ottoman Empire's recent history and genocidal actions against its minority subjects, especially the Armenians, and its transformation into a Turkish Republic. He concludes, "In the Nazi vision of the New Turkey, this meant a state that had, on a grand scale, 'solved' its minority question, in a 'final' manner. And in these discourses on the New Turkey, the resulting new national body, emerges as a kind of 'postgenocidal wonderland.'"[54] This sinister context helps explain at least to some degree the post-genocide and post-independence mindset of Giulkhandanian who, as one of the leaders of the ANG, supported Abeghian's campaign to alter Nazi views on Armenians.

Abeghian was instrumental in the efforts to slide the pendulum to the other side of the racial binary, in effect, the effort to "Aryanize" Armenians. He moved to Berlin with his family in 1922, the same year

---

[51] Stefan Ihrig, *Justifying Genocide: Germany and the Armenians from Bismarck to Hitler* (Cambridge: Harvard University Press, 2016), 302, 305.
[52] Ibid., *Justifying Genocide*, 305, 306, 312, 315-17.
[53] Hitler cited in Ihrig, *Justifying Genocide,* 318.
[54] Ihrig, *Justifying Genocide*, 320.

that the Armenian Soviet Socialist Republic became an infinitesimal part of the Soviet Union. In 1926, he joined the faculty of the University of Berlin (Friedrich-Wilhelms-Universität) where he remained a professor of Armenian Studies during the Nazi regime until 1945. Abeghian devoted a great deal of his time and efforts to promoting German-Armenian friendship through the association established by Johannes Lepsius and through the publication of its German-language organ, *Hayastan* (Armenia).[55] The weekly newspaper involved close collaboration with the Commissioner for Settlement to Southwest Africa, Paul Rohrbach. Abeghian endeavored to counteract the conflations of Armenians and Jews through a number of articles, for instance, on Armenian culture and German-Armenian ties. His essay on "Nordic types among Armenians" appeared in *Armeniertum-Ariertum* (Armenianism-Aryanism), under his editorship in 1934. The book consisted of several chapters on Armenian history, culture, as well as pseudo-science by prominent Germans, all with the goal of proving the "Aryan" origins of Armenians. Abeghian also sought the intervention of Rohrbach and others.[56]

Although Harutyun Hayrapetyan exonerates Abeghian, stating, "It is above suspicion that the issue of the Aryan origins of Armenians was largely an object of political exploitation rather than pure ideological reality," several factors point to a less apologetic interpretation of Abeghian and by association Giulkhandanian: his successful career at the University of Berlin during the rise and subsequent rule of the Nazis, his close association with Rohrbach – "an advocate of the Social Darwinian

---

[55] This periodical should not be confused with the Armenian Legionnaires' paper with the same name. Harutyun Hayrapetyan, "Artashes Abeghyan. Mets banasern u hasarakakan gortsich'ĕ" [Artashes Abeghian: The great philologist and public activist], (117-133), 124. Institute for Armenian Studies – YSU, www.armenianreligion.am/images/menus/1202/Hayrapetyan_Harutyun.pdf. (Accessed May 1, 2019).

[56] Hayrapetyan, "Artashes Abeghyan," 126-127. In turn-of-the-century Europe, the Aryan discourse tied to the Armenians was most passionately debated among art historians based in Vienna and spearheaded by Josef Strzygowski. Giulkhandanian and company must have been aware of these political debates disguised as scholarship. For a comprehensive study on this discursive link between Aryanism, art, and the Armenians, see Christina Maranci, *Medieval Armenian Architecture: Construction of Race and Nation* (Leuven: Peeters, 2001); and idem, "Armenian Architecture as Aryan Architecture: the Role of Indo-European Studies in the Theories of Josef Strzygowski," *Visual Resources* 13 (1998): 363-80.

and racial theories that underpinned it"[57] – and his own views as reflected, for example, in a letter written in 1938.[58] In this letter, Abeghian complains that, on occasion, information which appeared in *Hayrenik Amsagir* about Germany (read Nazi Germany) and the contemporary situation was "exaggerated and false." Having made this somewhat apologetic assessment, he moves on to address the conflation of Armenians with Jews in German media, which "wash them in the same bowl." He adds that he and others are working to show the fallacious nature of such assessments, that Armenians "have cultural and other important ties with Germany and Germany has an interest in preserving those ties," and that they are taking steps – from individual meetings to publications – to "'prove' our being Aryan and not having any connection to Jews." Abeghian follows the last phrase with "As if that pain were not enough for our people" (*mer zhoghovrdin ayd ts'avn ēr pakas ardēn*), most certainly referring to the genocide of World War I.[59] Thus, to some degree the collaboration of Giulkhandanian and his ANG comrades reflect both a post-genocide trauma and genuine concern about what could befall Armenians as well as an equally strong anti-Semitic bigotry. Abeghian's academic credentials, network, as well as his mere presence in Berlin propelled him to the forefront of a crusade to "Aryanize" the Armenians; however, he did not

---

[57] See David Olusoga and Casper W. Erichsen, *The Kaiser's Holocaust: Germany's Forgotten Genocide and the Colonial Roots of Nazism* (London: Faber & Faber, 2010), 112.

[58] "Mer ashkhatakits'neru namaknerĕ" [Our colleagues' letters], *Hayrenik' Amsagir* 42, no. 3 (March 1964): 11-18. Artashes Abeghian's letters from Berlin, 1923-1938 – written Berlin, March 25, 1938.

[59] "Mer ashkhatakits'neru namaknerĕ," 11-18. Artashes Abeghian's letters from Berlin, 1923-1938 – written Berlin, March 25, 1938 – 16, 17. Following the Allied bombings of Berlin, which destroyed Abeghian's home, he fled with his family. They lived for a short period in Stuttgart, "where thousands of other Armenian Displaced Persons had gathered" and where Abeghian lectured at the school of Funkerkaserne DP (Displaced Persons) camp. He settled in 1947 in Munich "where he taught Armenian Studies at the University of Munich until his death in March 1955." Thomassian, *Summer of '42*, 151. See also *Azat Hayastan – Freies Armenien* 2/3 (September-October, 1943): 27, which addresses the "unfair attacks" on Armenians appearing in Vienna's *Neues Weiner Tagblatt* (New Viennese Daily) and the Armenian National Committee's protest, resulting in the publication of Abeghian's article "Hayastan ew hayer" in the same paper. The article provides information on Armenian origins, language, history, and culture based on what Abeghian characterizes as "irrefutable historical and scientific" evidence.

act alone and was supported by comrades such as Giulkhandanian, especially in the leadership of the ANG.

Collaboration? Or Collaboration!

While self-preservation and political strategizing compelled some Armenians to invent an Armeno-German racial discourse, there is no question as to the Armenian effort in the French Résistance against the Nazis as well as during the so-called "great patriotic war" after Hitler's invasion of the Soviet Union in June 1941.[60] The most well-known example of the former is the FTP-MOI (Francs-tireurs et partisans – main-d'œuvre immigrée) comprised of European immigrants in Paris and responsible for political violence against Nazi individuals and targets. The group's military commissioner was genocide survivor Missak Manouchian who was executed along with others by the Nazis in 1944. Manouchian's group may have been one of the most – if not the most – active in the French resistance movement against the Nazis. Manouchian commanded about fifty fighters who carried out at least two dozen successful attacks in the second half of 1943.[61]

Hundreds of thousands of Armenians also fought in the Soviet military and even served in leadership roles, such as General Hovhannes Khachaturi Baghramyan (Ivan Khristoforovich Bagramyan) and three admirals who took part in the creation of a Soviet tank corps in early 1943.[62] While a substantively higher number of Armenians contributed to the Allied war effort, a few of those who lived in Germany and occupied France collaborated with the Axis, specifically the Nazis. In particular, although the ARF as a party remained officially neutral, many of its cells supported the Allies while a few individuals threw in their lot with the Axis – a political maneuvering that in hindsight is ethically questionable. Despite "a letter [written by J. (Zhirair) Missakian] in *The Times* (London) of July 19 1941," as noted by Walker, "indignantly rebut[ting] the idea that any of the Armenian people entertained pro-Axis sympathies," charging Turkish intrigue in the matter, a few ARF members in Paris and Berlin did indeed collaborate with the Nazis.[63] This collaboration included

---

[60] For discussion of French resistance and Armenians, see also Sahakyan, "Institutions, Politics and Identities," 256.

[61] For a study on Manouchian, see Philippe Robrieux, *L'Affaire Manouchian* [The Manouchian Affair] (Paris: Fayard, 1986).

[62] Walker, *Armenia*, 355, 356.

[63] Ibid., 356, 357.

the establishment, in late 1941, of an Armenian battalion active in the Crimea and North Caucasus with Wehrmacht approval. The battalion was led by Kanayan and included "a small number of committed recruits, and a larger number of Armenians from the prisoners of war taken by the Nazis in their sweep eastwards." It numbered between 8,000 and 20,000 or perhaps, more closely, 11,000.[64] A year later, in December 1942, Alfred Rosenberg, head of the Nazi party's Office for Foreign Policy and Ideology Reich Minister for the Occupied Eastern Territories starting in 1941, officially recognized the ANG, led by its president Artashes Abeghian in Berlin and its vice-president Abraham Giulkhandanian in Paris, as representing the "interests of Europe's Armenians to the German leadership and its real and major purpose was to help Armenian prisoners of war and to protect Armenian national interests."[65] The raison d'être of the ANG was to serve as a government in exile.[66]

In a study published soon after WWII, George Fischer provides an analysis of Soviet émigré communities in Europe and Soviet POWs, led by former Red Army Lieutenant General, Anxirei A. Vlasov, fighting for Nazi Germany.[67] Of particular interest to the present study is his exposition

---

[64] Thomassian's research more closely aligns with Joachim Hoffman's at 11,000. Joachim Hoffmann, *Kaukasien 1942/43: Das Deutsche Heer und die Orientvölker der Sowjetunion* [Caucasus 1942/43: The German Army and the Oriental Peoples of the Soviet Union] (Freiburg: Rombach, 1991), 323 cited in Thomassian, *Summer of '42*, 146.

[65] Hayrapetyan, "Artashes Abeghyan," 129.

[66] See also Eduard A. Abrahamyan, "Battalion Zaytun of the German Army," http://www.armenian-history.com/Nyuter/HISTORY/ARMENIA20/Battalion_ Zaytun_of_the_German_Army.htm (Accessed 1 May, 2019). Abrahamyan states that national committees starting "in the middle of 1944 ... were officially acknowledged as governments, and national legions were renamed into United national liberating units."

[67] George Fischer, *Soviet Opposition to Stalin: A Case Study in World War II* (Cambridge: Harvard University Press, 1952). Fischer lived in Moscow as a child and worked with the U.S. army's Counter-Intelligence Corps after WWII. He was well informed because of "his mother's work for the International Refugee Organization in Munich" and immersed himself in Munich émigré and refugee communities "where monarchies and Social Democrats fought bitterly to represent the 'true' Russia." He saw to Harvard University's interview project with émigrés and acted "as the 'spiritual father' of the Institute for the Study of the History and Culture of the USSR in Munich, funded by the CIA." See David C. Engerman, *Know Your Enemy: The Rise and Fall of America's Soviet Experts* (Oxford: Oxford University Press, 2009), 52-53.

of anti-Soviet émigré groups who "entered into a 'marriage of convenience' with Nazi Germany," as they sought separation from the Soviet Union and independent statehood. Taking advantage of the nationalist goals of these communities, Rosenberg advocated the creation of the POW legions and the national committees, like the ANG headed by Abeghian and Giulkhandanian. According to Fischer, Rosenberg promoted "seizing upon the independent aspirations of all these peoples in an intelligent and purposeful way . . . to transform them into state forms . . . and to build them up against Moscow." [68] In addition to Giulkhandanian and Abeghian, other members of the Committee included Garegin Nzhdeh and Vahan Papazian.

ANG's *Azat Hayastan* (1943) and the stridently and more explicitly fascist weekly, *Hayastan* (1942-43), published by the Armenian Legion, comprised of POWs fighting under the German flag, began publication within a particularly important context of the German offensive in Stalingrad in mid-1942, followed by a Soviet counteroffensive in November 1942, resulting in the start of German withdrawal from the Caucasus in January 1943. In early February, German forces lost at Stalingrad and surrendered; in mid-1943, British and American air raids hit Germany, followed by Italy's capitulation to the Allies and its declaring war on Germany in October. Both Armenian-language newspapers, at the time, framed collaboration with Nazi Germany as a nationalist struggle against Bolshevism and in favor of Armenian independence. They did have their differences, however. *Hayastan*'s pro-German stance was cruder and frequently incorporated photos of and speeches by Nazi officials, including Hitler himself.[69] It was also primarily written by

---

[68] Fischer, *Soviet Opposition to Stalin,* 10-11, 19-22.

[69] Thomassian proposes several reasons for the motives of Armenian and other POWs fighting for Germany: self-preservation, starvation, poor conditions, opportunism, anti-Bolshevism. See Thomassian, *Summer of '42*, 73-80, 83. The editors of *Hayastan* and *Azat Hayastan* seem to have had cordial relations and pursued similar goals. The ANG was responsible for taking care of the Eastern front Armenian POWs. In the second and last issue of *Azat Hayastan*, the editorial board congratulates *Hayastan* for completing its first year of publication with fifty issues and wishes it "successes" and "ardor and strength to carry out their idealist [gaghap'arakan] work with the same animation." Apparently after the eleventh issue, the editorship was transferred to the Armenian POWs. See "'Hayastan' shabat'at'ert'ĕ," [The weekly *Hayastan*], *Azat Hayastan* 2 (Sept-Oct 1943): 22; "Azgayin keank'" [National life], *Azat Hayastan* 2 (Sept-Oct 1943): 27. The responsible editor of *Hayastan* is listed as Leg. S. Hovik although the National

legionnaires, was quite militaristic, and often referred to historical battles and heroes – like the Mamikonians of the fifth century – to emphasize the struggle for the nation: "We are fighting for our nation."[70] When in the summer of 1943, the legions were redirected away from the battle against the Soviets and commanded to fight Germany's other enemies, as observed by Fischer, a shift took place in the morale of the legions. He explains that the redirection of troops "deprived them of much of their rationale. By dispersing them far and wide, the move drastically reduced whatever hopes and illusions they may have retained of becoming more and more an independent opposition movement."[71] This development as well as the dissolution of the ANG in October 1943 explains why *Hayastan* ceased publication in 1943 after a two-year run and extreme political rhetoric.

The issue of the collaboration of some members of the ARF – such as Giulkhandanian, Abeghian, and Nzhdeh – with Nazi Germany has received largely partisan attention. In his discussion of this collaboration, Vahe Sahakyan focuses in particular on the efforts of two individuals: John Roy Carlson (Arthur Derounian) and Sarkis Atamian. In *Under Cover,* Carlson writing in 1949 exposes pro-Nazi activities, organizations, and individuals in the United States and although he neither focuses nor singles out the ARF he does mention meeting two ARF members with pro-Nazi sympathies. In an unrelated article, "The Armenian Displaced Persons: A First-Hand Report on Conditions in Europe," however, he does present a litany of charges against the ARF "made by the pro-Soviet opponents." The ARF was charged simultaneously with fascism, political opportunism, terrorism as well as for being "agents of foreign powers" and "Turk-ophiles."[72] Sahakyan writes, "Carlson's article… provided a detailed report on the formation of the Armenisches Nationales Gremium in Berlin, of its ranks, filled mostly with Dashnaks and their affiliates, of its program and activities during the War." Although Giulkhandanian was named as a member of the ANG, which collaborated with the Nazis, the Committee's president Abeghian and Kanayan were his targets.[73] Carlson is emphatic

---

Library of Armenia's online catalog names Vigen Shant, son of Levon Shant, as editor.
[70] *Hayastan* 8-9 (32-32) March 7, 1932, 1.
[71] Fischer, 51. See also Abrahamyan, "Battalion Zaytun of the German Army."
[72] Sahakyan, "Institutions, Politics and Identities," 291-92, details up to 295.
[73] Ibid., 295, John Roy Carlson, "The Armenian Displaced Persons: A First-Hand Report on Conditions in Europe: A First-Hand Report on Conditions in Europe," *Armenian Affairs* 1, no. 1 (1949-50): 26.

in his damning charges against these "quisling-minded Dashnags," adding with no small degree of rebuke: "These European Dashnags, with headquarters in Berlin, appealed to, and bargained with Hitler's emissaries for an 'independent' Armenian state. That they had to boot-lick Nazi masters goes without saying...Once committed to it, there was no alternative to the price for 'independence' except subservience to Hitler."[74]

On the opposite side, ARF has had its defenders, including Armenian-American ARF member Sarkis Atamian, who in a 1955 publication, *The Armenian Community: The Historical Development of a Social and Ideological Conflict*, intended to provide a "'scholarly' vindication for the Dashnakts'ut'iwn [ARF] and its anti-Soviet political course."[75] Atamian portrays the ARF "as a victim of the pro-Soviet attacks during the years of WWII, rejecting any possibility that the Dashnakts'ut'iwn could have thought to benefit from the Nazi victory" and emphasizing the official pro-Allies policy of the party.[76] Contrary to Carlson's representation of the ANG as "Naziesque," Atamian links it to the anti-Stalinist movement of mostly Soviet POWS – including Armenians – captured by Germany and, thus, disassociates it from the ARF.[77] While never mentioning Giulkhandanian or the others on the Committee, Atamian centers solely on Kanayan, "whose role was to win '...Nazi leniency toward the Armenians in the Caucasus'" and who saved the lives of several thousand Armenian displaced persons.[78] He points to his release after his arrest by US authorities as vindication of his innocence.[79] For Atamian, the lofty goal of a "United, Free and Independent Armenia" was paramount and the reason behind both its anti-Soviet stance and its support of the Allies, even

---

[74] Carlson, "Armenian Displaced Persons," 17-21.

[75] Atamian was a member of Garegin Nzhdeh's Ts'eghakron starting in 1933. According to Sahakyan, "Regarding Garegin Nzhdeh and the Ts'eghakron movement, Atamian first of all argued that Nzhdeh had been expelled from the party because of his racist views, and, secondly, that Ts'eghakron had nothing to do with racism." See Sahakyan, "Institutions, Politics and Identities," 299; Atamian, *Armenian Community*, 390-391. See also Sahakyan's discussion on Ruben Darbinian. Sahakyan, "Institutions, Politics and Identities," 295-302.

[76] Sahakyan, "Institutions, Politics and Identities," 298-299; Atamian, *Armenian Community*, 387.

[77] Carlson, "Armenian Displaced Persons," 26, Sahakyan, "Institutions, Politics and Identities," 300; Atamian, *Armenian Community*, 399, 401.

[78] Sahakyan, "Institutions, Politics and Identities," 300; Atamian, *Armenian Community*, 401.

[79] Sahakyan, "Institutions, Politics and Identities," 300; Atamian, *Armenian Community*, 402.

the Soviet Union.[80] For other defenders of the ARF collaborators, the principal aim of men, such as Kanayan and Nzhdeh, was the preservation of Armenian – POW and civilian – life.[81]

The reconstruction of the post-WWII narrative regarding Giulkhandanian, but most ostensibly Kanayan and Nzhdeh, resembles closely – although on a more minor stage – another "memory project." Benjamin Tromly's study on the process by which the collaboration of the Vlasov movement led by "a turncoat Red Army general" with Nazi Germany was reinvented points to the similarities of memory projects during the same period, "in which peoples and states passed over or reworked memories of violence, occupation and collaboration that were potentially divisive or compromising."[82] Tromly lists three interwoven elements of the narrative: "anti-Stalinism, democracy, and struggle against Nazism."[83] It is the "first thesis... that collaboration with the Germans had been a product of anti-Stalinist convictions widespread among the Soviet people" that also resonates with the Armenian reinvention that privileges (and even privileged during World War II) the national existential struggle against Bolshevik erasure of Armenian culture, identity, and, of course, freedom.[84] Much like the Vlasovite memory project, the post-war Armenian nationalist narrative, which survives with few exceptions today, of Armenian collaboration with Nazi Germany shared "the myopia and partisanship characteristic of the genre."[85] For that reason, it is imperative to approach the evidence with a critical eye.

In this regard, the ANG's organ, *Azat Hayastan,* may provide clues regarding Giulkhandanian's and the ANG's goals and views. Each member of its editorial board and the ANG – Giulkhandanian, Abeghian, and Nzhdeh – spoke to his strength and to an aspect of ANG's agenda in the pages of the newspaper. Their views are clearly expressed in the first issue, which appeared in August 1943 and elaborated on the goals and approach of the ANG and its organ, giving us a reasonably good idea of

---

[80] Sahakyan, "Institutions, Politics and Identities," 300-301; Atamian, *Armenian Community,* 216-218.

[81] For a detailed discussion, see Thomassian, *Summer of '42*, 35-37.

[82] Benjamin Tromly, "Reinventing Collaboration: The Vlasov Movement in the Postwar Russian Emigration" in Gelinada Grinchenko and Eleonora Narvselius, eds., *Traitors, Collaborators and Deserters in Contemporary European Politics of Memory* (London: Palgrave Macmillan 2018), 90.

[83] Tromly, "Reinventing Collaboration," 99.

[84] Ibid., 87, 99-100.

[85] Ibid., 102.

the direction that editor Giulkhandanian as well as Abeghian and Nzhdeh wanted to take the paper. In the editorial, Abeghian introduces the ANG and its organ by setting up a narrative of a "clash of civilizations": on one side were "the world's satiated and gluttonous" (*ashkharhis kushterĕ ew hghp'ats'atsnerĕ*) – led by England – and on the other were "the [economically] deprived and [nationally and politically] harmed" (*zrkowats u anirowats*) – headed by Germany. Given England's and Russia's "egoist and knavish diplomacy and violent force" toward Armenians, the choice for Abeghian was to make common cause with Germany. For the ANG then, "The preservation of the Armenian people's physical existence and its unfettered progress as well as the Armenian fatherland's liberation and prosperity is the uppermost commandment."[86] In an effort to further rationalize the alignment with Germany, he adds that the same approach has also been adopted by Armenia's Caucasian neighbors. Abeghian sums up the ANG's two fundamental commandments as the following: first, the recognition of Armenia as its own particular country in the orbit of European peoples – thus the name of the organ, *Azat Hayastan* (Free Armenia). A free Armenia would be realized with the "German Reich's effective aid and under its strong protection." Second, "The creation of such political conditions in which it is possible to preserve and to advance unfettered the supreme national values – language, literature, art, economy, government, court, and all culture and public life with all their branches." Abeghian then lists a number of topics the editorial board planned to pursue in forthcoming issues: primarily anything that would be in the interest of Armenians and Armenia, Armenian-German relations in the past and present, the two peoples' bonds and mutual political, cultural, and economic interests, as well as literary and artistic subjects.[87]

---

[86] See also *Azat Hayastan* 1 (August 1943), 1.

[87] "Azgayin Khorhurd," 1-2; Similar ideas are expressed in A. Aramian, *Azat Hayastan* 2 (September-October 1943): 4-5. For Free Armenia, see also A. Aramian, *Azat Hayastan* 2/3 (September-October 1943): 7-8. For a discussion of Armeno-German relations, including during the Crusades and Israel Ori's and Joseph Emin's early modern liberation efforts seeking German assistance, see Artashes Abeghian, *Azat Hayastan* 2/3 (September-October 1943): 1-5. See also idem, "Israel Orin ĕst Krusinski ew Hanway..." [Isreal Ori according to Krusinski and Hanway...], *Hayrenik' Amsagir* 14, no. 11 (1936): 51-63. For a list of ANG's action items, see Carlson, "The Armenian Displaced Persons: A First-Hand Report on Conditions in Europe," 19. Carlson includes several excerpts from a 12-point agreement between Nazi Germany and the ANG, made public on February 15, 1943. It includes the following: "the Armenian National Council

With Giulkhandanian's article, "Khortakel en ew hoginerě..." (They have shattered the souls too...), the paper's focus moves to the Soviet Union, reflecting Giulkhandanian's deep-seated anti-Bolshevik stance. In this issue, he writes about the "soviet man" whose spirit has crumbled under threat of death, prison, unending investigations, forced lies, and so forth to such a degree that he is "gradually losing his high moral virtues, often becoming ... a machine..." In his categorization of the "soviet man" – collaborator, worker and peasant, and ordinary citizen – we see a glimpse of Giulkhandanian's earlier socialist bent as he hails the working class, especially the peasant, as the "healthiest" because he is perceived to be least under the destructive influences of the Bolsheviks, concluding that it is on them that the future Free Armenia must lean. He underscores that this development is only possible with the destruction of the Bolshevik yoke.[88] Obviously, his socialist leanings had not been completely submerged under the weight of anti-Bolshevism and Nazism. Nevertheless, an article covering the speeches of Alfred Rosenberg (ideologue of the Nazi party and Minister of the Eastern Occupied Regions) and Otto Dietrich (German SS, Hitler confidant, and Press Chief) at a press conference in Vienna (June 1943) clearly indicates the impact of Nazi ideology on Giulkhandanian's treatment of the "soviet man." While his article directly quotes Rosenberg, who is reported to have said, "Bolshevism seeks to

---

undertakes to be an agent between Germany and the Armenians; .... The Armenian National Council will do everything to facilitate the work of its patron government, including the national wealth of the land, taking into consideration the economic reconstruction of Armenia and the interest of the two peoples; .... Realizing the historic, political, economic and cultural intimate ties between Great Germany and her protectorate, Armenia, the Armenian National Council will consider it its high duty to strengthen these mentioned ties and to render them unbreakable. For this purpose are already called, and hereafter will be called, those auxiliary Armenian forces which are now active and fighting with the Germans for final victory and liberation...

The Armenian National Council is an agent in the present period of transition. Its jurisdiction and activity cease the moment when, under the leadership of Germany and the help of the Armenian National Council, a new government is created in Armenia.

An avowed task of the Council was to select – with Nazi approval, of course – Russian-Armenian soldiers from the prisoners-of-war camps. Many of these later joined special units of the Wehrmacht composed of similar anti-Soviet minority troops." See Carlson, "Armenian Displaced Persons," 19.
[88] *Azat Hayastan* 1 (August 1943): 2-3. See also *Azat Hayastan* 2/3 (September-October 1943): 10.

annihilate in man that which exists as human," Giulkhandanian also recounts that Rosenberg addressed Hitler's victory over the Soviets by repelling their attack, pushing them East, and "sav[ing] Europe."[89]

Nzhdeh picks up on this anti-Bolshevik theme in the second and last issue of the organ, calling the 1917 revolution "a revolution of spiritual bankruptcy" and a "pathologic apparition" and Bolshevism a nihilistic and "errant doctrine."[90] It is his "*Meṛnelu kamkʿē: Hay lēgēonakannerin*" (The will to die: to the Armenian legionnaires) that lays bare, however, perhaps most clearly of the three, the author's character and ideology.[91] Nzhdeh's fervent nationalism is reflected in his discussion of a homeland, where he writes, "The fatherland is a spiritual reality – it is a thing 'from the soul and for the soul'" (*voguts' ew vogu hamar*). Resurrecting the legendary memory of Vardan Mamikonian, he reminds his readers – which he assumes to be largely legionnaires – of the Mamikonians' vow: "for them their vow to die for fatherland was not solely a desire, an oath, but will... The will to die ... is valor and happiness to die for one's fatherland." It is not for Nzhdeh a matter of the fatherland demanding such sacrifice "but because the conscious death is felt as supreme desire to subdue the eternal, to become immortal." And just like the fifth-century Mamikonians who fought the more powerful Sasanian army and empire to preserve their Christian faith and autonomy, so too the legionnaires might die, but they will not be defeated.[92] Indeed, he continues, their battle is not only for fatherland but also for the race (*tsʿegh*). Speaking directly to them, he prescribes, "so that your race and fatherland live, have the will to die for them." For Nzhdeh, the "Armenian man" (hay mard) is worthless (*anpētkʿ*) if he does not have that will, and moreover, whoever is against the cultivation of that will is "an internal enemy to our race (*tsʿegh*) and fatherland." In this way, Nzhdeh leaves no room for dissent. He carves out only a single path: through the will to die the nation lives and the

---

[89] The article, however, also reports on the speeches of Dietrich and Zuterman whose focus lands on Jews and the Allies. Zuterman, identified as the vice-president presiding over the last session of the press conference, lists four Nazi ideals and goals: (1) "Liberate the peoples from the international Jewish poison;" (2) "Free the world from witnessing the danger of communist terrorism;" (3) "Emancipate working humanity from capitalist exploitation;" (4) "Emancipate the world from English imperialism." *Azat Hayastan* 1 (August 1943), 16, 17.

[90] G. Nzhdeh, *Azat Hayastan - Freies Armenien* 2/3 (September-October 1943), 5-7.

[91] Ibid.

[92] Ibid., 3.

legionnaire becomes an "eternal" hero like the Mamikonians. Any alternative path is treachery to the nation.[93]

It is worth pausing for a moment to address the use of the Mamikonians, especially Vardan who rebelled against Sasanian attempts to impose Zoroastrianism, not only in this article but also in another by Abeghian and others in the legionnaires' *Hayastan*.[94] The decisive battle at Avarayr (in today's Maku, Iran) in 451 C.E. ended with the devastating defeat of Mamikonian's forces but was followed, three decades later, by an agreement (Nvarsak, 484 C.E.) between the Armenians and the Sasanians that provided freedom of worship and some autonomy to Christian Armenia. The narrative that developed about Avarayr "became the paradigm of resistance in Armenian history" and "although Avarayr was a military defeat, it was (and is) celebrated as a 'moral victory.'" Beginning in the late nineteenth century, it took on national and nationalist overtones in Armenian collective memory.[95] Thus, in the WWII context, Nzhdeh's and others' references to the Mamikonians' martyrdom was explicit: "they may die but not be defeated – that is how the Mamikonians

---

[93] Ibid., 4. Although the term "mard" may be used more broadly in a gender-neutral way to refer to (hu)man, Nzhdeh's militaristic language and his legionnaire audience among other factors make it unlikely that he had both men and women in mind in his nationalist harangue.

[94] See, for example, *Hayastan* 17 (8 November 1942) and *Hayastan* 23 (December 20, 1942).

[95] Razmik Panossian, *The Armenians: From Kings and Priests to Merchants and Commissars* (London: Hurst & Co, 2006), 48. Sebouh Aslanian, drawing from Victor Turner, talks about the Battle of Avarayr as a "root paradigm." In particular, he focuses on Arshag Chobanian's published essay of 1898 wherein Chobanian equates "the Hamidian massacres and the War of Vardanants' as immortalized by the author Eghishe. The forced conversion of Armenians to Islam and the massacre of those who refused are for Chobanian repetitions, in symbolic time, of Vardan's resistance to Yazdigerd II's policy of forced conversion to Zoroastrianism. Even more resonant with deep continuity with Avarayr is the heroic resistance Armenians in Zeytun put up against the Ottomans only a year prior to the publication of his essay." See Sebouh Aslanian, "The Vardanants' Paradigm: Some Notes on the uses of Eghishe's work on the War of Vardan in two contributions to the Armenian Press in 1898 and 1999," unpublished paper. See also Daniel Ohanian, "An Ancient Hero in Modern Times: Remembering General Vardan Mamikonean (d. 451) in 1909 Istanbul," unpublished paper. Thanks to both authors for their intellectual generosity.

were."[96] This kind of self-assurance contrasts starkly with the dependence on German succor.

Germany as Savior: The Law of the Third Force

The celebration in 1943 of the anniversary of the first Republic's independence, which was proudly reported in Giulkhandanian's edited *Azat Hayastan*, clearly demonstrates the association of the ANG with top Nazi officials. The article gives an account of 200 officials, including representatives of the Eastern ministry's SS leadership and foreign ministry as well as top military officers, university professors, and members of the press. The program included remarks by Abeghian who spoke of the collaboration of the Bolsheviks and Allies who "hand in hand" had divided Armenia and the South Caucasus among themselves. Abeghian talked of feeling "betrayed" by so-called "friends" while the Soviets "sacrificed the Armenian people with their selfish politics." He underscored that the only path to the "emancipation of our fatherland [Armenia] from the yoke of the oppressors" and the advancement of the "Armenian Nation" lay in "the assistance of Great Germany."[97]

In many aspects, the ANG's appeal for German assistance was very much reminiscent or part of what nationalist historian Rafael Ishkhanian called the "law of the third force."[98] According to him, "When we look

---

[96] Nzhdeh, *Azat Hayastan - Freies Armenien* 2/3 (September-October 1943), 3.

[97] "We Armenians nourish [*tatsel*] certain hopes and have expectations from Germany's final victory..." in "Azgayin Khorhurd," 21-22 (21). Israel Ori appears again in this article. The ANG-Nazi German bonds are also reflected in other articles and translations of speeches by Nazi leaders. For example, the translation of Hitler's speech on German-Italian relations is followed by another on Italian treachery. Here the reference is to Italy's declaration of war on Germany on October 13, 1943. See *Azat Hayastan* (Sept-Oct 1943): 23 and "Potolioyi karavarut'ean davachanut'iwně" [The Badoglio government's treachery], *Azat Hayastan* (Sept-Oct 1943): 24. Also included in the last issue is a report by a Dr. Arzumanian on Italian Armenians who, according to the author, enjoy equality in Italy as "Aryan"s *Azat Hayastan* 2 (Sept-Oct 1943): 27.

[98] Rafael Ishkhanian, "The Law of Excluding the Third Force," in Gerard Libaridian, ed., *Armenia at the Crossroads. Democracy and Statehood in the Post-Soviet Era: Essays, Interviews and Speeches by the Leaders of National Democratic Movement in Armenia* (Watertown, MA: The Blue Crane Books, 1991), 9-38. Armenian original first published in Paris-based *Haraj* (October 18, 19, 20, and 21/22, 1989), 9-38. Ishkhanyan was a proponent of the autochthonous origins of the Armenians. See his *Hayeri tsagumě ew hnagin patmut'iwně* [The

carefully at our [Armenian] political history during the last 300 years, we see that with one or two exceptions it was always based on reliance on the third force" – that is, an almost unrelenting reliance on a force outside itself ("first force") and its neighbors ("second force") – for assistance and liberation.[99] Ishkhanian's essay is a call for self-reliance and the "exclusion of the third force."[100] In his brief survey of Armenian history, he focuses particularly on appeals to Russia and "credits" Israel Ori's (1658-1711) early modern efforts for the Russian orientation but notes its persistence through the nineteenth and early twentieth centuries from the Treaty of Berlin to WWI. He points to only one exception, that is, the founder of the first Republic of Armenia Aram Manukian who "rul[ed] out reliance," "develop[ed] a dialogue with neighbors based on an accurate accounting of one's resources," and achieved "the greatest victory of the Armenians... without the third force" in May 1918.[101] Although it goes unmentioned by Ishkhanian, it is Ori's German orientation that is the more common refrain in ANG's references to WWII Armenian-German collaboration. Ori, the son of a *melik* (regional ruler) from Zangezur, spent a significant portion of this life seeking the military support of European powers to liberate eastern Armenia from Safavid Persian rule and to create an independent state. To this end, one of the European powers he pursued was Prince Johann Wilhelm of the Palatinate (southwestern Germany), even marrying and entering into the service of the Palatinates and offering the Prince the crown of a liberated Armenia.

Although Giulkhandanian, in an ARF regional congress in 1906 convened in Tiflis, had expressed his lack of faith in Europe, "which has fed us only words; I do not believe Europe; its intervention seems improbable," he continued to place his faith in Russian assistance. He proclaimed, "we must work toward having Russians subjugate Asia Minor," further adding, "We must convince the Russian people through

---

origin of the Armenians and their ancient history] (Beirut: Altapress, 1984), published four years later in Armenia as *Hay zhoghovrdi tsagman ew hnagin patmut'ean harts'er* [Problems concerning the origin of the Armenian people and their most ancient history] (Yerevan: Hayastan Publications, 1988). See also a discussion of the "autochthonous model" by Sebouh Aslanian in his "'The Treason of the Intellectuals': Reflections on the Uses of Revisionism and Nationalism in Armenian Historiography," *Armenian Forum* 2, no. 4 (2002): 1-38 (29-34).

[99] Ishkhanian, "Law of Excluding the Third Force," 12.

[100] Ibid., 38.

[101] Ibid., 13-14, 19-22, 38.

propaganda that the ground of its future successes is Asia Minor... In a renewed free Russia, the Armenian people may advance, progress, and create for itself a fortunate situation."[102] After the Bolshevik revolution of 1917 and especially the loss of the independent Republic of Armenia to the Soviets, Giulkhandanian relinquished Russia in favor of another third force – this time, Germany.

Conclusion

The evidence clearly suggests that Giulkhandanian did not seem to share all of the views or experiences of Hervé with whom this essay began. He certainly did not share Hervé's opposition to Nazism despite Hervé's own "ambiguity on the issue of antisemitism." Giulkhandanian, unlike Hervé, also did not support an "alliance with the Soviet Union during the 1930s." He may, however, have shared his interest in Italian fascism.[103] No doubt, Giulkhandanian was affected and acted in a complex set of constantly shifting political contexts in the short span of four decades between 1905 and 1943. Certainly, when he found himself in Nazi-occupied Paris in the early 1940s, the world had come a long way from the time he began his political career on the shores of Baku's oil fields and in the revolutionary and leftist fervor of early 1900s South Caucasus. To some degree, Giulkhandanian was a man of his time and a man of his space, who operated in a tumultuous world of radicalism, revolution, and war and whose considerations and actions were often dictated by conditions on the ground rather than inflexible ideology. We began this essay with Hervé's justification or explanation of why he had swung from a position of socialism, anti-militarism, and anti-nationalism to one that espoused the authoritarian nation. As we noted, Hervé defended himself by claiming, "I am persuaded that it is not I who has changed, but the circumstances."

It is plausible that Giulkhandanian, too, had not necessarily changed but that the world around him had. It is also possible that he was a pragmatist beleaguered with the trauma of genocide as well as loss of territory and an independent state. Moreover, it is equally likely that he became and remained anxious and concerned about Armenian lives in WWII Europe and coupled with the above he chose to place his hopes on a "third force" – Nazi Germany – which he believed could help the Armenians repel the reviled Bolshevik enemy from Armenia and restore

---

[102] *Niwt'er*, 2: 276, 277.
[103] Loughlin, "Gustave Hervé's Transition," 19.

the independence interrupted by Sovietization. However, these do not sufficiently explain Giulkhandanian's "about-face." He did not leave behind a memoir that addresses this precise question of why, if at all, he changed, nor did he speak about it as did Hervé. What we have is only fragmentary outward traces of his deeds and actions in the forty-year period under consideration, thus leaving it up to scholars to infer from his involvement in various causes, his editing of assorted journals, and his close relationships with injudicious persons the deeper ideological transformation beneath the surface of the archival traces that mark his life.

The last piece of the puzzle that brings us closer to answering the question with which we began – why does Giulkhandanian seem to change, especially from nationalist-socialist revolutionary to national socialist collaborator – must be sought in Giulkhandanian's and his comrades' (that is, Abeghian and Nzhdeh) unequivocal anti-Semitism that embroiled the ANG in a campaign to remove Armenians from any association with Jews by "establishing" the Aryan origins of Armenians. Giulkhandanian and his comrades' collaboration with Nazi Germany exposes an enormous lapse of judgment not so uncommon to its time. Granted, the miscarriage of judgment in the form of collaboration, cooperation, and collusion with Nazi Germany took place under pressing circumstances; nevertheless, with historical hindsight the decisions and subsequent actions of Giulkhandanian and the ANG amounted to an ethical failure and moral bankruptcy, too often dismissed in scholarship and in collective memory at the cost of facing history.

Fig. 1 – Abraham Giulkhandanian
(1875-1946)

Fig. 2 – The Abeghian family, May 1922, likely Istanbul. Photo among Giulkhandanian family papers. The note on the backside of the photo, which says, "Family Dr. Abeghian and me on the left," is written by Giulkhandanian's son Ruben who appears in Fig. 1, on the passport. The photo was received by the ARF Archives from Rouben Giulkhandanian (France).

Fig. 3 – Abeghian is second from left; Giulkhandanian is in center, sitting and looking to his right. The backside of the photo bears a rough sketch and identities of individuals in photo.

Fig. 4 – Armenian Republic passport for Abraham Giulkhandanian, wife Haykanush, and son Ruben, residing in Istanbul, departing for Germany through Romania, 20 September 1922.

Fig. 5 – Certificate of origin for Abraham Giulkhandanian, issued by the Office of Armenian Refugees, Paris, 11 May 1933.

Photos courtesy of Armenian Revolutionary Federation Archives, Watertown, Massachusetts. Thanks to George Aghjayan, Director of the ARF Archives, for all his assistance.

Rethinking the Establishment
of the First Republic of Armenia:
Reactions of the Ottoman-Turkish and
Armenian Press in Istanbul (May-October 1918)

Ari Şekeryan

The historiography on the establishment of the First Republic of Armenia has primarily focused on the political developments of the time and the political reactions of the Armenian government.[1] Analysis of the Ottoman Turkish and Ottoman Armenian press regarding the establishment of the First Republic has thus far been lacking in the established literature. This article attempts to analyze and conceptualize the political positions of the Ottoman Turkish and non-partisan Armenian

---

[1] The literature on the historiography of the establishment of the First Republic of Armenia is rich, with a number of authoritative works having been written on the subject matter. The following is a selective list of the works: Richard G. Hovannisian, *Armenia on the Road to Independence, 1918*, (Berkeley: University of California Press, 1967); Idem, *The Republic of Armenia*, 4 vols. (Berkeley: University of California Press, 1971–1996); Ronald Grigor Suny, *Looking toward Ararat: Armenia in Modern History* (Bloomington: Indiana University Press, 1993); Simon Vrats'ean, *Hayastanĕ bolshewikean murchi yew t'rk'akan sali mijew* [Armenia Between the Bolshevik Hammer and the Turkish Anvil] (Beirut: Hamazgayin Tparan, 1953); A.A. Harutyunyan, *T'urk'akan intervents'ian Andrkovkas 1918 t'. yew ink'napashtpanakan krivnerĕ* [Turkish Intervention in the Transcaucasus and the Self-Defense Battles] (Yerevan: Haykakan SSH GA Hratarakch'ut'yun, 1984); A. Kh. Karapetyan, *1920 T'vakani Hay t'urk'akan Paterazmĕ yew sovetakan ṛusastanĕ* [Soviet Russia and the Armeno-Turkish War of 1920] (Yerevan: Hayastan, 1965); Aleksandr Khatisian, *Hayastani Hanrapetut'ean tsagumn u zargats'umĕ* [The Birth and Development of the Republic of Armenia] (Beirut: Librairie Hamaskaïne, 1968); Galust Galoyan, *Hayastanĕ yew mets derut'iwnnerĕ 1917-1923 t't'* [Armenia and the Great Powers 1917-1923)] (Yerevan, 1999); Dzatur P. Aghayan; *Hoktemberĕ yew hay zoghovrdi azatagrakan payk'arĕ* [October and the Liberation Struggle of the Armenian Nation] (Yerevan: Yerevani Hamalsarani Hratarakch'ut'yun, 1982).

press in Istanbul vis-à-vis the proclamation of the First Republic of Armenia, benefitting from a collection of the Ottoman Turkish and non-partisan Armenian press, which has until now remained mostly untouched by scholarship. The main premise of this article is that during the months of May to October 1918, both the Ottoman Turkish and non-partisan Armenian dailies welcomed the establishment of the Armenian state; however, this support remained conditional upon the Republic establishing healthy relations with the Ottomans and abandoning its territorial aspirations. Furthermore, the non-partisan Armenian dailies put forward that the Ottoman Armenians who were living within the bounds of the Ottoman Empire possessed no political aspirations of secession from the Ottoman lands. I shall provide evidence from the Ottoman Turkish and non-partisan Armenian newspapers to elaborate on this argument.

This article benefits from a collection of Ottoman Turkish and Armenian newspapers published in Istanbul from May to October 1918, such as *Vakit* (The Times), *İkdam* (Perseverance), *Haftalık Gazete* (The Weekly News), *Tasvir-i Efkar* (Picture of Ideas), *Tanin* (Resonance), *Ati* (Future), *Sabah* (Morning), *Alemdar* (The Flag-Bearer), *Verjin Lur* (The Latest News) and *Zhamanak* (The Time). In addition to the press, documents from the Prime Minister's Ottoman Archives are included in the analysis.

At the beginning of the World War I in 1914, more than thirty Armenian newspapers, journals, and periodicals were being published in Istanbul. After the declaration of the participation of the Ottoman Empire in the war, the Ottoman government embarked upon a campaign of prohibition against the Armenian press, closing twenty-five newspapers and journals, leaving only *Biwzantion* (Byzantium), *Zhamanak*, and *Verjin Lur* in business. The reason was simple: these Armenian newspapers were not affiliated with any political organizations, making them essentially 'neutral' in the eyes of the state.[2] Regarding the Armenian press, it must be underlined that the publications of the Armenian political parties such as the publications of the Armenian Revolutionary Federation (ARF) were banned by the Ottoman government during the World War I. For this reason, only the reactions of the non-partisan dailies such as *Verjin Lur* and *Zhamanak* are included in this article. Another non-partisan daily, *Biwzantion,* is not included in the analysis because the archive of the

---

[2] A. Kharatyan, *Arevmtahay mamuln ir patmut'yan avartin (1900-1922) (1900-1922)* [The Western Armenian Press at the End of its History] (Yerevan: Patmut'yan instit'ut', 2015), 12-13.

newspaper was not accessible during the time this research was conducted. Since the ARF-affiliated *Chakatamart, Kilikea, Goyamart* and other newspapers such as *Arewelean Mamul, Horizon, Hay Dzayn, Hay Ts'aw, Zhoghovurt, Zhoghovurdi Dsaynĕ* and *Erkir* were published after October 1918, they are excluded from this article.

Verjin Lur was published in Istanbul from 1914 to 1930.[3] Owned by Hrachia Der Nersesian, the paper's editorial board consisted of Armenian intellectuals Hagop Der Hagopian, Hovhannes Asbed, Levon Saterian, Ardashes Kalpakjian, Vahan Toshigian, and the famous Armenian author Yervant Odian.[4] The daily officially remained 'neutral and independent,' with no political affiliation. However, the arguments supported in the daily's columns were often in line with Ramkavar Liberal Party policies.[5] *Verjin Lur* was one of the most popular dailies among the Armenian community in Istanbul, with a circulation of ten thousand during and after WWI.

Zhamanak, which continues to be published today in Istanbul, was first published in 1908 by Misag Kochunian. It was largely popular among the members of the Armenian community, with many leading Armenian authors serialising their novels in the columns of *Zhamanak*. The circulation of the daily was the largest among all the Armenian newspapers. *Zhamanak* is an eminently important primary source for this article because it had an uninterrupted print run in 1918.[6]

The Ottoman Turkish dailies that were included in this analysis represented both pro-CUP, pro-Turkish Nationalist and anti-CUP camps within Ottoman Turkish society. For instance, while the publications of the *Vakit, İkdam, Haftalık Gazete, Tasvir-i Efkar, Tanin* and *Ati* dailies

---

[3] Garegin Levonyan, *Hayots' parberakan mamulĕ liakatar ts'uts'ak hay lragrut'yan* [The Periodical Press: A Complete Catalogue] (Yerevan: Hratarakut'yun Melk'onyan Fondi, 1934), 81.

[4] Mildanoğlu, *Ermenice Süreli Yayınlar, 1794-2000* [The Armenian Periodicals 1794-2000], 131.

[5] Kharatyan, *Arevmtahay mamuln ir patmut'yan avartin (1900-1922)*, 391. The Ramkavar Liberal party was founded in 1908 by a group of liberals who were formerly attached to the Armenakan party. The party operated as the Constitutional Democratic Party from 1908 to 1921. It was popular among upper class Armenians of Istanbul. In 1921, during the Armistice years, the party renamed itself as the Ramkavar Liberal Party. The Ramkavar party defended the idea of liberalism. Although it supported the unity and independence of Armenia, it advocated achieving this goal through negotiation and dialogue rather than violence.

[6] Mildanoğlu, *Ermenice Süreli Yayınlar, 1794-2000*, 97.

were close to the CUP and the Turkish national movement, *Sabah and Alemdar*'s publication policies were anti-CUP and anti-Turkish national movement.[7] Editorials, opinion articles, as well as news items were examined for this purpose. Even though each issue of the above-mentioned dailies from May to October 1918 were scanned, only those issues where articles appeared about the establishment of the First Armenian Republic are included in this article.

Following the signing of the Treaty of Brest-Litovsk in March 1918, Russian power and influence in the South Caucasus entered dormancy, resulting in the emergence of a power vacuum in the region.[8] The Russians agreed to withdraw their troops from *Elviye-i Selase*[9] (Three Provinces) and return control of the region to the Ottomans.[10] The dismantling and outright destruction of state institutions, as well as the departure of Russian troops from the region, led the nations of the South Caucasus – Georgia, Azerbaijan, and Armenia – into turmoil. Caught in a trap before the army of the Ottoman Empire, the three nations had no choice but to establish an

---

[7] Nuri İnuğur, *Basın ve Yayın Tarihi* (İstanbul: Çağlayan Kitabevi, 1982), 337–63.

[8] The Treaty of Brest-Litovsk was a peace agreement signed between the Bolshevik government and the Central Powers (German Empire, Bulgaria, Austro-Hungarian Empire and the Ottoman Empire) on March 3, 1918, which ended the participation of the Russians in World War I. With this peace treaty, the Ottomans took control of Kars, Ardahan, and Batum regions on the eastern border. See Donald Bloxham, *The Great Game of Genocide: Imperialism, Nationalism, and the Destruction of the Ottoman Armenians* (Oxford: Oxford University Press, 2005), 150; Razmik Panossian, *The Armenians from Kings and Priests to Merchants and Commissars* (London: Hurst & Co., 2006), 245.

[9] *Elviye-i Selase* (Three Provinces) was a geographical term used for the area of Kars, Ardahan, and Batum. This area was left to the Russian Empire during the war in 1877-1878. During the Turkish-Armenian War in 1920, the Ankara government managed to bring Kars and Ardahan back under Turkish control; Batum was left to the Bolsheviks.

[10] Haidar Bammate, "The Caucasus and the Russian Revolution (from a Political Viewpoint)," *Central Asian Survey* 10, no. 4 (1991): 10; Bülent Gökay, "The Battle for Baku (May-September 1918): A Peculiar Episode in the History of the Caucasus," *Middle Eastern Studies* 34, no. 1 (1998): 33; Richard G. Hovannisian, "Armenia and the Caucasus in the Genesis of the Soviet-Turkish Entente," *International Journal of Middle East Studies* 4 (1973): 131; Peter Sluglett, "The Waning of Empires: The British, the Ottomans and the Russians in the Caucasus and North Iran, 1917–1921," *Middle East Critique* 23, no. 2 (2014): 201; Richard G. Hovannisian, "The Allies and Armenia, 1915-18," *Journal of Contemporary History* 3 (1968): 145.

interim autonomous government which could defend the rights of the people of the South Caucasus.[11] The Transcaucasian Commissariat formed a legislative assembly, the *Seim* (Diet), which consisted of members from the national councils of Georgia, Azerbaijan, and Armenia, with additional members from the Russian Constituent Assembly.[12] Though this ostensible alliance had been formally established, the Georgians sought assistance from Germany in order to secure the protection of their lands, while the Azerbaijanis did the same with the Ottoman Turks, who held close historic and cultural ties with the Muslim Turkic populations of the Caucasus and Central Asia.[13] It was the Armenians who lacked external support, with no state showing signs of providing any until October 1918.[14] In this atmosphere of uncertainty and insecurity in the Caucasus, the Transcaucasian government announced the conscription of its population; however, the response from the masses was rather muted.[15] The Azerbaijanis were reluctant to participate in a war against the Ottomans, and the Georgians were not concerned with an Ottoman offense, with the exception of the Batum area. The Armenian National Council attempted to mobilize the Armenian population in response to the Ottoman offensive, but the window of opportunity had passed, and the Ottoman troops soon took control of Kars, Ardahan, and Batum. On April 22, the Federative Republic of Transcaucasia was founded.[16] However, only one month later, the Georgians decided to leave the Federation and

---

[11] Gökay, "The Battle for Baku (May-September 1918): A Peculiar Episode in the History of the Caucasus," 34.

[12] Bammate, "The Caucasus and the Russian Revolution (from a Political Viewpoint)," 8.

[13] Richard G. Hovannisian, *Armenia on the Road to Independence, 1918* (Berkeley: University of California Press, 1967), 183. The German-Georgian agreement was reached in May 1918 at Poti. Germans were allowed to use the railways and ports of Georgia and even occupy certain strategic points. The Georgians sought to protect themselves from the Bolshevik threat, choosing to create an alliance with Germany. See David Marshall Lang, *A Modern History of Soviet Georgia* (Westport: Greenwood Press, 1962), 206–8.

[14] One of the disadvantages of the Armenian Republic pointed out by Hovannisian. See Richard G. Hovannisian, "Caucasian Armenia Between Imperial and Soviet Rule: The Interlude of National Independence," in *Transcaucasia: Nationalism and Social Change*, ed. Ronald Grigor Suny (Ann Arbor: The University of Michigan, 1983), 259–61.

[15] Bammate, "The Caucasus and the Russian Revolution (from a Political Viewpoint)," 10.

[16] Ibid., 13.

declared their independence on May 26, which was followed shortly after by proclamations of independence from Armenia and Azerbaijan on May 28.[17] While the Armenian forces succeeded in stopping the May 1918 advance of the Ottoman troops at Sardarabad, forty miles from the capital of Yerevan, the Batum Conference ended on June 4, 1918, consummating an absolute victory for the Ottomans. According to separate agreements signed by the three republics, the Ottoman Empire recovered the previously established Turco-Russian borders of the 1878 Berlin Treaty.[18]

The First Republic of Armenia was recognized only in the areas not occupied by Ottoman troops, constituting approximately ten thousand square kilometers; the nation was confronted with a massive humanitarian crisis due to famine, disease, and thousands of refugees who had fled the areas occupied by the Ottoman Turks.[19] The prospect of famine was so grave in Armenia as indicated by reports written in the following months that there were more than 500,000 Ottoman Armenian refugees in the Republic, as well as 50,000 in the North Caucasus, living in abject poverty and on the brink of starvation.[20] Even in Yerevan, approximately 150 people died each day from hunger and typhus, and in the second largest city, Gyumri, the rate was one hundred per day. In total, 1,000 people died each day within the borders of Armenia. Reports stated that there was a shortage of both doctors and medicine, and people were reduced to collecting dead animals in the streets for food.

The situation was so grim that H. Manugian, an Armenian correspondent, wrote that Caucasian Armenians were waiting to die in front of the cemetery gates; instead of an 'Independent and United Armenia,' the Armenians would see "an independent and mass cemetery."[21] In another report, it was stated that three thousand people were dying of hunger and disease per day in Armenia. Though lacking

---

[17] Ibid., 13; Anna Mkhoyan, "South Caucasus from 1918 to 1921: History and Historical Parallels with the Contemporary Era," *Nationalities Papers* 45, no. 5 (2017): 911.
[18] Gökay, "The Battle for Baku (May-September 1918): A Peculiar Episode in the History of the Caucasus," 37; Tatul Hakobyan, *Armenians and Turks: From War to Cold War to Diplomacy* (Yerevan: Lusakn, 2013), 15–17. For the agreement between the Armenian and Ottoman governments, see BOA, HR.SYS. 2876–3, 5 June 1918.
[19] Hovannisian, "The Allies and Armenia, 1915-18," 146; Hakobyan, *Armenians and Turks: From War to Cold War to Diplomacy*, 15–17.
[20] *Chakatamart,* January 22, 1919, no. 57.
[21] *Chakatamart*, February 18, 1919, no. 84.

money, the government was able to distribute rations of meat, rice, and water.[22] These reports were written in January 1919, about five months after the signing of the Armistice of Mudros, thus at a time when the Ottoman Empire had withdrawn its forces from the region and the Allied powers had pledged assistance to the Republic. One can imagine the extent of the famine, disease, and suffering through the months of May to October 1918.[23]

The Establishment of the First Republic of Armenia and the Reactions of the Press in Istanbul

The establishment of the Armenian state in the Caucasus was welcomed by both the Ottoman Turkish and non-partisan Armenian press in Istanbul; however, the two viewed the occasion from separate vantages with separate concerns, reflecting their different political positions. The Ottoman government did not raise any objections regarding the establishment of a republic within certain designated borders and thus supported the creation of the infant state. Even though the majority of the Ottoman Turkish dailies endorsed the stance of the Ottoman government regarding the establishment of the Armenian state in the Caucasus, Turkish intellectuals were uncomfortable with the potential territorial claims entailed, which could include the return of cities such as Kars, Erzurum, Van, and Bitlis. Therefore, such Turkish authors aired their concerns surrounding the aspirations of the Armenian politicians and urged the Ottoman government to be careful in their approach to the Armenians. At the same time, the majority of Turkish intellectuals welcomed the establishment of an Armenian state, thinking that the political activism of the Armenian diaspora would come to an end if the Ottomans established healthy relations with the Republic and, furthermore, brought it under the influence of Ottoman foreign policy. Therefore, it is possible to argue that the position of the Ottoman Turkish press and Turkish intellectuals in regards to the announcement of the First Republic of Armenia in 1918 was dually motivated. There was a fear of losing lands to the Armenian state, which had good relations with the Allied powers, leading the Ottomans to

---

[22] *Alemdar*, March 22, 1919, no. 91.
[23] See Hovannisian, "Caucasian Armenia Between Imperial and Soviet Rule: The Interlude of National Independence," 261–62; George A. Bournoutian, *A Concise History of the Armenian People: From Ancient Times to the Present* (Costa Mesa, Calif.: Mazda Publishers, 2002), 297–98; Hakobyan, *Armenians and Turks: From War to Cold War to Diplomacy*, 49–52.

attempt to exert influence on the Republic in the hopes of controlling territorial demands of the established Armenian state.

The non-partisan Armenian dailies and intellectuals in Istanbul were nonetheless trying to prove that the Ottoman Armenians had remained loyal to the Ottoman Empire since the beginning of the war and urged the newly established Armenian state in the Caucasus to become friends of the Ottomans and re-establish the relations that the Armenians and Turks had for centuries. I shall argue that while analyzing the position of the non-partisan Armenian dailies, it should be taken into account that in May 1918, at the time of the establishment of the Armenian state, the war was still underway and no state had proffered support to the Armenians. Under the pressure of Ottoman public opinion, the Armenian intellectuals writing in *Verjin Lur* and *Zhamanak* refrained from making bold statements, opting instead to side with the Ottoman state. In the final section of this paper, we shall see how the position of these Armenian intellectuals and dailies changed dramatically in only a week's time following the signing of the Armistice of Mudros in October 1918.

The Ottoman Turkish Press

As mentioned above, the primary aim of the Turkish policy concerning the Armenian state was to bring it under the influence of the Ottomans in order to avoid any territorial loss. As a means to temper the territorial claims of the Armenian state, the Ottoman Turkish press and Turkish intellectuals focused on the Ottoman Armenians, admonishing them to remain faithful to the Ottoman state, for if the Ottoman Armenians pursued secessionist aspirations, the territorial claims of the Armenian state would be legitimized in the eyes of the international community.

To illustrate the position of the Ottoman Turkish dailies, one may consider an editorial published in *İkdam*. Entitled "The Armenia," this editorial provides insight into Ottoman public opinion regarding the Armenians and the Armenian state. *İkdam* argued that the Armenians were free to do as they pleased within the borders of their country, but any attempt to intervene on behalf of the Ottoman Armenians would be considered an attempt to meddle in the internal affairs of the Ottoman Empire. The daily counseled the Ottoman Armenians that they had no bond with the Armenian state in the Caucasus. *İkdam* went on to argue that the only difference between Ottoman Turks and Armenians was religion, even claiming that Ottoman Armenians were indeed "Christian Turks" and "Ottomans who were following the Orthodox church." In conclusion, the editorial warned the Ottoman Armenians that they should show complete loyalty to the Ottoman state if they wanted to continue to "live" and "prosper" in the "glorious" empire rather than remain a member of a tiny, mountainous state in the Caucasus.[24] The argumentation of *İkdam* provides important clues for our discussion here. As has been underlined, the Turkish public and policy makers had two primary concerns regarding the Armenian state: the potential support of Ottoman Armenians to the Armenian state and, inversely, the potential signaling of support by the Armenian state to Ottoman Armenians. Therefore, the majority of Turkish intellectuals proclaimed to Ottoman Armenians that they had lived in "brotherhood" with the Turks in the past and thus should not "backstab" their birth state. It is important to note here that the deportations and genocide that occurred during the wartime were nearly absent in the discussion – be it the Armenian press or the Ottoman Turkish press. *İkdam*'s concluding remarks also bear significance in the sense that it defined the newly established Armenian state as being "tiny" and "a mountainous state without any natural resources." This "tiny, mountainous, and poor Armenian state" was acceptable to the Ottoman Turkish public.

Vakit reminded Armenians of the total lack of support from the Allied powers in response to their request for military assistance, prompting them to question, "What shall we do? Our cannons could not reach Mt. Ararat."[25] As a result, the daily advised Ottoman Armenians to pledge loyalty to the Ottoman Empire in order to be seen as equal subjects. *Vakit* welcomed those Armenian dailies publishing articles in support of the idea of Ottomanism.[26] A few days later, *Vakit* again emphasized that, with the exception of the Ottoman Empire, no state in the world – including neither Britain nor France – supported the establishment of a free Armenian state. The Allied powers showed no sympathy toward the Caucasian Armenians, and the Germans prioritized the protection of Georgian rights in the region.[27] In contrast, according to *Vakit*, the Ottoman government had welcomed the establishment of the Armenian state in the Caucasus, immediately recognizing its sovereignty. Furthermore, *Vakit* proposed that the Ottoman government give assistance to the newly established Republic, as doing so would grant the Ottomans a degree of influence over the Armenian diaspora communities. According to the daily, if the

---

[24] *İkdam*, June 24, 1918, no. 7678; *Verjin Lur*, June 24, 1918, no. 1297.

[25] *Vakit*, June 27, 1918, no. 249.

[26] Ibid.

[27] Hovannisian, *Armenia on the Road to Independence, 1918*, 183.

Ottoman government won the sympathy of the Armenian state in the Caucasus, it would serve to dilute the anger and enmity of the global Armenian diaspora directed towards it, as well as serving a dual purpose— by providing basic aid to the Armenian state, the Ottoman government could help establish a stable structure on its eastern border and avert the ambitions of the Ottoman Armenians to unite with their compatriots. [28] *Vakit* wrote:

> There is the Armenian nation that, if its need for independence is not satisfied, will not stop causing havoc and will not abstain from doing anything. The main target of this anger will be us... The only way to free the Armenian nation from such an irresponsible situation is to make them landlords. If they become landlords, they would stop political riots and engage in trade and agriculture. In this way, we would get rid of both an insecure structure on our Eastern border which wants to interfere at every instance, and those Armenians who secretly lobby against us in foreign countries and provoke our own Armenian citizens. [29]

This skeptical approach of the Ottoman intellectuals can be seen in a letter addressed to Talat Pasha which was published in *Ati* daily, addressing the political agenda of the government regarding the Armenian state. *Ati* sent a letter to Talat Pasha urging him about a possible "Armenian danger." According to the daily, considering that the Armenians had previously engaged in armed conflict even when lacking an officially recognized military, the Ottoman state was understandably concerned that if the Armenian state established and organized an army of 25,000 people, it could result in serious consequences, including the potential of becoming "a second Bulgaria or Macedonia." *Ati* heeded Talat Pasha to view the establishment of the Armenian state with the greatest of caution, as it could become "a satellite of the USA or Britain in the region," "causing problems" for the Ottoman state. [30] Additionally, the daily ran an editorial on the declaration of the Armenian Republic in the Caucasus, warning the Ottoman Armenians not to engage in any further revolutionary activity:

---

[28] *Vakit*, September 3, 1918, no. 316.
[29] Ibid.
[30] *Ati*, June 23, 1918, no. 1785.

> Some of our fellow citizens, who assume themselves as Armenians of Armenia (*Ermeniyye*), started to speak of 'you' and 'we'... Armenians, who constitute a minority in almost every part of our state, are Ottomans in the first place... An Armenian should consider Ottomanism superior to his Armenianness. For Armenians, there is life and prosperity in forgetting the Tashnagts'ut'iwn [ARF] past.[31]

The argumentation that the Armenian revolutionaries were engaging in "harmful activities" against the Ottoman state was put forth by not only the *Ati* daily. One of the prominent Turkish intellectuals of the time, Ahmed Emin, in his lead article published in *Vakit*, claimed that these "harmful activities" of the Armenian revolutionaries affected the life of the greater Armenian community and that the massacres which happened during the wartime were a result of the activities of the Armenian revolutionaries. According to him, the primary responsibility for the "Armenian massacres" lay with the Armenian revolutionaries and the British Empire, with that of the Russians and the Ottoman government being secondary. He highlighted that the Armenian state was established within the natural borders of the Armenian nation; as such, if the Armenian government would abide by these borders and not pursue a policy of territorial annexation of Ottoman lands, nor provoke the Ottoman Armenians to rebellion, the Ottoman state would remain as the friend of the Armenians and would provide any assistance needed.[32]

In addition to Ahmed Emin and the *Ati* editorial, Yunus Nadi, another prominent intellectual of the time, also drew parallel arguments in his articles. In a front-page article published in *Tasvir-i Efkar*, he argued that the Armenian state would not have been founded without the help of the Ottoman state and, furthermore, that without the support of the Ottomans, the Armenians could not guarantee their existence in the Caucasus. However, he maintained that the "revolutionary Armenians" living in Europe were publishing propagandist articles in Western newspapers, claiming that the Ottoman state had annihilated the Ottoman Armenians during the wartime and now sought to destroy the new Armenian state in the Caucasus. In his view, the "Armenian question" had been successfully addressed by the "measures" taken by the Ottoman state during the wartime and the subsequent establishment of the Armenian state in the

---

[31] *Ati*, June 25, 1918, no. 174.
[32] *Vakit*, June 27, 1918, no. 249.

Caucasus.[33] It is noteworthy that, beyond a strategy to keep the Ottoman Armenians aligned with the Ottoman state while at the same time urging the Armenian state not to provoke the Ottoman Armenians, the Ottoman Turkish public viewed the establishment of an Armenian state as the end of the Armenian question. Thus, the Ottoman Turkish intellectuals argued that the establishment of a "Great Armenia," intended to include the *Vilayet-i Sitte* and Cilicia regions, was concluded with the creation of the Armenian state within the current borders. According to *Tasvir-i Efkar*, the Armenian troops "occupied" the city of Yerevan, and the newly established Armenian state possessed irredentist aims, demanding the annexation of certain regions of Georgia, Azerbaijan, and the Ottoman state to its authority; therefore, the daily cautioned the Ottoman government to be vigilant in its dealings with the Armenian state.[34]

Similar to the ideas presented in *Ati, Vakit*, and *Tasvir-i Efkar,* an editorial published in *Haftalık Gazete* claimed that Armenian foreign policy was guided by two paramount goals—first to annex the Borchalo region from Georgia, and then that of the Karabagh region. The daily claimed that Armenians were trying to win the support of the Ottoman government and Ottoman public opinion in order to achieve these objectives, putting forward that the policy of Armenia was "tetrahedral and insincere," as the Armenians were simultaneously juggling relations with the British, Russians, and French, in addition to the Ottomans. According to *Haftalık Gazete*, the Armenians should not forget that the establishment of the Armenian state was a "benevolent gesture" from the Ottomans and that the existence of the Armenian state "would always be attached to the protection of the Ottomans."[35]

The argumentation of the Ottoman Turkish intellectuals and press regarding the establishment of the Armenian state rested on two key points. Firstly, they stated that the Armenian state had been established within its natural borders, and therefore the territorial claims were not based on demographic realities such as being majority on those lands. The second point was that Ottoman Armenians were subjects of the Ottoman Empire, and as such, the Armenian state should not incite Ottoman Armenians to interfere in the domestic politics of the Ottoman state. By establishing friendly relations with the "diminutive" Armenian state, suggested Ottoman intellectuals, the government would be positioned to achieve a number of significant outcomes. Through improving relations,

---

[33] *Tasvir-i Efkar*, June 29, 1918, no. 2500; *Verjin Lur*, June 29, 1918, no.1302.
[34] *Tasvir-i Efkar*, July 6, 1918, no. 2507.
[35] *Haftalık Gazete*, August 29, 1918.

the Ottomans would be able to navigate the territorial claims of the Armenian state diplomatically. Such friendly relations with the Armenian state would also aid in "controlling" Ottoman Armenians. Finally, in demonstrating their support of the Armenian state, Ottomans would showcase to the Allied powers that they were not the enemies of the Armenians and that they had not pursued a policy of annihilation of the Armenian population in wartime. This reasoning can be seen, for example, in the pages of *İkdam*, which criticized articles published in Europe on the Armenian genocide, claiming that the Ottoman state had from the beginning supported the establishment of an Armenian state in the Caucasus and had recognized its sovereignty at once. Therefore, the daily asserted that it was outrageous to suggest that the Ottomans had wanted to annihilate the Armenians, instead ascribing blame to the British Empire for the massacres.[36]

The position of the non-partisan Armenian dailies: *Verjin Lur* and *Zhamanak*

While the Ottoman Turkish press was pressuring the Ottoman government to act with caution in establishing relations with the Armenian state and to urge Ottoman Armenians to distance themselves from "revolutionary activities," the non-partisan Armenian dailies were publishing articles expressing the "loyalty" of Armenians to the Ottoman state and showing support for the Ottoman policy toward the Armenian state.

To illustrate the political position of the non-partisan dailies at the time, an opinion article published in the *Zhamanak* daily may be taken as an example. On 25 June, the *Zhamanak* daily declared that the Armenian state should invest in developing friendship with the Ottomans, stating that the Armenian government was already aware of this reality, as they sought to include Turkish and Georgian members in the Cabinet of the Armenian State in order to establish healthy relations with the Ottoman Empire, Georgia, and Azerbaijan.[37]

To further illustrate the position of the non-partisan Armenian dailies in Istanbul, we can examine a dispute where one Armenian daily, *Verjin Lur*, accused another Armenian daily, *Zhamanak*, of irresponsibility in its coverage. *Zhamanak* published an article on the history of the Armenian

---

[36] *İkdam*, September 24 1918, no. 7764.
[37] *Haftalık Gazete*, July 4, 1918.

Kingdom of Cilicia, which ruled the region for roughly three centuries.[38] While the article in *Zhamanak* bore no particular agenda, *Verjin Lur*'s editorial severely criticized *Zhamanak*'s decision to print the article, claiming that it disturbed the "healthy relations between the Ottoman Turks and the Armenians." *Verjin Lur* admonished *Zhamanak* to exercise greater caution when publishing such an article, as it could be perceived by the Ottomans as a call to re-establish an Armenian kingdom in the Cilicia region.[39] The reaction of *Verjin Lur* illustrates the position and concerns of the intellectuals belonging to this camp. Even though *Zhamanak* was also a non-partisan daily and it did not publish the article with the intention of advancing a political agenda, *Verjin Lur* sent a clear message that the Armenian dailies should be careful not to spread the appearance of distrust in Turkish-Armenian friendship in their publications.

With regard to the establishment of the Armenian state, *Verjin Lur* assured the Ottoman public in an editorial that the Armenians living in the Ottoman Empire had no political attachment to the Armenian state in the Caucasus and, as subjects of the Ottoman Empire, the Armenians had been and would remain loyal to the Ottoman state.[40] Further commenting on the statements of Prime Minister Kachaznuni and Foreign Minister Alexander Khatisian regarding the intention of the Armenian government to establish friendly relations with the Turks, *Verjin Lur* wrote that the only logical course of action for the Armenian government would be to ally with the Turks, who endured as the most powerful state in the region.[41]

Avedis Surenian, one of the daily's editors, indicated in his lead article, published 22 June 1918, that the most viable strategy for the Armenian state was to be friends of the Ottomans and that the Ottoman Armenians should resume their position as "loyal subjects" of the Ottoman Empire.[42] In a follow-up article, he underlined that a "judicious" Armenian state should work to gain the goodwill of the Ottomans because it would be deleterious for the Armenian state to additionally have an enemy army on the western borders when they were already enmeshed in troubles with Azerbaijan in the east and Georgia in the north. According to him,

---

[38] BOA, HR.SYS 2886 – 5, 14 July 1918.
[39] *Verjin Lur*, July 20, 1918, no.1320.
[40] *Verjin Lur*, June 21, 1918, no. 1296.
[41] *Verjin Lur*, September 18, 1918, no. 1370.
[42] *Verjin Lur*, June 22, 1918, no. 1295.

resolving the issues with Azerbaijan would be easier if the Armenian state first improved its relations with the Ottomans.[43]

The Arrival of the Armenian Delegation (June 1918)

In addition to the reactions of the non-partisan Armenian dailies and intellectuals, the statements of representatives of the Armenian state – and how they were covered in the Ottoman Turkish and non-partisan Armenian press – also carry importance. Following the escalation of rhetoric in the Ottoman Turkish press that the newly established Armenian state could not be relied upon for their loyalty, a representative of the Armenian state, Khatisian, in his statements given to Turkish reporters, revealed the Armenian state's strategic goal of maintaining healthy relations with the Ottomans in order to directly affect its relationship with Azerbaijan. He argued that since Azerbaijan was a satellite state of the Ottomans, improving relations with the Ottomans would increase the chance of finding a resolution to the border disputes with Azerbaijan.[44]

Tasvir-i Efkar published a letter by Khatisian but made the point of describing its contents as "insincere." In his letter, Khatisian attempted to assure readers that the Armenian state's primary objective was to secure the friendship of the Ottoman state and that it did not aspire to annex any Ottoman lands. Secondly, he argued that the Armenian state in the Caucasus had no rights to interfere on behalf of Ottoman Armenians who were living in the Ottoman Empire and declared that Ottoman Armenians held no attachments to the Armenian state in the Caucasus. He explained that the problems of Ottoman Armenians were the result of internal problems within the Ottoman state and were in no way related to his government. In his concluding remarks, Khatisian advised the Ottoman Armenians to move on from the wartime genocide and re-establish friendly relations with the Ottoman Turks, so as to continue to live in brotherhood within the Ottoman borders.[45] Along the same lines, one of the representatives of the Armenian state, Avedis Aharonian, in an interview, ensured that the aim of the delegation[46] in Istanbul was to build

---

[43] *Verjin Lur,* August 3, 1918, no. 1331.

[44] *Tasvir-i Efkar*, June 22, 1918, no. 2493.

[45] *Tasvir-i Efkar*, July 6, 1918, no. 2507; *Verjin Lur*, June 23, 1918, no. 1296.

[46] The Armenian diplomats that visited Istanbul were Avedis Aharonian, Alexander Khatisian, Sdepan Gorganian, Harutyun Agabalian, Levon Lisitsian, Kevork Khatisian, Hagop Kocharian, Dikran Mirzaian, Arshag Harutyunian, and Mikael Babajanian. See *Verjin Lur*, 20 June 1918, no. 1295.

fraternity with the Ottoman state, making clear that any problems of Ottoman Armenians fell under the domain of the Ottoman state, and, therefore, they had no authority to intervene on behalf of the Ottoman Armenians.[47] It is important to interpret the statements of the Armenian politicians as tactical decisions, for during the period of May to October 1918, the defeat of the Ottoman Empire was not yet certain, and no Western power had openly declared support for the Armenian state. Furthermore, the fledgling Armenian state engaged in territorial disputes with their two neighbors, Georgia and Azerbaijan. Armenian politicians simply wanted to prevent the Ottomans from becoming a third hostile state against their recently established Republic.

During their visit to Istanbul, members of the Armenian delegation embarked upon a campaign to rehabilitate their image in the eyes of the Ottoman Turkish public, pursuing every opportunity to appear in the columns of the Ottoman dailies in order to reshape what had become a hostile public perception of the Armenian state. In an interview with the *Vakit* daily, the members of the Armenian delegation reminded readers that the Ottomans had been the first to recognize the Armenian state, noting the importance that this "gesture" carried for Armenians, as well as making clear that their primary goal for the Istanbul Conference was to cement the bond between the two states again. At the same time, the Armenian delegation had come to Istanbul to accomplish two significant political agenda items. First, they sought to secure the Ottoman government's guarantee to allow the safe return of Armenian refugees who had fled to the Caucasus during the genocide. Second, they pursued a trade deal on the importation of certain necessities from Turkey, such as wheat, flour, and meat.[48] Even though the delegation's principal mission was to achieve these goals, it used the occasion to state its territorial demands, that is the Borchalo region from Georgia and the Karabagh region from Azerbaijan. The announcement of the Armenian delegation was published in the *Haftalık Gazete* daily, exhibiting the stance of Armenian foreign policy towards Georgian, Azerbaijani, and Turkish politicians. The delegation presented its case in the following manner: once the Armenian state had been granted the borders as outlined by the delegation, it would then begin to integrate the Armenian communities scattered throughout the Caucasus. In turn, this would decrease the activities of "Armenian revolutionaries" outside Armenia – following the return of the Armenian

---

[47] *Sabah*, June 28, 1918. no. 10280; *İkdam*, June 30, 1918, no. 7684; *Haftalık Gazete*, July 4, 1918.
[48] *Vakit*, September 22, 1918, no. 329.

diaspora communities to live within the borders of Armenia, the delegation argued, the propagandist activities against the Ottomans would come to an end, enabling the continued development of friendly relations between the two nations.[49] The Armenian delegation explained that the population within the proposed borders of the Armenian state would be composed of seventy percent Armenians together with thirty percent non-Armenians, including Kurds, Azerbaijanis, Russians, Georgians, and Turks.[50] Mikael Babajanian stated in an interview that relations between Armenians and Turks in the Caucasus were improving, giving as evidence that the Armenian government had allocated two posts in the Cabinet to be occupied by Turks. Furthermore, use of the Turkish language was permitted in governmental buildings, an act of good will towards the Turkish minority.[51] He affirmed that the Armenian government was invested in taking steps to facilitate peaceful cohabitation between the ethnic minorities and the majority within the Armenian state.[52]

A letter from Boghos Nubar to Clemenceau elicited strong reactions from Turkish intellectual circles. The Ottoman dailies further argued that the "diaspora Armenians" and the "Armenian revolutionaries" residing in Europe were fomenting dissent against the Ottoman state and that the Ottoman Armenians and the Armenians in the Caucasus should publicly refute the claims of Armenians in Europe.[53] Thus, the Ottoman public exerted pressure upon Armenians living within Ottoman lands to state that they were not of the same opinion with those Armenians in Europe. Patriarchal locum tenens Archbishop Kapriel Jevahirjian, in response to the escalating anger of Turkish intellectuals, argued that the Armenian community in the Ottoman Empire had not involved itself in politics during the wartime and had never sought revenge for the Armenian massacres. He underlined that he prayed for the two nations to live again in brotherhood, as they had for centuries under the auspices of the Ottoman state. According to Archbishop Jevahirjian, Armenians should not dwell on the "past events" and instead focus on "re-establishing" friendly relations with the Turks.[54] In addition to the statements from Archbishop Jevahirjian, the representative of the Armenian community in the Ottoman state, the representative of the Armenian government, Khatisian, clarified

---

[49] *Haftalık Gazete*, August 29, 1918.
[50] *Haftalık Gazete*, August 1, 1918.
[51] *Verjin Lur*, August 27, 1918, no. 1351.
[52] *Verjin Lur*, August 29, 1918, no. 1353.
[53] *İkdam*, August 11, 1918, no. 7723; *Haftalık Gazete*, August 29, 1918.
[54] *Tasvir-i Efkar*, October 29, 1918, no. 2545.

in an interview that Boghos Nubar occupied no official position within the Armenian government; therefore, his words could not be taken as the official position of the Armenian state. When asked how the Armenian delegation regarded Boghos Nubar's statement, he emphasized that Armenians did not aspire to reclaim lands from the Ottoman Empire and that the primary aim of the delegation in Istanbul was to discuss the return of Armenian refugees to Ottoman lands, as they were living under terrible conditions in the Caucasus.[55]

In response to the sentiments expressed in the Ottoman Turkish dailies, the non-partisan Armenian dailies sought to regain the "trust of the Ottoman Muslims" by publishing articles and opinions expressing the "loyalty of the Ottoman Armenians" towards the Ottoman state. With the ongoing war and political uncertainty at hand, Armenian intellectuals writing in *Verjin Lur* and *Zhamanak* dailies did not want to give Ottoman Turkish society any reason to incite hatred against them. *Verjin Lur* published a lead article written by Avedis Surenian, in which the author echoed thoughts previously expressed in the Ottoman Turkish press: "We enthusiastically shake the brotherly hand that they extend to us... being the children of the same country, the Turk and the Armenian are forever equal and together... both would live happy. We greet with gladness this brotherly cordial expression."[56]

Throughout the war, the Ottoman Armenian community suffered as the target of genocide. With a considerable number of Armenian intellectuals either imprisoned, deported or killed, and the majority of the Ottoman Armenian population scattered throughout the Empire, the Armenian community was left decimated. Thus, the pro-Turkish stance of the two non-partisan Armenian dailies did not represent the whole Armenian community in the Ottoman Empire. Even though there was justifiable anger within the Armenian community toward the Ottoman state and Turkish/Muslim society, the two non-partisan dailies strategically chose to wait until the end of the war and the beginning of the occupation of Ottoman lands by the Allied powers to reveal their political position. An editorial published in the 6 July 1918 edition of *Verjin Lur*, for instance, strongly supported Turkish-Armenian friendship:

> Let's think for a moment. Who are the closest elements in
> this country? And is it even possible to distinguish Turks and
> Armenians from each other, these two elements who mostly

---

[55] *Haftalık Gazete*, August 29, 1918; *Verjin Lur*, 30 August 1918, no. 1354.
[56] *Verjin Lur*, June 26, 1918, no. 1299.

have similar appearance, behavior and pronunciation… Don't we find Armenians and Turks most similar to each other in the plays of Mnagian, Burhaneddin and Benlian, who represent Turkish social life? Starting with our grandees, we wish to see each Armenian working for this [Turkish-Armenian brotherhood]. We call upon Armenian deputies, officials, leading merchants, intellectuals, teachers and editors to put extremely serious efforts towards the strengthening of Turkish-Armenian brotherhood.[57]

The Signing of the Armistice of Mudros (October 1918)

Following the removal of the CUP government in October 1918, the tone of the non-partisan Armenian dailies quickly began to change. Seeing the fall of the government as a bright light finally appearing at the end of the tunnel, the dailies gave voice to a wave of long-restrained criticism towards the CUP government. This turn of events altered the discourse of the dailies: they became more vocal in demanding fundamental democratic rights. They asked that the new cabinet, on behalf of Armenian victims and survivors, return their constitutional rights immediately.[58]

On the very day of the signing of the Armistice of Mudros, the atmosphere of elation was palpable in the Armenian community. On November 1, 1918, *Verjin Lur* announced the Armistice with the headline, "The Whole Capital Celebrates and Goes into Raptures," and the lead article, titled "Today's Enthusiasm: The Flags of the Entente Fly Splendidly," opened with a passage reflecting the Armenian political transformation: *"Kristos haryaw i merelots"* (Christ is risen from the dead!). As has been discussed above, only a matter of months before the signing of the Armistice of Mudros, *Verjin Lur* had called upon Armenian intellectuals and the public to support Armenian-Turkish friendship and be "loyal citizens" of the Ottoman State.

The flags of Greece, Italy, France, and Britain were flown on the streets of Pera, with Christians greeting each other, "Christ is risen from

---

[57] *Verjin Lur*, July 6, 1918, no. 1307. Born in Istanbul in 1839, [Mardiros] Mnagian helped found the Ottoman theatre, writing and translating hundreds of plays. [Serope] Benlian was a famous Armenian theatre actor born in Istanbul in 1835. He spent his career travelling the cities of the Ottoman Empire – from the Greek Islands to Edirne, from Cairo to Adana – to bring plays to the stage. Burhaneddin [Tepsi] was a Turkish theatre actor and writer born in 1882 in Tarsus, Adana.

[58] *Verjin Lur*, October 15, 1918, no. 1393.

the dead! Blessed is the resurrection of Christ!" According to an Armenian correspondent, the streets were full of people crying tears of joy. The Armistice of Mudros, perceived as salvation for the Ottoman Armenians, was likened to the resurrection of Jesus, imbuing it with divine meaning. However, the correspondent feared the celebration would end like those held after the announcement of the restoration of the Ottoman constitution in 1908:[59] "The scene clearly reminded me of the Constitution announcement days ten years ago, which, sadly, later in faint hands became a dictatorship causing bloodsheds that this unlucky country suffered for four years."[60]

The Armistice opened a new stage in the history of Ottoman Armenians. The publications of the non-partisan Armenian dailies brought to the surface feelings from the Armenian community which had been suppressed during wartime – anger toward Muslim/Turkish society and the CUP government in particular. Nevertheless, as we have seen, only just a month before the war ended, these two dailies were still publishing articles promoting Turkish-Armenian friendship and the idea of "peaceful coexistence" in the same country. The pro-Turkish/pro-Ottoman approach of *Verjin Lur* and *Zhamanak* drastically changed with the signing of the Armistice of Mudros once it was clear that the threat had subsided.

---

[59] The Ottoman constitution (*Kanun-i Esasi*), ratified in 1876, was restored following the Revolution of 1908, also known as the Young Turk Revolution. The Ottoman Armenians were ardent supporters of the CUP during their fight for the declaration of the constitution, and following the revolution, many public celebrations were organized by the Armenians and Turks under the motto '*liberté, égalité, fraternité.*' However, following the revolution, in 1909, the Armenians of Adana were massacred during the counter-revolutionary uprising. For the Young Turk Revolution and the political position of the Ottoman Armenians regarding these developments, see Bedross Der Matossian, *Shattered Dreams of Revolution From Liberty to Violence in the Late Ottoman Empire* (Stanford: Stanford University Press, 2014); Idem, "From Bloodless Revolution to Bloody Counterrevolution: The Adana Massacres of 1909," *Genocide Studies and Prevention* 6 (2011): 152-73; Ohannes Kılıçdağı, "Socio-Political Reflections and Expectations of the Ottoman Armenians after the 1908 Revolution: Between Hope and Despair" (Ph.D. thesis, Boğaziçi University, 2014); Ohannes Kılıçdağı, "The Bourgeois Transformation and Ottomanism Among Anatolian Armenians after the 1908 Revolution"; Ari Şekeryan, ed., *1909 Adana Katliamı: Üç Rapor* [1909 Adana Massacre: Three Reports] (Istanbul: Aras Yayıncılık, 2014).

[60] *Verjin Lur*, November 1, 1918, no. 1407.

Conclusion

The reactions of Ottoman Turkish intellectuals and the press regarding the establishment of the Armenian state must be understood within the framework of the politics of the Great War. By August 1918 – after the August 8 defeat of the German army on the *Schwarze Tag*, which saw the British unleash a crushing tank and armored attack at Amiens[61] – it was clear that the only path left for the Ottoman Empire was to negotiate a surrender.[62] Ottoman politicians and intellectuals anticipated that the newly established Armenian state would work with the Allied powers and demand the annexation of the Empire's eastern provinces. With this particular concern in mind, the Ottoman government strove to create the appearance of collaboration with the Armenian state in order to wield influence over it. However, being a friend of the Armenian state was not part of the real political strategy of the Ottoman government, during both wartime and the postwar period. Therefore, even though the Ottoman government had not protested the establishment of the Armenian state in the Caucasus, it did take measures to control the extent of the Armenians' demands. The prevention of a possible collaboration between the Armenians in the Ottoman Empire, the Armenians in diaspora, and the Armenian state was at the core of the Ottomans' political strategy.

The non-partisan Armenian dailies in Istanbul, on the other hand, supported the arguments of the Ottoman Turks, and the Armenian intellectuals published articles in these dailies calling for the Armenian government to cooperate with the Ottomans and not pursue territorial claims. This was an act of self-preservation in order to protect its physical existence and avoid enduring any further violence, such as had been wrought during the course of the war. Due to the security concerns, these dailies had expressed support for the Ottoman policies. However, following the signing of the Armistice of Mudros and the occupation of the Ottoman lands by Allied troops, the position of these dailies transformed drastically. This change in political position can be traced in the articles, news items, and editorials published during the Armistice years from October 1918 to 1922.

As has been demonstrated with evidence from the Ottoman Turkish and non-partisan Armenian dailies of Istanbul, the reactions by these

---

[61] Gwynne Dyer, "The Turkish Armistice of 1918 2: A Lost Opportunity: The Armistice Negotiations of Moudros," *Middle Eastern Studies* 8 (1972): 314.
[62] Idem, "The Turkish Armistice of 1918: The Turkish Decision for a Separate Peace, Autumn 1918," *Middle Eastern Studies* 8 (1972): 144.

dailies during the months of May to October 1918 regarding the establishment of the Armenian state in the Caucasus aligned closely, though the former had political reservations and the latter existential concerns. It is crucial, however, to conceptualize the political positions of the Armenian community and the Ottoman state within the broader context of the Armistice years from October 1918 to September 1923. In that sense, this article fills a gap in the recent historiography by bringing the press sources into the discussion and by focusing on a short yet important period to analyze the reactions of Ottoman Turkish and non-partisan Armenian dailies vis-à-vis the establishment of the First Republic.

Fig. 1 – *Verjin Lur*

Fig. 2 – *Zhamanak*

Fig. 3 – *İkdam*

Fig. 4 – *Vakit*

Fig. 5 – *Haftalık Gazete*

The Role of Women in the Social and Political Life of the Republic of Armenia (1918-1920)

Seda D. Ohanian

After having lost its statehood in the Middle Ages, Armenia gained independence in May 1918 amidst very complicated geopolitical and military conditions, becoming the first modern Armenian state, known as the Republic of Armenia (*Hayastani Hanrapetut'iwn*). At the time, the territory comprised only 12,000 sq. kilometers. However, it would gradually expand, be strengthened, and become a viable democratic republic. In this regard, the Parliament Speaker, Avetik Sahakian, after reviewing the tragic events that led to the formation of the independent Republic and in the presence of the Turkish envoy as well as other countries' diplomatic representatives, concluded optimistically, on August 1, 1918 at the opening session of *Hayastani Khorhurd*, that the "doors of the jail will open and our borders will expand with the iron force of life, with the defense of our just and indisputable right to the occupied lands."[1]

From the very beginning, Armenia was faced with countless obstacles and misfortune. Nevertheless, its people and leadership struggled to overcome those difficulties – domestic and foreign alike – and succeeded in laying the foundations of a modern state. Hence, to achieve this goal, certain steps had to be taken to establish, first and foremost, a legal structure for the fledging Republic. In this chaotic situation, Armenia laid its legislative foundations for a parliamentary system of government.

At the time, elections were out of the question. Thus, the Armenian National Council (established in Tbilisi in 1917 and then moved to Yerevan in July 1918) agreed to triple its membership and serve as an interim legislative body. This Council (*Khorhurd*), convened on August 1, 1918, and elected Avetik Sahakian as the Speaker of the Parliament. The Council worked until June 1919, when normal elections were held and members of Armenia's Parliament (Khorhrdaran) were elected from both

---

[1] Rouben Ter Minassian, *Hay heghap'okhakani mĕ hishataknerĕ*, hator 7 [The memoirs of an Armenian revolutionary, vol. 7] (Los Angeles: Horizon Press, 1952), 146.

Eastern and Western Armenians residing in the newly born Republic of Armenia.

Although the crisis surrounding the Act of May 1919 about the declaration of an Independent, Free, and United Armenia by the Government of Armenia on May 28, 1919 was still at its peak, especially due to the opposition (in particular the National Delegation in Paris), this Parliament carried on its tasks until the Sovietization of the Republic on December 2, 1920.

The statute for elections to the Parliament – a modified version of the procedures used in 1917 for elections to the All-Russian Constituent Assembly – was adopted by the government on March 12, 1919.[2] This statute – duly edited to conform to Armenian reality – was named "Law for Armenia's Parliament Elections" and enfranchised all adult citizens, twenty-years-old and over, regardless of religion, race or sex, including Western Armenian refugees, who resided in different parts of the Armenian Republic. According to this law, the entire country became a single electoral district and selected the eighty members of Parliament, of which twelve were Western Armenians based on the Act of May 1919.

When the Parliament convened on August 1, 1919, exactly one year after its inaugural session, the atmosphere was quite different. World War I was over and the Turkish invasion of Eastern Armenia's territories (according to June 1918 Batum Agreement) had been repulsed and amidst promising hopes, the young Republic, defying all kinds of odds and seemingly never-ending war conditions, managed to survive and even expand its borders. The first session was opened by Avetik Sahakian, whose "faith in the Armenian people and their fledging state remained inexhaustible."[3]

In order to prepare draft legislation and introduce it to the Parliament, twelve parliamentary committees were duly created through open voting during the third session of the Parliament (August 7, 1919).[4] At the time, women did not have the right of suffrage in most countries across Europe (see table below), whereas in the newly born Republic of Armenia, out of eighty MPs, three women, all intellectuals in their own right, were elected

---

[2] Richard G. Hovannisian, *The Republic of Armenia*, vol. I: *The First Year, 1918-1919* (Berkeley and London: University of California Press, 1974), 471.

[3] Ibid, 476. See also Simon Vratsian, *Hayastani hanrapetut'iwn* [The Republic of Armenia] (Beirut: Tparan Mshak, 1958.), 276.

[4] Armenian National Archive, Minutes of RA Parliament Meetings 1918-1920, Yerevan, 2010, 239.

to the Parliament. These ladies actively participated in three of the twelve committees.

For example, Dr. Katarine Zalian-Manukian served on the Immigration and Reconstruction Committee and also participated in the six-member Medical-Sanitary Committee. The other two prominent figures, Berjouhi Barseghian and Varvare Sahakian,[5] were members of the Scholastic-Educational Committee.

Women's Suffrage Internationally

- 1893 New Zealand (21+)
- 1918 Great Britain (30+ if women had University degree and owned property)
- 1919 Armenia (20+)
- 1920 USA (21+)
- 1928 Great Britain (21+)
- 1934 Turkey (22+)
- 1944 France (21+)
- 1945 Italy (21+)
- 1952 Greece (21+)
- 1971 Switzerland (18+)
- 1979 The UN Convention on the Elimination of All Forms of Discrimination against Women (CEDAW) affirms the right of women to vote

---

Most studies on this period deal with the role of male figures in the Parliament, whereas analysis of the role of women in the legislative institution remains in its infancy. Therefore, the aim of this article is to shed some light on these women's participation in the development of parliamentary activities. In addition to those mentioned above, there were other women, who although were not directly involved in these activities, played an important role in the development and social life of the Republic.

In July 1915, after the *"incomprehensible"*[6] retreat of the Russian Army, hundreds of thousands of Armenians of the Vaspurakan (Van)

---

[5] Armenian National Archive, 239-42; *Hayastani Ashkhatavor*, August 13-14, 1919.

[6] The six or seven retreats of the Russian Army from the liberated Western Armenian regions were not justified, since at the time of each retreat there were no enemy forces in the vicinity. The Russians aim and final goal was to have an Armenia without Armenians.

region and other parts of Western Armenia followed the retreating troops. After a long and deadly march, they finally settled down throughout the Ararat Valley. These people, suffering from various kinds of contagious diseases, were naturally in need of physical and psychological assistance. Zalian-Manukian served these people with the outmost dedication. It was at this time that she met her future husband, the founder of the Republic of Armenia, Aram Manukian, who had arrived in Yerevan with the incoming Western Armenians.

Zalian-Manukian, born in Ghurdughuli[7] (Armavir), worked in the American Pediatric hospital there from 1915-1917. She was also active in the organization of the resistance at Sardarabad and participated in the battle. She was elected to the Parliament a few months after her husband's death. When Armenia was Sovietized, she found refuge at her sister's house. Shortly afterwards, she went on to live with Aram's relatives in Krasnodar. In 1927, upon hearing of the dire need for doctors in Armenia, she came back to Yerevan and again dedicated herself to her profession. She passed away in 1965.

As mentioned above, Zalian-Manukian was a member of the Medical-Sanitary Committee and worked a great deal for the development of medical and sanitary services for the people in general and the army in particular. Due to the efforts of the members of this Committee, an intermediate medical school with enrollment open exclusively for women, was opened in January 1920. After graduation, they worked at hospitals to serve the army.[8]

One of the many achievements of this Committee was the construction of new hospitals. At the beginning of 1919 there were three hospitals with only three hundred beds in Armenia. At the end of the same year, there were thirty hospitals with one thousand six hundred beds, five medical centers, and five nursing centers. In 1920 more hospitals and medical centers were established throughout the country, in Yerevan, Alexandropol (Gyumri), Kars, Jalal Oghli (Stepanavan), among other places. Medicine was supplied to the needy free of charge and with a fifty percent discount to the working class. At the time, tropical diseases such as malaria were spreading all over the country. In order to fight against

---

[7] This name was in use in Soviet Armenia until 1935 when it regained its historical name *Armavir*.

[8] *Haṛaj*, January 1, 1920. See also Sona Zeitlian, *Hay knoj derě hay heghap'okhakan sharzhman měj* [The Role of the Armenian Woman in the Armenian Revolutionary Movement] (Antelias, Lebanon: Tparan Kat'oghikosutān Hayots' Metsi Tann Kilikioy, 1968), 162.

this epidemic, a special committee named the "Tropical Diseases Committee" was formed in Yerevan, which had a specialized hospital to treat and cure people suffering from this illness. Treatment of the epidemic was confined not only to Yerevan, but was also carried out in Igdir, Etchmiadzin, Akhta (Hrazdan) and other parts of the country.[9]

As mentioned above, thousands of survivors of the Armenian Genocide found refuge in the newly formed Republic, which, despite difficult socioeconomic conditions, assumed responsibility for sheltering and feeding these destitute Armenians. However, the burden was too heavy for the young government to carry without the help of various diasporan philanthropic organizations. To overcome these problems, a group of public figures initiated the formation of the Armenian Red Cross Society, which was approved by the government during its meeting on February 17, 1920.[10] This was duly ratified by the Parliament on March 19, 1920, and subsequently recognized as a state entity[11] by the International Red Cross in Geneva.[12] The founding members of the Central Board were:

Dr. Hovhannes Ter Mikayelian	E. Ter Sargsian
Dr. S. Kamsarakan	A. Gyulkhandanian
Mrs. O. Araratian	S. Kanayan
Dr. Hovhannes Hovhannesian	Dr. P. Hovhannisian
Dr. Katarine Zalian-Manukian	Dr. N. TerDavtian
Dr. Mandinian	

Chapters of the Red Cross were also operational in Kars, Vagharshapat, Alexandropol, Jalal-Oghli (Stepanavan), Gharakilisa (Vanadzor), and Igdir. In April 1920, the Armenian Red Cross received the blessing of Kevork V, Catholicos of All Armenians.[13]

The prevailing grave conditions of the country and the people did not impede the founders of the Red Cross Society from fulfilling their

---

[9] *Ashkhatank'*, December 8, 1919.

[10] Armenian National Archive, *The Meetings of The Government of the Armenian Republic 1918-1920* (Yerevan 2014), 402.

[11] Armenian National Archive F.199, L.1, A.128, 56. According to this document, the Board members were considered government employees (letter dated April 8, 1920 from Armenia's Red Cross addressed to the Prime Minister).

[12] *Hayastani Koch'nak*, March 18, 1922, 377.

[13] *Nwireal Hayuhineru Arak'elut'iwnĕ*, Armenian National Archive, F.154.

obligations. In a dramatically short time, they were involved in meritorious activities with the help of various diasporan organizations.[14]

The main task of the Red Cross was to help the army in those critical times. For this purpose, and in the short time before the Sovietization of the state, it established two hospitals with all the necessary equipment along with a nutrition center, bath-house, and wash-house, among other services. The society spared no effort to achieve these goals.

After the Sovietization of the Republic, the activities of the Armenian Red Cross Society were temporarily halted but resumed in November 1921 under the close surveillance of the Soviet authorities until the end of the 1930s.[15]

Zalian-Manukian was also a member of the Immigration and Reconstruction Committee. The government allocated a fair sum of money (36,200,800 Russian rubles) for the Kars immigration project, of which 15 million rubles were used to transport and supply one month's living expenses for the immigrants in their new environment. Moreover, an amount of 17,486,800 rubles was allocated as a remuneration fee for governmental organizations, and medical-sanitary purposes. A further sum of 9,744,100 rubles was allocated to transport 20,000 Armenians from Azerbaijan, Nukhi, Aresh, Shamakh, and Geokchai to Armenia. Furthermore, one million rubles were allocated for other transportation

---

[14] It was obvious that the Soviet authorities would try to belittle the activities of this purely humanitarian organization during the independence period by declaring the date of its formation as 1921. Although in some Soviet-era publications the date was mentioned as 1920, it was argued that, "...the members were from quite insignificant circles, who did not have wide contacts with the people and therefore did not enjoy their respect and authority...". However, after scrutinizing all archival documents, it is now clear that this organization had attained a substantial activity in the short time since its formation and succeeded substantially in overcoming the grave socioeconomic conditions of the people of Armenia, especially the most vulnerable sector: the refugees. See *Hayastani Karmir khach'i ĕnkerut'yan gortsuneut'yunĕ 1920-1930-akan t'vakannerin: p'astat'ght'eri ev nyut'eri zhoghovatsu* [The Activities of the Red Cross Society of Armenia in the 1920-1930s: Collection of Documents and Subjects] (Yerevan: Patmut'yan institut, 2018).

[15] Ibid. The last documents in the Armenian National Archive are dated May 25, 1936, Yerevan, reporting about Armenian Red Cross activities during the year 1935 and a letter by Dr. A. Aharonian dated 1937(?) (Armenian National Archive, F.154, L. 3, A. 23, papers 51-52 and F.420, L.6, A. 2, P.56, respectively).

charges and 3,600,000 rubles for living expenses. Finally, another sum of 944,000 rubles was allocated for organizational charges.[16]

The second important figure, Berjouhi Bardizbanian-Barseghian, was born in Edirne (Adrianople) in 1886 to a well-off family. She was educated in Philipopolis (Plovdiv, Bulgaria) under the tutelage of the prominent revolutionary Rostom (Stepan Zorian), one of the three founders of the Armenian Revolutionary Federation, and his scientist wife Liza Zorian. This fact gave her a chance to meet several Armenian revolutionaries visiting the city, who were either going to "Erkir"[17] or going further on to Europe. One of those activists, Sarkis Barseghian (a.k.a. Vana Sarkis), was to become her future husband. It seems that the young revolutionary literally enchanted her. Upon the latter's suggestion, she organized a group of young Armenian girls, and taught them Armenian literature and history in order to spread the ideals of the revolution. She moved to Geneva to study literature and pedagogy. After graduation, she devoted herself to teaching in Giresun and Van, where Barseghian was the headmaster. They got married in 1909 and moved to Istanbul in 1914. On April 24, 1915, Sarkis was arrested in Istanbul,[18] exiled and brutally killed alongside his friends and compatriots in the Syrian deserts. Bardizbanian-Barseghian stayed for a while in the city, hoping in vain that one day her husband would return. While in Constantinople, she was informed of several kidnapped Armenian children and young girls. She put all her energy into discovering the whereabouts of these unfortunate Armenians and paving the way to liberate them from their captors, mostly Turkish high-ranking officers. She was instructed and guided by another dedicated Armenian woman, Zaruhi Meghavorian-Sagheyian (or simply Zaruk to her close friends). In most cases, they succeeded in this extremely dangerous task. She described the details of these operations in a memoir entitled "*Khandzvadz Ōrer*" (Scorched Days), published in *Hayrenik'* monthly from October 1938 to July 1939.

After losing any hope of her husband's return, she left for Bulgaria with her infant child and then for Tbilisi, where she taught at the Hovnanian and Gayanian schools. After the proclamation of Armenia's independence, she moved to Yerevan where she was elected a member of Parliament as a representative of the Western Armenians and participated in the School-Education committee.

---

[16] Vratsian, *Hayastani hanrapetut'iwn*, 354.

[17] The name "Erkir" meaning "Homeland" was given to Western Armenia by the Eastern Armenian revolutionaries.

[18] Zeitlian, *Hay knoj derě hay heghap'okhakan sharzhman mēj*, 157.

Barseghian was very active in this committee. One of the many bills she drafted and submitted to the Parliament advocated teaching the Armenian language to all government employees, since most of them could not speak their mother tongue. For this reason, all official correspondence and acts were carried out in Russian, which was not an acceptable practice in independent Armenia, and the bill was an effort to rectify the situation. Although the substitution of the Armenian language for Russian in official functions (as suggested by Barseghian's bill) was perhaps the most difficult administrative measure to implement,[19] nevertheless, the Parliament passed the bill after thorough discussion of all its articles.

It must be underlined that Armenian was not taught as a language in schools under tsarist occupied areas where Armenians lived. This was due to the anti-Armenian policy of the tsarist regime. It is worthy to note that, Armenians were illiterate in their mother language. Therefore, in an effort to reverse this situation, the committee in charge of education strongly suggested opening public schools and community colleges to raise the level of literacy among the Armenians of Yerevan. These kind of schools were supposed to be opened in almost all the cities of Armenia. The curriculum included Armenian language, mathematics, and humanitarian subjects and were offered free of charge.[20]

In this regard, we read in one of the newspapers published at the time in Yerevan, that according to a suggestion made by the head of school affairs in Goris (a city in the region of Syunik), evening classes were opened for all government officials and public organization employees to attend these classes and better their skills in all things Armenian.[21]

The government was trying to implement a gradual nationalization process, yet this fact aggravated certain sectors of the society, particularly Western Armenians, who demanded that Armenian language should be dominant in all public and governmental circles. The media in particular targeted those institutions where the nationalization process was slow. To find a solution to this problem, a meeting was held on April 17 with the participation of editors-in-chief of certain newspapers, such as Hemayak Manukian (*Ashkhatank*), Vahan Khoreni (*Hayastani Ashkhatavor*), Zaven Korkotian (*Hayastani Kooperatsy*), and A. Avetisian (*Van Tosp*). The

---

[19] Richard Hovannisian, *Armenian People from Ancient to Modern Times*, vol. II (New York: St. Martin's Press, 1997), 315.
[20] Armenian National Archive, 1918-1920, 58th meeting, January 3, 1920, 420. See also *Haraj*, January 8 and 9, 1920.
[21] *Haraj*, January 11, 1920, 4.

participants took the following decisions: 1) Call on all government and public organizations to speak and write in Armenian only; 2) Refuse all writings, news, declarations and advertisements in any language other than Armenian, except when the party concerned was not Armenian but this ought to be accompanied by an Armenian translation; 3) Demand that Armenian be the official language of the Republic and to permit the use of any other language as a secondary language; 4) Establish a "Nationalization" department in all the newspapers, where news would be printed in Armenian; 5) To consider the establishment and continuation of "The Nationalization Committee" whose members would be the participants of the current meeting. This committee would occupy itself with practical questions, such as advising and helping the rapid nationalization of the institutions.[22]

It is probable that the activities of the above-mentioned committee and the School-Education committee as well as Barseghian's bill about the Armenianization (*Hayats'um*) of the officials and ordinary citizens of Armenia alike made the deputy minister of Internal Affairs, Sarkis Manasian, address the following circular to all governmental offices:

> ...I propose that from now on all correspondence and paperwork from regional, public and country commissioners, from all officials of government institutions be in Armenian and explain this to all whom this may concern. When employing new officials, priority must be given to those who read, write, and speak Armenian fluently. In addition to the above, all registrations by junior officials in the courts should be carried out in Armenian and if the accused person is not Armenian, then the proceedings may be conducted and registered in Russian. Please arrange that all permits, commands, permissions, etc., and in general all correspondence be written in Armenian.[23]

At the end of the year, most of the government institutions and public organizations were nationalized. Moreover, after lengthy and strenuous discussions between the parliamentarians, the Armenian language was declared the official language of the country on December 24, 1919.[24]

The School-Education Committee further researched and presented to the Parliament several bills, which later on became laws only after thorough and detailed scrutiny of all the pertaining articles. For example,

---

[22] Vratsian, *Hayastani hanrapetut'iwn*, 351-352.
[23] Ibid.
[24] *Haraj*, December 31, 1919.

in April the Parliament preliminarily confirmed the bill to replace the old-style parochial school system with compulsory six-year elementary education based on a new and progressive curriculum. Properties of these old schools would be passed onto the Ministry of Art and Public Education exclusively for schooling purposes. The curriculum should include Armenian language and history, geography, natural sciences, hygiene, singing, painting, gymnastics, and handicraft as per the program prepared by the Ministry of Art and Public Education.[25] In addition, during the years of independence, she promoted the very useful and extensive activities of the American Committee (Amercom) to the benefit of the government and the people.

After the collapse of independence, she was one of the thousands of refugees who were forced to leave their fatherland. She stayed in Sofia with her son for a while. She then left for Paris, where she worked at the Nansen Office. Literature was her passion until the end of her life. Some of her literary works have been translated into French and English. The short stories "Arpik" and "A Ring from My Chain" were printed in English in *Hairenik'* monthly.[26] They were considered one of the best literary works of the year by American critic A. O'Brien.[27] Barseghian passed away on May 18, 1940, after long years of battle with brain cancer.

The third woman in the Armenian Parliament was Varvare Tadeosian-Sahakian, the wife of Avetik Sahakian, nicknamed "Hayr Abraham" (Father Abraham), who was also intimately known as "Mayr Abraham" (Mother Abraham). She was born in the province of Lori where she received a multifaceted education. She enlisted in the Armenian Revolutionary Federation (ARF) at an early age and after marrying Sahakian became his closest associate. At this time, they suffered the loss of their son Armen, due to dysentery. However, they bore this calamity with great strength and fortitude.

As mentioned above, Tadeosian-Sahakian participated in the School-Education Committee of the Parliament, researching and presenting bills in this field. One of those bills was about opening concurrent classes and

---

[25] Vratsian, *Hayastani hanrapetut'iwn*, 366. It is worth mentioning that another segment of the destitute Armenian people, the school children of the Vaspurakan region, repatriated without statehood in totally strange surroundings. They were sheltered at the remote tent-cities of Baquba and afterwards Nahr Omar in Iraq, receiving almost the same education which their fellow pupils of the same age were receiving in their own free and native fatherland – the Republic of Armenia.

[26] Zeitlian, *Hay knoj derě hay heghap'okhakan sharzhman mēj*, 159.

[27] Ibid.

kindergartens. This was to be made possible through available funds, since one hundred of the projected five hundred primary schools were not yet opened and the Parliament had already voted to allocate funds for their opening. Therefore, she suggested using these still available funds to open concurrent classes in the rest of the already opened schools, which were overcrowded. She also added that there were not enough buildings to absorb all the children who were left out of schools. Furthermore, she argued that it was meaningless to rent new buildings for this purpose, since the problem could be solved through her proposal. Tadeosian-Sahakian also thought that the balance of the opened credits could be used to open new kindergartens for young children. By this step, she explained, they could take them off the streets.[28] Most of them were, of course, the children of Western Armenian refugees. By this step, these misplaced children could be included in the educational institutions and become useful citizens in the future. The opposition members in the Parliament (Social Revolu-tionary Party, which had four seats) questioned the government as to why schools have not yet been opened in the villages. They further stated that the bill in question lacked necessary information to back it up. Therefore, the opposition members proposed returning the bill to the government to reconsider and present it again to the Parliament. Although Tadeosian-Sahakian gave certain information about the number of schools, the discussions continued and resumed.[29]

These discussions were carried on to the next session of the parliament (December 2, 1919) and Nikol Aghbalian, Minister of Education and Art, offered detailed information and explanations. The bill, originally pre-pared and presented to the Parliament by Tadeosian-Sahakian, was passed with certain amendments and returned to the government with a recommendation that the said ministry should ask for a new loan to cover the expenses for opening the suggested adjacent classes and similar kindergartens.[30]

It is worth mentioning that at the beginning of 1919 there were only 133 elementary schools with 383 teachers and 11,136 students. After Aghbalian took over the Ministry of Education and the conditions in the country became more tolerable, it was possible to increase the number of schools (excluding the regions of Zangezur and Lori) to 456, with 1,047

---

[28] Armenian National Archive, Minutes of RA Parliament Meetings 1918-1920, Yerevan, 365.
[29] Armenian National Archive, 366. See also *Haṛaj*, December 3, 1919.
[30] Armenian National Archive, Minutes of RA Parliament Meetings 1918-1920, Yerevan, 366-367.

teachers and 41,188 students. The same progress was evident in regard to secondary and higher educational schools. In 1918-1919 there were six high schools with 177 teachers and 3,137 students, and in the following year, 1919-1920, there were twenty high schools with 305 teachers and 5,162 students, one university, eight professors and 200 undergraduate students. However, this was not the limit of the educational activity. In the years 1919-1920, community colleges and public educational courses were taught in Yerevan, Alexandropol, and elsewhere, in addition to the abovementioned professional schools. There were also agricultural schools in Alexandropol and Nor Bayazid. There were also plans to establish pedagogical, technical, co-operative, musical, geological, pharmaceutical, and military schools.

The writers were protected and financially subsidized by the government even if they lived and worked in Tbilisi. A certain amount was allocated to publish the writers' works: 3,200,000 rubles and the same amount for translation of scientific books; 1,000,000 for the protection of the relics of antiquity, and 35,920,000 rubles for the reconstruction of the schools. Prince Arghutian-Yerkaynabazuk offered 20,000 volumes of literary and scientific works for newly established libraries. Before the fall of the Republic of Armenia, serious steps to expand these activities were planned.[31]

After the Sovietization of Armenia, Tadeosian-Sahakian's husband was also imprisoned along with his compatriots and members of the government. They were freed on February 18, 1921 by popular uprising. Following the final handover of power to the Bolsheviks on April 2, 1921, Sahakian, along with his wife and their two sons, Armenak and Suren, and thousands of other people, walked for 33 days all the way to Tabriz, which was the first station of their forced exile. They stayed there for six years. Their elder son Suren studied in Prague, while the younger one, Armenak, went to Paris, where he studied chemistry and at the same time worked in a printing house.

In 1928, Sahakian was offered a job in Tehran as agronomist-entomologist and the family stayed there for a year. Afterwards, in 1929, he was offered a similar job by the British Mandate government of Iraq. However, Tadeosian-Sahakian could not endure the extremely hot climate in Iraq and consequently moved to Beirut in 1930. In 1932, their younger son Armenak passed away after succumbing to typhus, which was a serious blow to the couple. In 1933, exactly one year later, her husband also passed away. This was the last and fatal blow to Tadeosian-Sahakian,

---

[31] Ter Minassian, *Hay heghap'okhakani mě hishataknerě*, vol. VII, 280-83.

who passed away a few years later after struggling with stomach cancer. She was buried beside her loved ones in Beirut.

Notwithstanding all these difficulties and misfortunes, Tadeosian-Sahakian never ceased participating in the social life of diasporan society. She was active in laying the foundation of many chapters of the Armenian Relief Society in Lebanon and anywhere her presence was needed. She emphasized that the Armenian Relief Society should not be just an exceptionally philanthropic organization, but rather be the torchbearers for the young generation.[32]

In addition to the three women above, the celebrated writer and public activist Zabel Hovhannesian-Yesayan also attended the sessions of the Armenian National Council of Baku in September 1918, alternately with Roupen Kajperouni.[33]

There were also other women who occupied important posts in the Parliament. Of these, it is worth mentioning Ellen Byuzand (Yeghsabet Stamboltzian) who was the officer in charge of the Parliament offices from November 1919 until the collapse of the Republic on December 2, 1920. Byuzand was arrested by the infamous Cheka with other Armenian women of different ages, who were kept captive until their release after the popular revolt of February 18, 1921.[34]

Byuzand was born in Alexandropol (today's Gyumri) in 1895 and was educated at the Hovnanian school in Tbilisi. She completed her education in law in Rostov. Like most of her contemporaries, she joined the ARF at a very young age. During the Armeno-Turkish war in 1920, she was at the battlefront (Zangibasar, today's Masis in the Ararat region) beside her fellow soldiers and earned the title of "*Armenia's Joan d'Arc*" by Simon Vratsian. After the final Sovietization of Armenia in April 1921, Byuzand was among the thousands of exiled Armenians who found refuge first in Persia then in Beirut, and finally settled down in Paris, where she started her full time writing career. She became a prominent figure in public life as well and was one of the founders of the Armenian Blue Cross (the local Armenian Relief Society organization) in France. As mentioned above, her article about the Armenian women imprisoned by the Cheka sheds light on the treatment of those women, young, married or elderly.

Several books and memoirs have been published about direct political and military events that took place after the Sovietization of the Republic, which eventually led to the February 1921 uprising and the arrests of

---

[32] Zeitlian, *Hay knoj derě hay heghap'okhakan sharzhman mēj*, 161.
[33] Vratsian, *Hayastani hanrapetut'iwn*, 157.
[34] *Hayrenik'*, August-Sept. 1965, 1-14 and 42-54 respectively.

prominent figures of the government. These memoirs omit the fact that Armenian women were also amongst those arrested, and do not mention names, identities, or even the reasons for their arrest. This task was reserved to Ellen Byuzand, who undertook revealing the names of the occupants of the women's cells in the central jail in her articles published in *Hayrenik'* monthly in 1965.

The list of Armenian women who dedicated themselves to the cause of strengthening the bases of the newly independent Republic and the government is certainly not limited to the above-mentioned figures. There were many who did not appear in the political arena. Of these we can point out is Zaruhi Meghavorian-Sagheyian, a fearless lady whose son was killed. She was a fervent, spirited, and devout person, engaged in freeing the young orphans of both sexes, who were snatched away from their parents, kidnapped, and kept in the houses of Turkish officers in Constantinople. She had several volunteer workers who verified and ascertained the houses where those unfortunate children were kept, and then informed Meghavorian-Sagheyian. The latter, in turn, took the necessary and decisive measures for their liberation. In most cases Meghavorian-Sagheyian succeeded in this most dangerous task and many children and young girls were freed from the yoke of their captors. She also helped Barseghian by sheltering her together with her infant boy in her humble house until the latter's departure from Constantinople to Bulgaria. After the declaration of the Independence she moved to Armenia and continued her selfless duties in the orphanages throughout the Republic.

During independence, Maro Stepanian and Sato Hakobian were also prominent figures. The latter, known as "Dashnakts'akan Sato," succeeded in transferring the ARF archive to a safer place right under the eyes of Cheka's officers. Sato Hakobian was the secretary of the ARF Yerevan committee and also the president of the ARF girls' chapter. She was also imprisoned and freed after the February 18, 1921 uprising.

Another prominent figure, who was actively engaged in the social life of the Armenians before and after declaration of the independence, was Dr. Heghiné Yeghyazarian-Papazian,[35] who was the daughter of a wealthy landlord – a patriotic figure himself. She was born in Yerevan in 1892. Their house was the meeting place of most of the revolutionaries passing through the city. Thus, from early childhood Heghiné was imbued with patriotism and became an activist herself, concentrating on national and

---

[35] Heghiné's image is mostly personified and embodied by "Sonia" in Malkhas' (Artashes Hovsepian) historical novel *Zart'onk'*.

public affairs. After studying medicine in Europe, she returned home before WWI and was recruited to serve as a doctor in the field hospitals.

In June 1915, after the liberation of Van, Yeghyazarian accompanied the medical team of Dr. Hamo Ohandjanian heading for Van. She was thrilled with the idea of serving the courageous people of Vaspurakan and enthusiastically took part in this patriotic expedition. The Russian Army, most unreasonably received orders to retreat again and with them hundreds of thousands of Armenians, who were compelled to leave their fatherland and migrate to Eastern Armenia. At this time, Yeghyazarian got infected with typhus and was almost dead when she reached Yerevan. After a difficult recovery, she worked at the hospital which was established at the St. Gayane Monastery in Etchmiadzin.

In 1916 Heghine and Koms (Vahan Papazian) were married. Afterwards, in 1917 Yeghiazarian-Papazian received a request from Costi Hambardzoumian[36] to take her medical team to Van. Again, after a few months and as a result of the second retreat, they too, joined the Armenians of Van to Igdir and then Yerevan.

In 1918, as the Turkish army was nearing Sarikamish, the Armenians started moving to the Northern Caucasus. Yeghyazarian-Papazian again was with the people providing them with every kind of help possible. She was taking care of the orphans too. The Papazians[37] were caught in the midst of the conflicts – communists against *kozaks* in the Northern Caucasus. They narrowly escaped and returned to Tbilisi, where Koms was nominated to take part in the conference organized by the National Delegation in Paris.

In addition to her activities as a doctor, Yeghyazarian-Papazian joined Zabel Yesayan, Rubina Ohandjanian, Melikian, and Zaruhi Masehian[38] in appealing to the respective parties in Europe to free the Armenian women and girls still suffering in the Turkish harems.

In 1919, Heghiné and Koms returned to Yerevan where famine, epidemics, and poverty were widespread all over the country and orphans

---

[36] Constantine (Costi) Hambartzoumian was elected as the governor of Van in October 1917, which lasted until the final and compulsory retreat of the Vaspurakan people and their leadership in March 1918.

[37] At that time Koms was the authorized representative of the Amercom (American Committee for Relief in the Near East, ACRNE and later Near East Relief).

[38] Zaruhi Masehian was Hovhannes Khan Masehian's sister. He was a member of the delegation appointed by the government of the Republic of Armenian to participate in the 1919 Paris Peace Conference.

were everywhere. She, together with Dolores Zohrab (the late Krikor Zohrab's daughter), was sent with a mission to check out the areas most affected by the epidemics and to offer as many services as they could to the people of those areas. Afterwards she served as a doctor in the orphanages, pediatric hospitals, and medical centers.[39]

In late summer of 1920, Yeghyazarian-Papazian was a member of the medical team that was sent to the Armenian army division under the command of Dro (Drastamat Ganaian). They were besieged by enemy forces and narrowly escaped and returned to Yerevan.[40]

Diana Agabegian-Apcar (baptismal name Gayane) was born in Rangoon, British Burma, on October 12, 1859. Her father was one of several New Julfans who migrated to Southeast Asia. Diana was one of seven children and the youngest in the family. She was raised in Calcutta and educated in a local convent school, becoming fluent in English, Armenian, and Hindustani. She married Apcar Michael Apcar, who was also a descendant of a New Julfan family. He became a successful merchant, especially in the import-export business of *shellac lacquer* pearls. In 1891, Diana and her husband moved to Japan, where they founded and expanded the family business. They had five children but only three survived. At the age of sixty-seven Diana experienced numerous physical problems: failing eyesight, hearing loss, and arthritis. She passed away on July 8, 1937, in Yokohama and was buried in a cemetery for foreigners beside her husband.

When the Republic of Armenia gained its independence, it was not recognized by any state. Through Diana's efforts, Japan became one of the first countries to recognize the new Republic. Recognizing and appreciating her efforts, she was appointed Honorary Consul of Armenia to Japan, which made Diana Apcar the first woman to hold a diplomatic post in the century. However, she was not actually recognized by the Japanese government. After Armenia's sovietization, her post was automatically terminated.

When her son took over the family business, Diana was left with more time to delve into her literary, humanitarian, and diplomatic work. She collaborated with various journals, among them *Armenia* (later *New Armenia*). She wrote extensively about the condition of the Armenians in the Ottoman Empire, emphasizing the moral duty of the West in an effort to raise the world's consciousness and save the "little ally," the Armenian people, from complete annihilation.

---

[39] Zeitlian, *Hay knoj derě hay heghap'okhakan sharzhman mēj*, 146-54.
[40] Ibid.

The fact that she was her homeland's Honorary Consul to Japan facilitated her work on behalf of the Armenian refugees, who arrived in Japan from Siberia and sought safe havens in remote and distant shores, particularly in the United States. She had an excellent grasp of the behind the scenes machinations of the Great Powers, which she thought were responsible for the calamities that befell her people.

Lola Sassuni, or Hripsime Metzaturian, also served her people before and after the proclamation of the Republic of Armenia. She was the cousin of the poet Misak Medzarentz. Her family moved from Akn to Constantinople in 1908. Like most of her compatriots she was involved in national-public activities. In 1917 she married Karo Sasuni and went to live in Tbilisi. She took part in taking care of the survivors, in particular the orphans of the Genocide, who were sheltered in Mush, Van, Khnus, and elsewhere. In 1918, on the eve of Armenia's independence, she joined Hamazasp's regiment and took part in the battle of Sardarapat.

After the proclamation of Armenia's independence, she was actively involved in the process of organizing Armenia's Red Cross Society. Metzaturian-Sassuni accompanied her husband who was appointed governor of Shirak province, and actively collaborated with the head of the orphanages of the region.

In 1920, she was arrested like most of her compatriots and was freed after the February uprising. In April, however, she and her husband were compelled to leave Armenia and find refuge in Zangezur. Afterwards, they were constantly on the move to Iran, Constantinople, Sofia, Vienna, Switzerland, Paris, Cairo, and finally Beirut, where the couple settled down.

Medzaturian-Sassuni continued her social activities and was one of the founders of the Armenian Relief Society in Lebanon. She passed away on October 2, 1969.

Conclusion

Judging from the above, it is obvious that female parliamentarians played a vital role beside their fellow male members of the parliament in shaping the first republic's social, political, and cultural life. At the beginning of the 20th century, while suffrage for women was slowly spreading throughout the world, a young republic in the South Caucuses was already ahead of the times. By running for election in 1919, Armenia's first three women MPs lay the foundation for eventually overcoming the stereotype, which was dominant amongst many societies regarding women's possible participation in the political life of nations.

The three women MPs, besides many more who were appointed to important and responsible positions in the new republic, were not celebrated feminist-activists like their counterparts in the West, but rather educated, intellectual, and socially active women, married to leading politicians. They were educated in various countries in Europe and fully supported the idea of a more prominent public role for women, emphasizing the importance of their participation in the political life of the Republic as well.

It is remarkable that Armenia's Parliament, during its short-lived existence, adopted more than 1,000 laws and legal documents, imposing the force of law over internal and external policies of the republic.[41] One of the most important national issues was the declaration of Armenian as a state language, in which Barseghian had a great role through her perseverance and insistence on the importance of using Armenian in all governmental and official correspondence.

After the collapse of the free and independent Republic, thousands of Armenians took the thorny path of exile. Although they were subjected to all kinds of sufferings – some of them were deprived of the simplest and most basic means of survival – yet they continued their activities in different parts of the world and proved once again their devotion towards their people. They put their lifelong experience into action to educate the new generation to grow up as good and useful Armenians, while at the same time hoping that the latter would and pass it on to the younger generation.

---

[41] Armenian National Archive, Minutes of RA Parliament Meetings 1918-1920, Yerevan. See www.parliament.am – "The History of Armenian Parliaments."

Fig. 1 –
Katarine Zalian-Manukian

Fig. 2 – Berjouhi Barseghian

Fig. 3 – Varvare Sahakian

Fig. 4 – Zabel Yesayan

Fig. 5 – Ellen Byuzand

Fig. 6 – Diana Apcar

Fig. 7 – Lola Sassuni

The Subversive Activities of Armenian Bolsheviks: A Critical Factor in Yerevan-Moscow Negotiations (1918-1920)[1]

Rubina Peroomian

Conscious of the fact that within the geopolitical situation after the all-Russian Revolution of March 8 (February 22), 1917, the fate of the Armenian people and the Armenian Cause was contingent upon the new reality in Russia, the Armenian Revolutionary Federation (ARF, Dashnakts'ut'iwn) initiated direct talks with the Provisional Government in Petersburg especially when it was quite evident that Ozakom, the governing body of the Caucasus, was unable and unwilling to work around Armenian interests.[2] Talks were carried out directly and through personal contacts by the Russian Armenian ARF leaders, Liparit Nazariants and Dr. Hakob Zavriev (Zavarian).[3] In these negotiations with the head of the government, Prince Georgy Lvov and Alexander Kerensky, replacing him shortly, important inroads were made.[4] The Bolshevik Revolution,

---

[1] This short essay is primarily based on a previously published study by this author, *Hayastanĕ H.H.D.-Bolshewik haraberut'iwnneri volortum, 1917-1921* [Armenia in the sphere of ARF-Bolshevik relations, 1917-1921] (Yerevan: Yerevani Hamalsarani Hratarakch'ut'iwn, 1997). But here, of course, recent findings, archival studies, and publications are used to reinforce the line of reasoning.

[2] Mikayel Papajanian, the only Armenian member of the Ozakom, appointed by the Provisional Government (March 22/9, 1917), had little knowledge of Armenian issues, while the Georgian and Tatar members worked to secure the best arrangement for their people.

[3] For details of negotiations in Petersburg and Moscow, see Liparit Nazariants, *Hay heghap'okhakan dashnakts'ut'ean ew khorhrdayin ishkhanut'ean mijew hamadzaynut'ean p'ordzer* [Attempts at agreement between the Armenian Revolutionary Federation and the Soviet government], in *Drōshak*, no. 8-9 (1928). Henceforth cited as Nazariants, *Hay heghap'okhakan Dashnakts'ut'ean.*

[4] The Provisional Government agreed to appoint a special commissariat for Western Armenia (April 26/May 9, 1917), detached from the Ozakom, with Zavriev as the vice-commissar taking charge of the Western Armenian affairs

November 7 (October 25), and the fall of the Provisional Government put a stop to these negotiations. In the next phase of relationship, that with the Bolshevik government (*Sovnarkom*), except for informal meetings between Nazariants and Leon Trotsky,[5] contact between the ARF and the Bolshevik government was indirect and depended a great deal upon the goodwill of such Armenian Bolsheviks who were engaged in joint projects[6] with the ARF and willing to play the role of mediators. Needless to say, most of their efforts were challenged and counteracted by the anti-ARF campaign of the Armenian Bolsheviks of the Caucasus and the

---

right away. Garo Sassuni attests to the great hope and enthusiasm of ARF activists engaged in rebuilding Armenian life in the Russian-occupied territories of Western Armenia and organizing the return of the Armenian refugees. See Garo Sassuni, *Tachkahayastanĕ R̦usakan tirapetut'ean tak 1914-1918* [Turkish Armenia under Russian rule, 1914-1918] (Boston: "Hairenik'" Press, 1927). As to the Caucasian affairs, there were prospects of creating ethnic boundaries with Georgian, Armenian, and Tatar concentrations, the realization of which was foiled because of an unsolvable dispute among the three. Simon Vratsian maintains that in this dispute there was a sense of agreement and cooperation between the Georgians and the Tatars, a phenomenon that lasted through the entire history of the three independent republics. See, Simon Vratsian, *Hayastani hanrapetut'iwn* [The Republic of Armenia], (Tehran: 3rd printing, "Alik", 1992), 23. Henceforth cited as Vratsian, *Hayastani hanrapetut'iwn.*

[5] Liparit Nazariants attests that Leon Trotsky, who had been a proponent of continuing the war, at least on the Caucasian front, considered the treaty of Brest-Litovsk (March 3, 1918) to be a misfortune for the Armenian people and was glad he did not have to sign it himself, for Georgy Chicherin had replaced him as People's Commissar for Foreign Affairs. See Nazariants, *Hay heghap'okhakan dashnakts'ut'ean*, 232. See also, Arshak [Jamalian] [Moscow] to Avetik [Sahakian], March 28, 1918, Armenian National Archive, Yerevan, fund 222, list 1, doc. 130. Henceforth cited as ANA.

[6] One such project stipulated the creation of an independent Western Armenia with boundaries defined by Avetik Shahkhatuni, approved by the 1916 ARF Congress, and submitted to the Provisional Government (see Vratsian, *Hayastani hanrapetut'iwn*, 22). It also addressed the idea of an Armenian canton in the Caucasus. Another joint project involved the preparation of a document substantiating the Armenian demands to be submitted by Vahan Terian in the Brest-Litovsk peace talks which began in December 1917. Of course, Vahan Terian, who participated in the peace talks as an adviser for Armenian Affairs, was not given a chance to speak. Lenin had his agenda and Armenian interests were the last thing on his mind and the first to be sacrificed.

Commissariat for Armenian Affairs.[7] The result was, thus, negligible, especially due to the fact that the Bolshevik government, or Lenin for that matter, engaged in quelling the internal tumult, withdrawing from the war at any price (by signing the ruinous treaty of Brest-Litovsk), and bringing Russian soldiers home, had temporarily pulled out of the Caucasus where the main players were the three political parties, the Social Democrat-Mensheviks, the Musavat, and the ARF.

A New Phase in the Relationship

After the Armenian declaration of independence on May 28, 1918, the breach between the ARF and the Armenian Bolsheviks grew wider. The Dashnakts'ut'iwn, being the key player in the formation of a free and independent Armenia and the Republic's administrative body, came under heavy criticism from the Armenian Bolsheviks for whom the idea of an independent state was preposterous. Stepan Shahumian, vehemently criticized the separation of Transcaucasia from Russia and the formation of an independent Republic and labeled its leadership as "a reactionarist body of petit-bourgeois."[8] In a letter to Lenin, dated June 23, 1918, he wrote, "Our international situation in the Caucasus is terrible indeed: independent Georgia, independent Azerbaijan, as though independent Armenia."[9] As to the Commissariat of Armenian Affairs, an article in the June 30th issue of *Komunist*, the Commissariat's organ in Moscow, titled "Independent Armenia," called the newly established independent Armenia "the realization of traitor dashnaks' centuries-old dream" and the free Armenia as "a grave that the Armenian large and petit bourgeoisie is preparing for the Armenian workers."[10]

---

[7] The Commissariat for Armenian Affairs, a branch of the Commissariat of Nationalities headed by Stalin, made it a point to thwart every move by the ARF toward rapprochement with Moscow leaders. They even managed to convince Lenin that the ARF had adopted a British orientation in the Caucasus and that cooperation with them was futile. See, Nazariants, *Hay heghap'okhakan dashnakts'ut'ean,* 232-233.

[8] Stepan Shahumyan, *Erker* [Works] (Yerevan: Haypethrat, 1958), 3:66-70.

[9] Ibid., 324.

[10] See A. N. Mnatsakanyan, ed., *Hoktemberyan sots'ialistakan mets revolyuts'ian yew sovetakan ishkhanut'yan haght'anakĕ Hayastanum: P'astat'ght'eri yew nyut'eri zhoghovatsu* [The great socialist revolution of October and the victory of Soviet rule over Armenia: A collection of documents and material] (Haykakan SSṚ GA Hratarakch'ut'yun, 1960), doc. no. 152, 234-235. Henceforth cited as

The ARF-Bolshevik, now in a larger context of Yerevan-Moscow, relationship entered a new phase. From day one after independence, Hamo Ohanjanian in Berlin and Hakob Zavriev and Artashes Chilingarian (Ruben Darbinian) in Moscow had tried in vain to persuade the Bolshevik government to recognize Armenian independence. The last attempt at formal negotiation, as Liparit Nazariants recorded, was foiled because Poghos Makintsian convinced the People's Commissariat of Nationalities to sabotage the meeting and hold the Dashnakts'ut'iwn responsible for the adverse events in Baku.[11] In fact, as a reaction to these events leading to the fall of the Bolshevik regime, some Bolshevik activists demanded the arrest of Mensheviks, Social-Revolutionaries, and Dashnaks in Moscow. However, as Nazariants attests, ironically, "only the Commissariat of Armenian Affairs heeded this demand and had the Dashnakts'akan leaders arrested."[12] The arrests were launched on August 27, 1918, the day of the arranged meeting between Nazariants, Zavriev, and Chilingarian with the Bolshevik representatives, Lev Kamenev (chairman of the Central Executive Committee of the All Russian Congress of Soviets), Varlam Avanesov (head of the Commissariat of Armenian Affairs), and Sahak Ter-Gabrielian. The latter had mediated with Lenin to authorize the talk between the two parties. The Bolshevik representatives failed to show up to the meeting that day. Nazariants and Zavriev along with some other ARF leaders were arrested and imprisoned and subsequently held hostage under the pretense of retaliation for the murder of Stepan Shahumian and the rest of the 26 Commissars. The prisoners were released in March 1919 but denied permission to leave Moscow. It was only in the spring of 1920 that Nazariants managed to get away. Zavriev, having contracted typhoid in prison, died shortly after his release.

It is significant that because of the extreme anti-ARF activities in the Commissariat of Armenian Affairs, Vahan Terian, the famous Armenian poet and Deputy Chair of the Commissariat, had resigned from his position. To him, opportunist elements like Gurgen Haykuni had infil-

---

Mnatsakanyan, *Hoktemberyan.* Dashnak is a derogatory word used in Bolshevik speech and writings for the Dashnakts'ut'iwn Party and its members.

[11] The anti-ARF or generally speaking the anti-Armenian independence campaign by the Commissariat of Armenian Affairs grew more intense after the fall of Baku Commune and Stepan Shahumian's murder. See Richard G. Hovannisian, *The Republic of Armenia,* vol. I, 1918-1919, (Berkeley: University of California Press, 1971), 395-396. Henceforth cited as Hovannisian, *The Republic of Armenia,* vol. I.

[12] Nazariants, *Hay heghap'okhakan dashnakts'ut'ean,* 233.

trated the Commissariat and were using every occasion to vent their hatred and animosity against the free Republic of Armenia and the Dashnak Party running its government.[13] During the Third International convened in Moscow in March 1919, Haykuni, who had replaced Terian on the Commissariat, spoke against the bourgeois nationalists in Transcaucasia, particularly Dashnakts'ut'iwn. For Haykuni, "national independences" were a perfidy of the counter-revolutionaries to destroy Bolshevism, the Republic of Armenia was "a mocking insult to the workers and peasants," and the Armenian government was "a pack of bandits." He reassured the Bolshevik leaders that the Armenian Communist Party would struggle until the ultimate victory of Bolshevism in Armenia.[14]

All the while, the Bolshevik government, still inattentive to the burgeoning republics on the southern borders of the former Russian Empire, was busy consolidating its power over Russia and continuing its secret negotiations with Turkey and Germany, while the Armenian government had ceased its attempts at rapprochement and its official call for negotiations. The latter was simply inundated with internal problems and the impossible task of building a Republic out of a "formless chaos" (*andzev kaos*) as Hovhannes Kachaznuni had described it. Another reason why relations with Bolshevik Russia were put on the back-burner was that many in Europe did not believe the Bolshevik regime would survive to become the true successor of the tsarist regime in Russia. That attitude influenced Armenian—or rather the ARF—leaders and drew them to seek the ultimate resolution of the Armenian Cause in Europe, hence their Western orientation. They also engaged in negotiations with non-Bolshevik forces in Russia clearly alienating the Bolshevik government in Moscow. That was a move that proved wrong in hindsight.

The Bolshevik government of Moscow and the anti-Bolshevik forces in southern Russia, however, did agree on one question, if nothing else, i.e. the intact preservation of the territories of the former tsarist Empire. Both Vasilii Maklakov, the anti-Bolshevik tsarist Russian Ambassador to France, and Boris Bakhmeteff, the Provisional Government's Ambassador to the United States, clearly conveyed this idea to Avetis Aharonian and the Armenian delegation to the Paris Peace Conference in a meeting on the sidelines of the conference on May 9, 1919.[15] The Soviets were

---

[13] Hovannisian, *The Republic of Armenia,* vol. I, 409–414.

[14] Ibid., 412.

[15] Avetis Aharonian, *Sardarapatits' minch'ew Sewr yew Lōzan* [From Sardarabad to Sèvres and Lausanne] (Boston: "Hairenik'" Press, 1943), 22–23. Henceforth cited as Aharonian, *Sardarapatits'.*

following the same policy when they signed an agreement in March 1919 with William Bullitt, President Woodrow Wilson's special envoy to the Paris conference. Under pressure from the Allied Powers, the Soviets agreed to accept the newly formed independent states within the borders of the former Russian Empire. Nonetheless, they managed by a clever twist to get the Allies to agree to withdraw from Russia and promise not to assist any state in rising against it. Assured of Allied non-interference, the Soviets could afford to temporarily tolerate the independent republics of Transcaucasia.

The Ninth ARF General Congress and its Directives

An important forum, where the internal and external policies of the party and for that matter the government of Armenia were being discussed and resolved, was convened in Yerevan on September 27, 1919. One of these resolutions clearly delineates the stance of the ARF or the Armenian government vis-à-vis the Soviets and the low priority assigned to Armeno-Russian relations. It reads: "Despite our complete goodwill toward the Russian people and the political revival of Russia, our diplomacy should resist the Russian government's attempts to spread Russian domination over the former Russian Armenia and hinder the realization of United Armenia."[16]

The resolution to struggle for the creation of a Free, Independent, and United Armenia[17] that was adopted in the same forum – and which was in fact a consecration of the proclamation of "the act of the declaration of the freedom of United Armenia" by the Armenian government's Council of Ministers on May 28, 1919[18] – resulted in another wave of Bolshevik discontent and condemnation. Anastas Mikoyan's statement on this occasion is an example. He wrote, "the Armenian Chauvinists are pushing forward the culpable and chimerical idea of creating a 'Great' Armenia

---

[16] *K'aghwatsk'ner H.H.D. 9rd ĕndhanur zhoghovi voroshumnerits'* [Excerpts from the decisions of the ARF 9th General Congress] (Yerevan: Urardia Press, 1920), 6.

[17] The text in V. Ghazakhetsyan et al. (compilers), *Hayastani hanrapetut'iwn, 1918-1920 t't'. (k'aghak'akan patmut'iwn), P'astat'ght'eri yev niwt'eri zhoghovatsu* [The Republic of Armenia, 1918–1920 (Political History): A collection of documents and material] (Yerevan: HH GAA "Gitut'yun" hratarakch'ut'iwn, 2000), 127.

[18] Ibid., 108.

within the boundaries of historical Armenia. Our Party cannot support the idea of neither a great nor a small Turkish-Armenia."[19]

It is ironic that while Armenian Bolsheviks were busy disparaging the idea of Armenian independence and slandering the Republic's ARF-dominated government, the ousted Ittihadist leaders in Moscow and Europe were negotiating to effect an accord between Bolshevik Russia and Kemalist Turkey and to secure Russian assistance to Turkey.

The Bolshevik-Young Turk-Kemalist Triangle and the Armenian Bolsheviks

The Bolshevik–Young Turk accord, signed in Baku on November 27, 1919, laid the foundation for the future scheme against the Republic of Armenia. New research in this domain and unearthed evidence provides details of an extended series of talks that began in Baku in the fall of 1919, whose goal was to liberate all Muslim countries from the yoke of Western European imperialism. This was followed by another treaty between the Bolsheviks and Kemalist Turkey signed on January 11, 1920. Vladimir Harutyunyan, a contemporary historian in Armenia, discusses Point 11 of this treaty, which reads, "Provide assistance to the movement being launched in the Caucasus against British and Russian Imperialism and the present governments of Georgia, Azerbaijan, and Armenia operating under their command and influence." The Armenian Bolsheviks Alexander Bekzadian, Isahak Dovlatov, Hakob Hakobian, Sargis Kasian, Anastas Mikoyan, and Askanaz Mravian were enthusiastic participants in those talks, and the all-out war against Armenia was being shaped under their nose. Harutyunyan concludes, "As we can see, Armenian Bolsheviks were indeed devoid of any nationalistic or even national attributes, and by their presence, they did not embitter but sweetened and strengthened the Bolshevik-Kemalist brotherly pact."[20]

---

[19] *Khawarum* [Eclipse], a pamphlet published by the Hovhannes Tumanyan Museum in Yerevan after the exhibition/illustration of the same title, 19; the quotation is dated December 1919.

[20] Vladimir Harutyunyan (compiler), *P'astat'ght'er Hayastani k'aghak'akan patmut'ean, Karsi marzě Hayastani aṛajin hanrapetut'ean kazmum (april 1919t'. – hoktember 1920t'.) Niwt'er yew p'astat'ghter* [Documents on the political history of Armenia, Kars province within the First Republic of Armenia (April 1919–October 1920): Materials and documents] (Yerevan: Modus Vivendi, 2016), 126. Henceforth cited as Harutyunyan, *Karsi marzě*.

Armenian leaders were concerned when rumors of such a pact reached Yerevan, but the Armenian Bolsheviks denied any such agreement. In order to verify its existence, the ARF Bureau sent three of its members, Arshak Jamalian, Simon Vratsian, and Ruben Ter-Minassian, to meet Hmayak Nazaretian, First Secretary of the Communist Party Bureau of Transcaucasia (KavBureau). Ter-Minassian later wrote that, by his silence, Nazaretian implicitly confirmed the existence of a secret accord, and that he explicitly stated that Moscow's new policy would entail increased propaganda and agitation in Armenia.[21] According to Vratsian, when the delegation put forth the idea of some kind of an agreement between the Bolshevik Russia and ARF the ruling party in Armenia, Nazaretian retorted contemptuously, "What agreement? The spread of the Soviet rule in Transcaucasia should be expedited."[22] Nazaretian's forecast was consistent with the resolution reached in a secret meeting of Armenian Bolsheviks in Yerevan in January 1920 to overthrow the Dashnak government and begin the process of the Sovietization of Armenia.[23] The Armenian committee, the ArmenKom of the Russian Communist Party, elected in that meeting in Yerevan, included Sargis Kasian, Askanaz Mravian, Ghukas Ghukasian, Avis Nourijanian, and Danush Shahverdian.[24] Nonetheless, the resolution was not put into effect at the time because the leaders of ArmenKom were aware of the fact that, with the limited numbers of their followers and thus lack of power in Armenia, they could not begin the process without outside help. Even according to Bolshevik sources, the number of those in Armenia who considered themselves Bolsheviks then did not exceed 400–600 souls.[25] Besides, they were uncertain as to whether a Soviet regime or proletarian rule would be premature in a backward country like Armenia where there were almost

---

[21] Ter-Minassian, *Hay heghap'okhakani mě hishataknerě*, hator 7 [The memoirs of an Armenian revolutionary, vol. 7] (Los Angeles: Horizon Press, 1952), 268. Henceforth cited as Ter-Minassian, *Hay heghap'okhakani mě hishataknerě*.

[22] Vratsian, *Hayastani hanrapetut'iwn*, 383.

[23] See Mnatsakanyan, *Hoktemberyan*, doc. no. 191, 303.

[24] See Vladimir Harutyunyan (compiler), *Hay bolshevikneri hakapetakan gortsuneut'yunę: 1919-1920t't'., P'astat'ght'eri zhoghovatsu* [Anti-statehood activities of the Armenian Bolsheviks, 1919–1920: Collection of documents] (Yerevan: Modus Vivendi, 2014), doc. 1-31, 86. Henceforth cited as Harutyunyan, *Hay bolshevikneri.*

[25] Ibid., 17. Reference is made to Shavarsh Amirkhanyan's *Mayisean apstambut'iwně Hayastanum* [The May uprising in Armenia] (Moscow, 1926).

no proletarian workers. According to Simon Vratsian, the idea of immediate Sovietization came from Avis Nourijanian.[26]

Bolshevik Anti-Governmental Propaganda and Agitations in Armenia

The number of Bolshevik propagandists and agitators did indeed increase in Armenia. Paradoxically, at the end of 1919, when the persecution and incarceration of Bolsheviks escalated in Georgia, ARF leaders gave Sargis Kasian, Askanaz Mravian, Sargis Khanoyan, Yegor Yerznkian, Avis Nourijanian, and others safe refuge in Armenia and entrusted them with responsible jobs in government and notably in the sphere of education, on one condition: that they should not engage in Bolshevik propaganda and activism. That condition was never met. The devoted Bolsheviks spread Communist ideas, established Communist cells, and instigated a population that was near starvation to revolt against the government and seek Russia's protection. They promised that Russia could fill the country with bread and sugar.

One such incident instigated by Bolshevik agitation occurred in Alexandropol in January 1920. Taking advantage of the people's complaints about the high price of bread, the Bolshevik activists Sargis Khanoyan, Yegor Sevian, and Bagrat Gharibjanian tried to turn popular discontent into mass protest. The government arrested and imprisoned the three agitators, which aroused a wave of protests in the Soviet media, criticizing the Dashnakts'ut'iwn and holding it responsible for the abject misery in Armenia. An article in April 1920 in the *Komunist* paper in Baku, reported, "Perhaps not in any corner of the world the army of the poor, the destitute, and the exploited is growing as rapidly as in Armenia." And, of course, "the government of dashnaks" is to blame.[27]

Despite all this, the government showed tolerance and leniency. After all, many ARF leaders were friends with Armenian Bolsheviks, shared the same ideology of Socialism, and had fought the Tsarist regime together.[28] Besides, they still naively believed that the goodwill they showed toward them could translate into good relations with the Moscow government.

---

[26] Vratsian quotes an article by Sargis Kasian in *Nor Ashkharh* monthly (1922). See Vratsian, *Hayastani hanrapetut'iwn*, 385.

[27] Quoted in Hovhannes Karapetyan, *Mayisean apstambut'iwnnerĕ Hayastanum* [The May uprisings in Armenia] (Yerevan: HSSṚ GA Hratarakch'ut'yun, 1961), 67, 69. Henceforth cited as Karapetyan, *Mayisian*.

[28] See Vratsian, *Hayastani hanrapetut'iwn*, 378.

The Armenian government failed to react when, according to information from Georgia, Ghukas Ghukasian had taken refuge in Armenia and was organizing Bolshevik cells in Alexandropol and spreading propaganda against the Armenian independent state.[29] Significantly, Ruben Ter-Minassian attributed this policy of tolerance not to political farsightedness, but extremism, which confuses the external political aspirations with internal political concessions.[30]

This policy lasted until the unrest of May 1, 1920, when the Bolsheviks, headed by Ghukas Ghukasian and the Armenian members of the Tbilisi-centered "Spartak" Communist youth organization, managed to turn the May 1 celebrations in Yerevan into an anti-government rally. They called upon "the workers, soldiers, and peasants of Armenia" not to be fooled by "freedoms" and "parliaments," but to "strive toward Russia," which would lead them toward their "bright future, Socialism."[31] Similar demonstrations were organized with more success in Alexandropol, Sarikamish, Kars, and Nor-Bayazed.

In order to quell the unrest, the ARF Bureau took direct control of the government and mobilized ARF members to ward off "the danger threatening the Armenian homeland and statehood."[32] The Bureau-cum-government was headed by Hamo Ohanjanian who was named Prime Minister. Of course, this action aroused discontent even within the leadership. Some, like Simon Vratsian (who would succeed Ohanjanian in November), called it *Dashnakts'ut'ean diktatura* (the ARF dictatorship).[33] In fact, with this action, the narrowly maintained separation of party and state was abolished. The action was also the cause of a deeper schism among the ARF leadership in which personal opinions and sometimes opportunistic preferences played a role. Hovhannes Kachaznuni's *Dashnaktsut'iwně anelik' chuni aylevs* [Dashnakts'ut'iwn has Nothing to do Anymore], Bucharest, 1923 and Vienna 1924, reveals some of these complexities. It touches upon realities such as that an elected parliament (August 1919) with ARF party members in an overwhelming majority, that is, a parliament without an opposition, was not a healthy way of ruling the country. The ARF took upon itself responsibilities that it had neither

---

[29] See ibid., 378-379. Vratsian quotes an article in *Khorhrdayin Hayastan*, May 14, 1927, where Askanaz Mravian describes Armenian Bolshevik activities.

[30] Ter-Minassian, *Hay heghap'okhakani mě hishataknerě*, 266-267.

[31] Mnatsakanyan, *Hoktemberyan*, doc. no. 164, 260–262.

[32] For the text of the declaration of mobilization, see the ARF Archives in Boston, section E, file 120, doc. 3.

[33] Vratsian, *Hayastani hanrapetut'iwn,* 390.

the means nor resources to handle. The ARF Bureau overpowered, controlled and pressured the parliament in its actions and decisions. Even the ARF's parliamentary faction followed the Bureau's directions.

Peaceful means to quell the insurgence had proven ineffective, and the Bureau-government resorted to force. There were arrests, incarcerations, even the execution of insurgent leaders. For this task, the government primarily commissioned Sebouh, the famous fedayee *khmbapet* [brigade master], and his troop of mostly Western Armenian former fedayees, and they were unforgiving. It was in this operation that Sebouh earned the moniker of "the executioner of Bolsheviks."[34] The unrest was suppressed and the country returned to normal, but the coup de force gave the Bolsheviks an opening to convince the Moscow government to act.[35] The Bolsheviks fled to Moscow or to the already Sovietized Azerbaijan with exaggerated reports of thousands imprisoned and thousands executed, and they inundated the Politburo and the Soviet press with letters of protest, demanding the accelerated Sovietization of Armenia and calling for the Red Army units in Azerbaijan to march into the country, overthrow the Dashnak government, and install the ArmenKom in power.[36]

As a result of this campaign, public opinion about the government's competence dropped, both in the interior and abroad. Contrary to this assessment, however, Simon Vratsian attests that public opinion in Armenia approved the measures taken to crush the unrest, and to support his view he cites the proclamations put out by the Social-Democrats Labor Party, the Populists, and the Ramkavars in Armenia.[37] All this was at a time when Bolshevik Russia, having consolidated its position nationally and internationally, had begun to move toward the Caucasus. In a March 17, 1920 telegram sent to Sergo (Gregory) Ordzhonikidze, the head of the Transcaucasian Military Revolutionary Committee, Lenin ordered him to accelerate the capture of Baku which he deemed extremely necessary.[38]

---

[34] Karapetyan, *Mayisean,* 275. For Sebouh's participation in the government's actions against the agitators, see Vratsian, *Hayastani hanrapetut'iwn,* 392.

[35] A detailed list of the names of those executed or otherwise killed in each city during the May uprising shows the total number of victims to be less than fifty. See Harutyunyan, *Hay Bolshevikneri,* doc. ii-72, 217–220.

[36] For more details on the May uprisings and the government's actions, see Vratsian, *Hayastani hanrapetut'iwn,* 314-414.

[37] Ibid., 392-394. Typically, the May 14 proclamation by the Social-Democrats Labor Party's Yerevan Committee, called the Armenian Bolsheviks' actions pleasing the Bolshevism-Pan Islamism alliance.

[38] See Lenin, V. I., *Erker* [Works], (Yerevan: 1969), 51:193.

KavBuro (Caucasian Bureau) was formed in April to facilitate the spread of the Bolshevik regime in the Caucasus, and the Red Army marched into Baku on April 27. Azerbaijan was Sovietized. It was time for the Armenian government to act, to set aside its Western orientation, which was supported and encouraged by the promises Allies made and developments in the Paris peace talks, and engage in direct negotiations with Bolshevik Russia whose presence in the Caucasus was already an absolute reality. The move had been overlooked long enough, for there was no consensus about its importance. There were those in the leadership who believed that rapprochement with the Bolsheviks would alienate the Allies. And there were others who thought this rapprochement could trigger a quicker response by the Allies in fulfillment of their promises. Unfortunately, they did not notice the change of political atmosphere and the inclination to favor Mustafa Kemal's Nationalist Turkey.

And Finally, Formal Negotiations in Moscow

An Armenian delegation headed by Levon Shant with Hambartsum Terterian and Levon Zarafian, two leftist ARF members, was formed and the delegation left Yerevan on April 30. Two Karabagh Armenians, Aramayis Yerznkian and Simonik Pirumian, accompanied the delegation as experts in issues pertaining to Karabagh in support of uniting Karabagh with Armenia.[39] Because of the lack of transportation the delegation reached Moscow after a long journey full of hindrances and only on May 28 did negotiations begin with Georgy Chicherin, the People's Commissar for Foreign Affairs, and his Armenian deputy Lev Karakhan.

During these negotiations, the Bolsheviks were primarily interested in receiving assurance from the Armenian government that the Armenians would not strike at Turkey when the Turks and the Bolsheviks began their joint operation to oust the European imperialists from Turkish soil. They also demanded that Armenia break with the Allies and authorize the Soviets to engineer the dismissal of agenda items concerning the Armenian Cause from the peace negotiations going on at Versailles. The Armenian delegation's initial impression was that the Moscow government had no intention to force a Soviet regime on Armenia in the

---

[39] It is ironic, that once in Moscow, these two Karabaghtsies changed course, severed their ties with the Armenian delegation and presented a distorted view of Karabagh Armenians who are waiting for the Bolsheviks and the Bolshevik regime to spread over Karabagh. See, Vratsian, *Hayastani hanrapetut'iwn*, 555, and Levon Shant's letter to Vratsian, dated June 18, from Marseille in ibid., 612.

near future. The impression was also that Chicherin was speaking from a position of power and with some arrogance and indifference. Hambartsum Terterian attests that the meetings usually occurred at night, that there were always two Nagant revolvers on Chicherin's desk with the barrels facing the Armenian delegation, and that the meetings were not recorded.

Important items tabled by the Armenian side, such as the Soviet government's recognition of the Republic of Armenia, a final agreement on Karabagh, Zangezur, and Nakhijevan – where fighting was raging between Armenia and Azerbaijan – as well as the issue of annexing Western Armenia to the Republic of Armenia were briefly discussed, but with no substantive outcome.[40] Chicherin fervently objected to this last issue, reasoning that according to Bolshevik tenets, the logic of historical belonging is irrelevant and that land belongs to the peasant cultivating it.[41]

Then, on July 1 the meetings were abruptly cancelled. Chicherin refused to continue negotiating with the "brutal murderers" of his Communist comrades. In a telegram to Yerevan, he protested the execution of hundreds of Communists, including "Comrade Mikoyan." Of course, as Vratsian states, Chicherin's reaction was based on false information. Mikoyan had never set foot in Armenia.[42] In fact, only two weeks before, on June 20, *Komunist,* Red Azerbaijan's organ in Baku, had published a memorandum addressed to the Armenian government to stop the "bloodshed" against Bolsheviks in Armenia carried out by Sebouh, the principal mauserist executioner. The memorandum cited an alarming number of peasants and workers tortured and killed, executed en masse. Three Armenians, Mikoyan on behalf of the Central Committee of the Communist Party of Azerbaijan, Kostanian representing the Russian Communist Party, and Nourijanian, representative of the military RevKom of Armenia were among the signatories.[43] Levon Shant's report to the Armenian government speaks of the efforts of the Azerbaijani and Armenian Bolshevik delegation from Azerbaijan especially sent to Moscow to abort the ongoing negotiations. Chicherin announced that the talks would continue in Yerevan with the Moscow government's

---

[40] Ibid., 453 for details of Armenian demands.

[41] For a detailed description of the negotiations, see Hambartsum Terterian, *Hayastani Hanrapetut'ean yew khorhrdayin r̦usastani banakts'ut'iwnnerĕ – Levon Shant'i patwirakut'iwnĕ* [The negotiations between the Republic of Armenia and Soviet Russia – Levon Shant's delegation] in *Hairenik'* monthly, No. 1-5, 1954.

[42] Vratsian, *Hayastani hanrapetut'iwn*, 452.

[43] Ibid., 451-452.

plenipotentiary representative, Boris Legran, member of the Central Committee of the Communist Party of Russia.

The talks stopped in Moscow. Chicherin had not been able to over-power the strong hatred and animosity of Bolsheviks in the Caucasus against the Bourgeois states of Georgia and Armenia. Moscow had to change its strategy of tolerating the existence of these two republics, even temporarily. Anastas Mikoyan, Avis Nourijanian, and other Bolsheviks in Baku and Moscow – and of course the Commissariat of Armenian Affairs – celebrated another success having convinced Chicherin to halt the negotiations. Chicherin had other reasons to cut the talks short: the Russo-Turkish pact was in the making and Soviet Azerbaijan was reluctant to relinquish the lands it was fighting to appropriate. The Armenian Bol-sheviks endorsed the Azerbaijani position in a statement by Amirkhanian, Poghosian, and Ghaltaghchian, recommending that the central government "demand that the regions of Ghazakh/Shamshadin in rebellion be either united with Azerbaijan or captured by the Red Army."[44] Furthermore, a letter to the Central Committee of the Communist Party, dated July 10, expressed dissatisfaction against Chicherin's concession in the division of Karabagh, Zangezur and Nakhijevan between Armenia and Azerbaijan. The letter insisted that the Armenian peasants of Zangezur and Karabagh were impatiently waiting to rid themselves of the yoke of the Dashnak government. Mikoyan was among the signatories.[45]

A telegram from Stalin to Sergo Ordzhonikidze, dated July 8, 1920, reveals the underlying Soviet position on this issue: "We should not endlessly oscillate between the two sides. We should support one, and in this case, it should be Azerbaijan with Turkey. I have spoken with Lenin. He does not object."[46] Stalin's message coincided with the date of the cessation of the talks in Moscow.

It is questionable how the Armenian delegation handled the negotiations. Levon Shant, Hambartsum Terterian, and Levon Zarafian were not seasoned politicians who could make decisions and close a deal without Yerevan's consent, and the lack of direct lines of communication between Moscow and Yerevan made things difficult. The only line

---

[44] *Khawarum*, 22. Reference is made to the ANA, fund 1022, list 4, doc. 68, no. 21.

[45] For the content of the letter and the names of the signatories, see Richard G. Hovannisian, *The Republic of Armenia*, vol. IV: *Between Crescent and Sickle, Partition and Sovietization*, (Berkeley, Los Angeles, London: University of California Press, 1996), 74.

[46] Ibid., 20.

available went through Tbilisi and were often sabotaged. Communications were withheld or delivered so late that they were outdated or no longer effective. As for Simonik Pirumian and Aramayis Yerznkian—two newly converted Bolsheviks—half-way through the talks, they secretly left Moscow with a 5,000-ruble grant from the Commissariat to expedite the Sovietization of Karabagh and Zangezur.

Secret Deals to Bring about the Demise of the Armenian Republic

Notwithstanding the formal negotiations, however, the future of Armenia was being forged not through talks in Moscow or Paris, but in the Russo-Turkish dealings in Moscow as well as the Congress of Eastern Peoples in Baku. Legran too with his aid, Sahak Ter-Gabrielian, had chosen to go to Baku instead of Yerevan to consult with Ordzhonikidze, with whose recommendation he advised Chicherin to annex Karabagh and Zangezur to Azerbaijan and move the Red Army to occupy Nakhijevan. The constant threatening to advance into Armenia coming from Turkey forced Legran to meet the Armenian government representatives and hold talks in Tbilisi before the Armenian delegation stranded in Moscow could return to Armenia. Indeed, Armenia was squeezed between "the Bolshevik hammer and the Turkish anvil" as Simon Vratsian quipped. Arshak Jamalian and Artashes Babalian, with Ruben Yuzbashian as adviser, were sent to Tbilisi to negotiate a treaty to stop military operations. A temporary agreement was signed between the two parties with heavy concessions on the part of Armenia. The date was August 10, ironically, the date when the Treaty of Sèvres was signed. With this agreement, Bolshevik Russia fulfilled its promise to Turkey. Karakhan had informed the Turkish representative in Moscow that the Red Army was ordered to occupy Karabagh, Zangezur, and Nakhijevan for Azerbaijan.[47] With the twist of fate, the signature under this agreement was the first official document which also meant Moscow's recognition of the Republic of Armenia.

The Russo-Turkish Treaty of Moscow was initialed on August 24, 1920, after which Mustafa Kemal authorized Kazim Karabekir to begin the military campaign against Armenia. The Congress of Eastern Peoples, convened on September 1, was attended by representatives of Mustafa Kemal's Nationalist Turkey as well as some Young Turk leaders. This was an important forum where the Armenian Bolshevik delegates Anastas

---

[47] Gabriel Lazian, *Hayastan yew hay datě* [Armenia and the Armenian Question], reprint (Tehran: "Alik" publishing, 1985), 251. The author quotes the memoirs of Ali Fouat Pasha, Mustafa Kemal's representative in Moscow, on this issue.

Mikoyan, Avis Nourijanian, Sargis Kasian, and Askanaz Mravian witnessed the Turkish-Azerbaijani-Russian conspiracy to bring about the demise of the Armenian Republic. In their fiery declarations, they claimed that the Dashnakts'ut'iwn, "with the help of bandit-mauserists.... buried the peasantry of Turkish-Armenia.... and is building a new Golgotha for the workers and peasants of Eastern Armenia."[48]

Mustafa Kemal's top-secret order to launch the attack on Armenia was issued on September 24, 1920. Operations began on September 28. It is significant that only a week before the attack, on September 20, the Central Committee of the Communist Party of Armenia had issued its own "top secret" message for limited distribution to the Communist bodies of Armenia with the order to destroy after reading:

> Kemalist Turkey is Soviet Russia's ally and is fighting for its national freedom against Imperialism. The victory of the Republic of Armenia over Turkey would be tantamount to strengthening Imperialism in the Near East and would jeopardize the victory of the Revolution in Transcaucasia and thus the Sovietization of the East. The Armenian Communist Bolsheviks should aim to expedite the defeat of republican Armenia, which will also expedite the Sovietization of Armenia. To that end, [we need to]
> 1. Dissolve the Armenian army....
> 2. Instigate and organize desertions in the army....
> 3. Persuade soldiers on the front not to fire at the advancing Turkish soldiers.
> 4. Persuade soldiers to disobey the orders of their commanding officers and destroy them if necessary.

This message was signed by Sargis Kasian, Askanaz Mravian, Avis Nourijanian, Shavarsh Amirkhanian, Isahak Dovlatian, and Ashot Hovhannisian.[49]

Indeed, these recommendations were put into effect point by point. And while the government was calling upon the nation to unite and defend the Republic, and while all the other political parties active in Armenia, as well as Gevorg V, Catholicos of All Armenians, supported the

[48] Mnatsakanyan, *Hoktemberyan*, doc. no. 243, 375–378.
[49] *Khawarum*, 11–12. Reference is made to the ANA, fund 1022, list 3, doc. 275, no. 1.

government's call for action,[50] the Bolshevik propaganda machine was working full blast to demoralize the army and destroy the Armenian resistance. Pamphlets and flyers were distributed, and fiery speeches were delivered to peasants and soldiers, encouraging them to ignore the call for mobilization, refrain from fighting, and return home. Bolshevik propaganda focused on two themes: the first revolved around the idea that Kemalist soldiers were not looters or slaughterers but simple peasants and workers, "brothers" coming "to liberate us from the yoke of Dashnak repression," while the second theme advocated putting down arms and embracing the Bolshevik regime which promised bread and sugar for the starving peasants. Armenian Bolshevik activists even cooperated with the Kemalist army, especially in Kars, providing them with intelligence in the hope that the Turks would capture the city and turn it over to the Bolsheviks.[51] In a message dated November 13, 1920, A. Ter-Martirossian and Mkrtich Khachikian wrote, "Liberated from the centuries-old Armenian yoke, the Alexandropol proletariat and the impoverished peasantry send brotherly and heartfelt greetings to the Turkish Communist Party. Long live Turkey's Communist Party. Long live the revolutionary Eastern Red Army. Long live Communism. Long live Soviet Armenia."[52] Vladimir Harutyunyan quotes N.E. Shutova, who explains the Armenian Bolsheviks' attitude toward territorial concessions to Turkey, "In order to be able to establish relations between Soviet Russia and Turkey, it is

---

[50] See Ghazakhetsyan, *Hayastani hanrapetut'iwn*, 300–301, for the texts of the joint declarations of Armenian political parties.

[51] For details of the fall of Kars, see Artashes Babalian, *Mi tari gerut'ean mēj* [One year in captivity], in *Hairenik'* monthly, vol. 2 (1924), 54-65. More recent publications include Ghazakhetsyan, *Hayastani hanrapetut'iwn*, 335, to see the article titled *"Bolshevik akentner"* (Bolshevik agents) which was originally published in *Haṛaj* (November 9, 1920). The article exposes the treacherous activities of the Armenian Bolsheviks who facilitated the Kemalist occupation of Kars. Vladimir Harutiunyan too sheds light on the details of the fall of Kars in *Karsi marzĕ Hayastani hanrapetut'ean kazmum, april 1919 – hoktember 1920, Karsi nahangapet Stepan Ghorghanyani husherĕ* [The marz (province) of Kars within the Republic of Armenia, (April, 1919-October 1920, The memoirs of Kars governor Stepan Ghorghanyan (Korganof)] (Yerevan: AniARC publication, 2018); in *Aṛajin hanrapetut'iwn, Karsi verchnakhaghĕ* [The First Republic of Armenia: the Endgame of Kars] (Yerevan: A Modus Vivendi publication, 2018); and in *Kars-Aleksandrapoli korustĕ 1920-in haykakan banaki spayi husherum* [The loss of Kars-Alexandropol in the memoirs of an Armenian army officer] (Yerevan: AniARC publishing, 2019).

[52] *Khawarum*, 38. Reference is made to the ANA, fund 1002, list 2, doc. 189.

indispensable first to solve the Armenian issue. For that matter, it is imperative to accept the importance of maximal territorial concessions to Kemalist Turkey on account of Armenia."[53]

Before briefly discussing the process of the Sovietization of Armenia, I need to backtrack and entertain three questions in order to fully illustrate the situation that led to Sovietization: How were the Bolsheviks able to spread so swiftly in Armenia? Why were they so successful in their propaganda among the masses? And finally, why did the ARF monopolize the government, if it did, only to have the Armenian Bolsheviks, and for that matter, seventy years of Soviet historiography label the free republic as "Dashnak Hayastan"?

It is a fact that the Bolshevik presence in the Caucasus was negligible. The Social Democratic Labor-Mensheviks controlled Georgia; Muslim Musavatists ruled over the Tatars; and the Dashnakts'ut'iwn was the power behind the Armenian Cause. The Dashnakts'ut'iwn was a majority in every national governance body, and in consecutive governments during the period of independence. In fact, after the declaration of Armenian independence, the first prime minister, Hovhannes Kachaznuni tried very hard to form a coalition government in Tbilisi. But the difficulties were many. The pool of intellectuals and political activists was limited. The Populist party leaders refused to participate and demanded that the ARF step aside and let them form the cabinet. They even suggested having two ruling bodies, one in Tbilisi and the other in Yerevan. "The Populists did not want to leave Tbilisi."[54] This idea stemmed from the fact that, as Vratsian states, neither the Populists, nor the Social-Revolutionaries and Social-Democrats were willing to take up residence in backward and destitute Yerevan and assume responsibility in that volatile situation. They would rather have the Armenian government operate from Tbilisi. Besides, the spirit of cooperation was lacking among the various Armenian political parties: to accept a portfolio in the government was seen as working under the command of the Dashnakts'ut'iwn. Therefore, the first cabinet was comprised solely of ARF members except for the minister of defense General Hovhannes Hakhverdian, a non-partisan. Grigor Ter-Petrossian, a non-partisan activist in Yerevan was invited as minister of Justice. It was only in November 1918 that the Populists agreed to participate in the coalition

---

[53] Harutyunyan, *Karsi marzĕ*, 147, fn. 345.

[54] Vratsian, *Hayastani hanrapetut'iwn*, 178; 178-182 contain details of the struggle to form a coalition cabinet in Tbilisi and the difficulties of transferring it to Yerevan.

government. The first Minister of Education, Mikayel Atabekian, was a Populist. However, after holding office for a few weeks, he returned to Tbilisi with the excuse of having important affairs to attend to, and he never came back to Yerevan. He was replaced by Gevorg Melik-Gharageozian, another Populist, who worked diligently until the resignation of all the Populist members of the cabinet in June 24, 1919 in opposition to the declaration of a Free, Independent, and United Armenia.[55]

Calling the Republic "Dashnak" was an invention of Armenian Bolsheviks who invested the word with all their hatred and animosity toward the Dashnakts'ut'iwn. It implied that the Republic was the mono-poly of the Dashnakts'ut'iwn, alien to the Armenian people's welfare, interests, and goals. That term and its implications was adopted and disseminated by Soviet historiography as a strategy to cover up Soviet transgressions, obscure the secret Russo-Turkish agreement and collabor-ation against independent Armenia, and blame the Dashnakts'ut'iwn for all the losses, including the loss of Turkish Armenia.

As to the rapid spread of Bolshevik or rather Communist ideology, the reason can be seen in the inability of the government to deal with unresolved internal and external problems jeopardizing public security. It can also be attributed to the dire economic situation and the absence of drastic measures to eradicate poverty, starvation, and joblessness to build a republic with a democratic structure and socialist ideology coveted by the ARF. In this situation, the Bolshevik propaganda – equality for all, Russian bread and sugar for the destitute, struggle against the wealthy class, rule of the working class, and brotherhood among nations – attracted not only the gullible, uneducated near-starving masses, but also idealistic youth. It was agreeable to the simple peasant youths to heed the sermon, put down their weapon, go home, and pick up their hoe and shovel.

Push for Sovietization of Armenia

On November 4, 1920, in a meeting of the Caucasian Bureau (KavBuro) of the Central Committee of the Russian Communist Party, with Stalin and Ordzhonikidze (then chair of the KavBuro) present, Shavarsh Amirkhanian, a member of the Central Committee of the

---

[55] Ibid., 266-267. Vratsian believes that the resignation was instigated by Boghos Nubar Pasha, the head of the Armenian National Delegation at Paris Peace Conference, who considered the declaration not in harmony with Armenian foreign policy.

Armenian Communist Party, reported that the situation in Armenia was grave and that in some areas virtually no government existed. He firmly stated that the situation was ripe for immediate Sovietization.[56] The final draft of Legran's agreement with the Armenian government was thus rejected and Amirkhanian's recommendation was sent to Chicherin for final approval. In fact, it was Amirkhanian who, together with Avis Nourijanian, would organize and supervise the execution by axe of imprisoned former leaders of Armenia on February 16–18, 1921, at the onset of the February uprising against Bolshevik rule in Armenia.

Legran was attempting to institute Soviet rule with the consent of the Armenian government without using force, so as to avoid the intervention of the Allies. But the coup de force came from the ArmRevKom in Baku supported by the Armenian detachment from the Red Army. With Ordzhonikidze's approval, these forces crossed the border on November 29, entered Ijevan, and declared Armenia Sovietized. ArmRevKom issued a proclamation citing the anarchy in the Armenian Republic and the people's anger at the adventurous and heedless actions of the Dashnak government, and reassuring the people that the Communist Party, with the help of the Red Army, liberator of all deprived nations, was leading the Armenian uprising to crush this bastion of the Allied Powers.[57]

How to explain the unseemly rush and excessive eagerness to destroy the country and rule over the ruins? Vladimir Harutyunyan writes, "It is one thing to struggle against one's own government and overthrow it, albeit by armed force.... However, it is another thing to destroy one's own independent statehood for the sake of foreign interests, and to receive instead the right of a local satrap to rule over the ruins of the once independent state. This is utter treason against statehood."[58]

Conclusion

Evidence shows that the Sovietization of Armenia was realized not at the behest of Moscow but because of the zeal and greed of the Armenian Bolsheviks for their personal gain, for the opportunity to rule the country, and for the sake of the victory of the Communist ideology and internationalism which they had so ardently espoused. Leonid Krasin, a high-ranking Soviet diplomat in Paris, had told Avetis Aharonian that

---

[56] Mnatsakanyan, *Hoktemberyan*, doc. no. 249, 397. See also Simon Vratsian, *Hayastani hanrapetut'iwn*, 496.

[57] ARF Archives (Boston), section A, file 11, doc. 59.

[58] Harutyunyan, *Hay Bolshevikneri,* 18.

Moscow had no interest in Armenia, but "the Armenian Bolsheviks have convinced us that the Armenian nation aspires to Communism." He had even stated, "We need an independent Armenia to separate Azerbaijan from Turkey."[59]

Of course, this general Soviet policy vis-à-vis Armenia was influenced by another gathering threat that changed the course of action, and that was Turkey's dangerous advance toward and aspiration to reach Azerbaijan. Mustafa Kemal was pursuing the realization of the Young Turk ideology of Pan-Turkism. An Armenia totally paralyzed by internal turmoil was incapable of defending its independence; indeed, it was on the verge of becoming a dismembered state totally dependent on Turkey. Stalin's telegram to Lenin, dated November 15, 1920, explained: "It is possible that in regard to Armenia we are already late, that is, Kemal will eat it and finish it sooner than we [can] get there."[60]

Armenia was Sovietized, and through subsequent treaties and rulings, Armenian territories were conceded to Turkey and Azerbaijan. The Sovietization was inevitable, and the ARF or the Bureau-government for that matter had its share of mistakes and miscalculations, but as Simon Vratsian, the last Prime Minister of Independent Armenia put it, "If the leaders of Armenia were free in their relationship with the Russians and did not meet at every instant the slandering and treachery of Armenian Bolsheviks, a major portion of the catastrophe that befell the Armenian nation would not have occured."[61] The historically inevitable Soviet Socialist Republic of Armenia would have been established with more respect to the rights of the people of Armenia and her territorial integrity.

---

[59] See Aharonian, *Sardarapatits'*, 122.

[60] Harutyunyan, *Karsi marzĕ*, 146, n. 344.

[61] Simon Vratsian, *Hayastanĕ bolshewikean murchi yew t'rk'akan sali mijew* [Armenia Between the Bolshevik Hammer and the Turkish Anvil] (Boston: A publication of A.R.F Central Committee of America, 1941), 146.

The Recognition of the First Republic of Armenia in South America (1918-1920)

Vartan Matiossian

The independence of Armenia in May 1918 was first met with caution and then with growing enthusiasm in the Armenian communities all around the world. South America was not an exception. The newly-created republic, thanks to the indefatigable will and continuous efforts of its representative, Etienne Brasil, did not shy away from seeking recognition and establishing diplomatic relations with several countries in the region.[1]

As it happens, the information about Etienne Brasil is scanty, and his life and work has remained shrouded in a certain cloud of mystery, to which we may add the facts of his residence in a faraway country and, logically, his non-Armenian name.[2] The future diplomat was born in 1882 and arrived in Brazil around 1908. He was a Catholic priest and took a position as professor at the archdiocesan seminary of Bahia, in the northeast of the country. He wrote ground-breaking studies on Brazilian natives in French, published in the Viennese ethnographic journal *Anthropos* (1908-1910) and signed Ignace Etienne. He would publish a flurry of textbooks and books on law, natural history, and philosophy until

---

[1] For an initial draft, see Vartan Matiossian, "Hayastani Hanrapetut'iwně yew Harawayin Amerikayi petut'iwnneř (1918-1920)" [The Republic of Armenia and the South American States: 1918-1920], *Haigazian Armenological Review,* vol. XX, 2000, 225-268; idem, *Harawayin koghmn ashkharhi. Hayeř Latinakan Amerikayi mēj skizbēn minch'ew 1950* [The Southern Corner of the World: The Armenians in Latin America from the Beginning to 1950] (Antelias: Richard and Tina Carolan Literary Prize, 2005), 41-63.

[2] Heitor Loureiro (São Paulo) has made the first detailed exploration of Brazilian archives and press in his doctoral dissertation, making very valuable inroads into Etienne Brasil's biography (Heitor de Andrade Carvalho Loureiro, "Pragmatismo e humanitarismo: a política externa brasileira e a causa armênia (1912-1922)," Ph.D. dissertation, Universidade Estadual Paulista "Júlio Mesquita Filho," 2016, 72-83. I am thankful to Dr. Loureiro for his useful comments on a previous draft of this paper.

the 1950s.[3] Leaving priesthood sometime in the early 1910s, he moved from Bahia to the capital, Rio de Janeiro, where he was a teacher at the French Lyceum by 1914.

Etienne Brasil had a doctorate in philosophy and a degree in pharmacy, and founded a school of pharmacy and tutored the children of many Brazilian and foreign officials. He was a member of various scholarly institutions. He later obtained a law degree and frequently represented local Armenians in government affairs and the courts.[4] By 1914 he established relations with the small circle of Armenians in Rio de Janeiro, according to a local correspondent to the weekly *Armenia* of Marseilles, who shed some light on his identity in an article published in 1917:

> Although he has forgotten the Armenian language by the force of circumstances, he has not forgotten the Armenians. He is an Armenian Catholic and a close relative to Patriarch Terzian; he pursued his education in Paris and forgot Armenian from an early age. But despite that, he never forgot his Armenian identity and here he has put his talent and enthusiasm to the service of the Armenian cause and the propaganda to the benefit of the Armenians for the past nine years, since he came to Brazil.[5]

It was reported in 1916 that Brasil's pro-Armenian articles appeared an average of two or three times a week, resulting in threatening letters

---

[3] See Narciso Binayan Carmona, *Entre el pasado y el futuro: los armenios en la Argentin* (Buenos Aires: [n. p.] 1996), 135. Interestingly, Etienne Brasil's brother, Bernard Ignace, was consul of Brazil in Bulgaria around 1921 (*Verjin Lur,* May 23, 1922). This points out, most likely, to the last name Iknadiosian, despite Binayan Carmona's claim that Brasil's actual name was Ignace Etienne (Binayan Carmona, *Entre el pasado,* 96), while the archives of the Republic, according to Richard Hovannisian, yielded the last name Etian; See Richard Hovannisian, *The Republic of Armenia. Vol III: From February to Sevres, February-August 1920* (Berkeley: University of California Press, 1996), 430.

[4] For a short curriculum vitae, which does not include any information prior to his Brazilian life, see Archives of the Republic of Armenia (ARA), Folder 400, Representation in South America, "Etienne Brasil"; Hovannisian, *The Republic,* 430.

[5] *Koch'nak,* September 15, 1917, 1123. Coincidentally, an article of Brasil was published in English two weeks later in New York (Etienne Brasil, "The War and Armenian Freedom," *The New Armenia,* October 1, 1917, 299).

from German residents.[6] In the same year, he organized an event to the benefit of the little Allies (Belgians, Serbians, and Armenians). An amount of 743 francs was raised for Armenians and sent to the editor of *Armenia,* Minas Tcheraz, who transferred it to Gevorg V, Catholicos of All Armenians, in Etchmiadzin.[7] A correspondent wrote:

> I can say that inasmuch a Tchobanian or a Basmadjian have been valuable and useful for the Armenian nation there, in France, Professor Etienne Brasil has been equally valuable and useful for us. (...) I do not think that any student or professor being in our Dr. Etienne's position who says 'I am Armenian' would be so interested in the pains of the Armenians.[8]

The impact of his activities grew considerably after Brazil broke diplomatic relations with the Central Powers in April 1917, which was followed by the declaration of war in October of the same year.

A group of Armenians sponsored the publication of Etienne Brasil's booklet *O Povo Armenio* ("The Armenian People," 22 pages),[9] which was released in the fall of 1917 and distributed free of charge.[10] Despite its brevity, the publication had a great impact in the press, since bibliography about Armenians was practically unavailable in Portuguese.[11] He followed suit with a similar, albeit more extensive volume entitled *Os Sirios* ("The Syrians," 69 pages) in 1918.[12]

Etienne Brasil was the driving force behind the Armenian Committee of Rio de Janeiro, formed with the main goal of securing the recognition of the fledging Republic. There were reportedly some 30 Armenians and Syro-Armenians (Arabic-speaking) living in the Brazilian capital, but

---

[6] *Hayrenik',* April 29, 1916, 5. Between 1910 and 1919, Brasil had published a total of 427 articles about Armenia and the Armenians (ARA, "Etienne Brasil"). On his pro-Armenian publications in that period, see Heitor Loureiro, "Reports from an Armenian Intellectual in Rio de Janeiro: Etienne Brasil and His Accounts on the Armenian Genocide," in *Genocide as a Spiritual and Moral Crime against Humanity. Proceedings of International Scientific Conference* (Moscow: Klyuch-S, 2017), 243-254.

[7] *Koch'nak,* November 25, 1916, 1253.

[8] *Koch'nak,* September 15, 1917, 1123.

[9] *Hayrenik',* January 13, 1918, 1.

[10] *Koch'nak,* September 15, 1917, 1123.

[11] *Armenia,* March 6, 1918, 2. The book reached Marseilles and Montevideo, for instance. See *Armenia,* January 9, 1918, 4; *El Día,* 13 de marzo de 1918, 5.

[12] See my article in *Haṛaj* (Paris), November 29, 1995, 2.

Etienne Brasil repeated that "we are just seven Armenians," for, it was reported, "he does not consider Armenian anyone who is not interested in the Armenian issue and the situation of his Armenian nation, and does not want to help his compatriots."[13]

The Armenian community of Brazil cabled U.S. President Woodrow Wilson on October 9, 1918, after the publication of his Fourteen Points.[14] E. Brasil wrote on November 3 to Ardashes Orakian, secretary of the Italian Committee for the Independence of Armenia, that "we have a small community that makes a lot of efforts. We have done active propaganda. Fifteen days ago we addressed a telegram to President Wilson. We are waiting for powers from the big Armenian centers and the Armenian Parliament to address the government of Brazil."[15]

On October 23, the Armenian Benevolent Union of São Paulo – a short-lived organization not to be confused with the local chapter of the Armenian General Benevolent Union, founded in the 1930s – asked the Armenian National Delegation of Paris about the position to adopt with regard to the Armenian Committee of Rio de Janeiro. Boghos Nubar, president of the Delegation, answered on December 5 that the latter totally agreed to its existence and that "it is necessary that you cooperate with that Committee from the standpoint of national interests."[16] Interestingly, on the same day, Etienne Brasil wrote to Avetis Aharonian, President of the Delegation of the Republic of Armenia, making note of a campaign of discredit of the Republic that had also impacted upon the Brazilian-Armenian community. He remarked:

---

[13] *Koch'nak*, September 15, 1917, 1123. The same number was given at the end of 1916 (*Hayrenik'*, November 5, 1916, 1).

[14] *Hayrenik'*, April 4, 1919, 1; *Pahak*, April 11, 1919, 3.

[15] Armenian National Archive (ANA), fund 448, catalog 1, file 56 (the letter is in French).

[16] Quoted in Yeznig Vartanian, *Prazilioy hay gaghutě. patmakan teghekut'iwnner ew zhamanakagrut'iwn* [The Armenian Community of Brazil: Historical Information and Chronology] (Buenos Aires: Sip'an, 1948), 58-59. Etienne Brasil had been shown a letter by Nubar – probably this one – where the Armenians of São Paulo were advised "not to do anything without consulting me and that the representative of the Armenian nation must be selected in Rio de Janeiro and not in São Paulo." The letter had impressed him favorably and triggered a positive shift in São Paulo Armenians' views about the Republic (Letter of Etienne Brasil to Avetis Aharonian, January 15, 1920, in ARA, Folder 400, Representation in South America).

> Coming to me, being free and independent from any party
> and any religion, I am intransigent in this question. Oceans of
> pretexts and sophisms cannot make forget a true Armenian *that
> today the Republic is our glory and our focus of hope.*[17]

Around the same time, an Armenian delegation met Dr. Epitácio
Pessoa, head of the Brazilian delegation to the Peace Conference, who
declared his sympathy for the Armenian cause.[18] The meeting had been
arranged by Mihran Latif (1856-1929), an Armenian engineer with an
extensive portfolio of relevant public works in Rio de Janeiro and well-
honed contacts in Brazilian circles. He was accompanied by Etienne Brasil
and Leon Apelian from Rio and Elian Naccache and Lazar Nazarian from
São Paulo. Brasil later wrote to Boghos Nubar about the importance of
showing a warm attitude towards Brazil and easing the entrance of its
products in Armenia.[19] The memorandum delivered to Pessoa stated in
part:

> The sons of Armenians who live in São Paulo, who have
> been born under the Brazilian flag and enjoy its protection,
> decided to have their voice reach you and ask that you speak on
> behalf of the homeland of their parents, with whose children –
> fraternizing with the same blood--they endured all sorts of
> suffering in a faraway country (...).
>
> (...) The future of Armenia depends on this conference of
> the civilized world, and the sons of Haig living in Brazil will
> have enormous gratitude to this blessed country when they have
> the opportunity to listen to the declaration of the representatives
> of this Republic, along with the uncountable expressions of
> sympathy already showed in favor of its independence by
> France, England, Switzerland, Italy, and especially the United
> States.[20]

Etienne Brasil also called upon King Albert of Belgium to defend the
Armenian cause at the Peace Conference.[21] He reported to have founded
the Armenian Union of South America, which would have three chapters

---

[17] Letter of Etienne Brasil to Avetis Aharonian, October 23, 1919, in ARA, Folder
400, Representation in South America (italics in the text).

[18] *Hayrenik'*, April 4, 1919, 1; *Pahak*, April 11, 1919, 3.

[19] *La Razón*, 23 de diciembre de 1918, 1.

[20] See the text of the memorandum in Vartanian, *Prazilioy,* 56-57.

[21] Kiud Mkhitarian, *Prazilahay gaghutĕ skizbēn minch'ew mer ōrerĕ* [The
Brazilian Armenian Community from the Beginning to Our Days] (Paris:
Mat'ikean, 1938), 14.

in Rio de Janeiro, São Paulo, and Buenos Aires, and would be chaired by M. Latif, following the suggestions coming from North America.[22] This Union, however, does not seem to have had a real existence. He also appears to have tried to establish cooperation with other Armenian communities. For instance, he wrote to A. Orakian in the abovementioned letter: "Please keep me informed of the number of Armenians in Italy, their activities, as well as the sympathies and promises of the Italian government. On my side, I will keep you informed of the developments."[23]

From head of the Brazilian delegation, Epitácio Pessoa would jump to the position of President of Brazil (1919-1922) after the elections of April 1919. He received Brasil, Apelian, and Naccache at the presidential palace on October 11. During the encounter, he promised to make all efforts "to establish good political and commercial relations with Armenia."[24] E. Brasil reportedly organized a group of Armenian and Brazilian merchants to develop trade between Brazil and Cilicia, which had recently been put under French mandate. Brazil was willing to make a trial effort by sending three ships to Egypt, but it was required that Armenian merchants purchased the Brazilian goods and guaranteed that they would load those ships in the return trip with merchandise that interested Brazil.[25] This and other similar projects of commercial cooperation, mentioned in Etienne Brasil's steady flow of letters to Aharonian, did not have any practical consequence.

In September 1919, Etienne Brasil suggested to Avetis Aharonian, president of the Delegation of the Republic of Armenia, to designate two delegates near the Brazilian diplomatic representations and the government "with a confidential character and at least unofficial."[26] A month later, he stressed the need for legal representatives, since the fact that Armenians were Turkish subjects created many practical difficulties.[27] Aharonian designated him diplomatic representative on December 24[28]

---

[22] *Hayrenik'*, April 4, 1919, 1; *Pahak*, April 11, 1919, 3.

[23] ANA, fund 448, catalog 1, file 56.

[24] Letter of E. Brasil to Aharonian, October 23, 1919, in ARA, Folder 400.

[25] Letter of Etienne Brasil to Avetis Aharonian, October 4, 1919, in ARA, Folder 400, Representation in South America. See also *Armenia,* November 12, 1919, 3.

[26] ARA, Folder 400, Representation in South America.

[27] Brasil to Aharonian, October 23, 1919, in ARA, Folder 400. See also Hovannisian, *The Republic,* 431.

[28] Letter of Etienne Brasil to Avetis Aharonian, January 4, 1920, in ARA, Folder 400, Representation in South America.

and Brasil received his credentials on January 29.[29] On February 16 Aharonian announced the designation of eight consuls and representatives, including "Doctor Etienne Brasil, of Armenian origin, designated diplomatic representative of the Republic of Armenia upon the government of Brazil in Rio de Janeiro."[30] In early April, the diplomat acknowledged reception of "credentials for Brazil and the other countries of South America."[31] Prime Minister and Minister of Foreign Affairs Alexander Khatisian wrote to him on April 17: "By note No. 1370, Mr. Aharonian informs me that he has designated you as representative of the Republic of Armenia in Brazil. By establishing you in that position, I am sure that you will try by all means to defend the interests of the Republic and keep its prestige high." Two days later, he asked him "to regularly send to our Ministry in Yerevan, at least once a month, a report containing all communications and news that may interest the Republic of Armenia."[32]

On February 9, 1920, Brasil had written to Uruguayan ambassador Manuel Bernárdez that the Armenian government had plans to designate Latif as ambassador extraordinary upon the South American nations.[33] In his correspondence with Boghos Nubar and Aharonian, he insisted about naming Latif Honorary General Consul, since, as Richard Hovannisian writes, "his mansion was a virtual embassy and he had enormous influence with government officials, including President Epitacio Pessoa."[34] Aharonian observed in June and July 1920 that it was not adequate to multiply such positions until the peace treaty with the Ottoman Empire clarified the status of Armenia. He suggested not to designate foreign citizens in September and recalled that the last word about diplomatic posts

---

[29] Ibid.

[30] ANA, fund 199, catalog 1, file 198, part A; *Haraj*, March 12, 1920, 3.

[31] Letter of Etienne Brasil to Avetis Aharonian, April 11, 1920, in ARA Folder 400, Representation in South America.

[32] ANA, fund 200, catalog 1, file 507. Strangely enough, Etienne Brasil's name did not appear in a list of diplomats of the Republic prepared in September 1920 (see R. Nahatakyan, "P'astat'ght'er Hayastani hanrapetut'yan patmut'yan masin" [Documents on the History of the Republic of Armenia], *Lraber hasarakakan gitut'yunneri*, 4, 1991, 160-161.

[33] Archivo General de la Nación del Uruguay, Fondo Ministerio de Relaciones Exteriores, Consular (AGN), Caja 168, Carpeta 416, "República de Armenia. Representación en el Uruguay." Thank you to Daniel Karamanoukian (Montevideo) for providing me with the documentation from Uruguayan archives.

[34] Hovannisian, *The Republic,* 430-431. See, among others, Etienne Brasil's letters to Aharonian of January 15 and February 4, 1920.

belonged to the government of the Republic.[35] In the end, Latif rejected his nomination, "finding the post very big and especially premature."[36]

Argentina's Recognition of Armenian Independence

Etienne Brasil's activities took fresh impetus with the de facto recognition of Armenia by the Allies in January 1920 and his official designation. This momentum was reinforced by the fact that his country of residence, Brazil, became a founding member of the League of Nations in the same month and a non-permanent member of the League Council, turning into the most prominent American member in the organization.

He would earn his first important result with the de jure recognition by Argentina, which came almost eight months after that of Georgia, probably due to the uncertainty surrounding Armenia throughout 1918-1919. Two weeks after independence, on June 10, 1918, Georgian Foreign Minister Akaki Chkhenkeli had made a petition of recognition to Luis Molina, Argentinean ambassador in Germany, followed by a letter to Molina on October 25 with an extensive memorandum about the history of Georgia, its political situation, and its borders. The Argentinean recognition of Georgia, however, was delayed until September 15, 1919.[37]

The recognition of Armenia was much more expeditious, probably due to the persistent action of Etienne Brasil, but also the Argentinean application of the theory of "democratic status," according to which, the progress of social consciousness towards the new order of national building unavoidably ended with a push to independence meaning to achieve full membership in the international order. "If that goal, on the grounds of the previously mentioned sociological conditions, was really the result of the free and spontaneous will of the peoples expressed in a democratic way, the Argentinean Ministry of Foreign Affairs went on to accomplish the recognition," international relations expert Lucio Moreno

---

[35] Hovannisian, *The Republic*, 432-433.

[36] Vartanian, *Prazilio,* 66.

[37] *Circular Informativa Mensual del Ministerio de Relaciones Exteriores y Culto*, septiembre de 1919, 444-455. On November 8, 1920, when in Paris on his way to the assembly of the League of Nations, Argentinean Foreign Minister Honorio Pueyrredón met his Georgian colleague Evgeni Gegechkori, who thanked him for the recognition of Georgia the year before (*La Prensa*, 9 de noviembre de 1920, 8).

Quintana, an official of the ministry at the time, wrote.[38] On the other hand, Argentina had remained neutral during the war, despite Allied pressure, and President Hipólito Yrigoyen (1916-1922) pursued an international policy that advocated for the establishment of an order of nations based on principles of fair and equal treatment.

Etienne Brasil transmitted the request for Argentinean recognition to Ambassador Mario Ruiz de los Llanos on February 20, 1920.[39] In early April, he reported that he had already delivered to Ruiz de los Llanos certain documents upon request of the Argentinean government and expressed his hope that "Argentina, free of any engagement with France, England, and the United States, will recognized us even before Brazil itself."[40] Later that month, he sent a letter to the influential daily *La Nación* of Buenos Aires, which wrote:

> Right now, he [Brasil] is in Rio advancing the same activity upon the Brazilian government, but, in his letter written to us, he promises to visit Argentina as soon as this country has recognized the new republic.
>
> In the same letter, Dr. Brasil expresses that, due to the great financial difficulties confronted by the new government of Armenia, right now it is not possible, as it would be desirable, that the newly-created Republic send a representative to each country of this continent. With the same intent of making savings, Dr. Brasil starts his bid in and from Rio, where he already lived when the Armenian government entrusted him with his mission.[41]

Nevertheless, barely ten days after the United States, Argentina became the second country in the world to grant Armenia recognition de jure. *La Época,* the daily of the governing Radical Party, wrote on May 2, 1920, that "a decree recognizing the Republic of Armenia was made public from the Ministry of Foreign Affairs. The government of Argentina is the

---

[38] Lucio M. Moreno Quintana, *La diplomacia de Yrigoyen. Relación técnica, objetiva y documentada de la política internacional argentina durante el período de gobierno 1916-1922* (La Plata: Compañía Impresora Argentina, 1928), 83.

[39] Letter of Etienne Brasil to Avetis Aharonian, February 20, 1920, in ARA, Folder 400, Representation in South America.

[40] Letter of Etienne Brasil to Avetis Aharonian, April 11, 1920, in ARA, Folder 400, Representation in South America.

[41] *La Nación*, 27 de abril de 1920, 4.

first that recognizes the independence of that new country."[42] On May 3, *La Prensa,* another influential daily, reported that, "by yesterday's decree, the Argentinean government recognized the independence and the sovereignty of the new state of Armenia. This resolution was notified yesterday to the consular agent of that new republic, who had taken steps, on behalf of his government, for the official recognition of that country."[43] Meanwhile, *La Época* reported that President Yrigoyen had already received telegrams of gratitude from Armenians of Argentina and Brazil.[44] On the same day, Brasil cabled to Aharonian: "Argentinean government communiques me recognition of Armenia. Send telegram of thanks to President Yrigoyen."[45] He simultaneously wrote to him that "yesterday, the Argentinean government has published the decree recognizing the Armenian Republic; I have received the communication one hour before the Official Bulletin." He attached the copy of a message by Ruiz de los Llanos, dated May 2, 1920, who notified him that, according to the communication he had just received, "the Argentinean government has recognized the Armenian Republic today."[46] In a letter written later in the month to the Inter-Party Body of Buenos Aires, he noted that "on the second of this month, I received from the Argentinean government the recognition of the Armenian government as a *free Nation.*"[47] Therefore, the recognition happened on May 2, but for unknown reasons the date

---

[42] *La Época,* 2 de mayo de 1920, 1. The U.S. Embassy also communicated the news on May 1 to the State Department (Hovannisian, *The Republic,* 432), which received the information on May 6 (*Hayrenik',* May 7, 1920, 3).

[43] *La Prensa,* 3 de mayo de 1920, 9. See also *La Nación,* 3 de mayo de 1920, 4; *El Día,* 4 de mayo de 1920, 3.

[44] *La Época,* 3 de mayo de 1920, 2.

[45] Copy of May 3, 1920, telegram from Etienne Brasil to Avetis Aharonian, in ARA, Folder 400, Representation in South America.

[46] Letter of Etienne Brasil to Avetis Aharonian, May 3, 1920, in ARA, Folder 400, Representation in South America. See also Hovannisian, *The Republic,* 432.

[47] See *Armenia* (Buenos Aires), January 17, 1955, 2 (italics in the text). The letter is undated and contains the line "Your letter dated 23..." (probably April). Interestingly, on June 8 Brasil wrote to the same address: "Please kindly send me two copies of the May 2 [*sic*] *Diario Oficial,* where the government of Argentina recognizes our government" *Armenia* (Buenos Aires), January 18, 1955, 2. More than three decades later, Stepan Shekherdemian, a Hunchakian key representative to the Inter-Party Body, handed the five letters written in Armenian to Sokrat Terzian, who published them in 1955 under the pseudonym S. Gran. The whereabouts of the original letters, as well as the minutes of the Inter-Party Body, which Terzian mentioned in his article, is unknown.

appeared as May 3 a month and a half later, when the decree signed by President Hipólito Yrigoyen and Foreign Minister Honorio Pueyrredón was published in the Official Bulletin:

> May 3, 1920
> Taking into account the applications of the representative of the temporary government of Armenia,
> the Executive Power of the Nation
> decrees
> Art. 1: To recognize the Republic of Armenia as a free and independent state.
> Art. 2: To communicate, publish in the Official Bulletin, and deliver to the National Register Board."[48]

Yrigoyen referred to the recognition of Armenia in his message of May 13, on the opening of the 1920 sessions of the Argentinean Congress:

> New states have sprung on the grounds of strong nationalities. The Executive Power took the initiative to recognize them every time that they introduced themselves with their clear personality and the expression of democratic ideals. For us, Armenia, Czechoslovakia, Georgia, and Polonia are already present in the international community.[49]

Alexandr Sizonenko, without offering further proof, has linked the recognition of Armenia and Georgia to the British policy in the Caucasus and to a putative anti-Soviet policy of the Argentinean government.[50]

According to press reports, Etienne Brasil wrote a letter of thanks to Yrigoyen,[51] while Aharonian had sent a telegram: "The delegation of the Republic of Armenia at the Peace Conference expresses its warm gratitude for the recognition of Armenia. I am convinced that our two peoples are called to cultivate friendly relations."[52]

---

[48] *Boletín Oficial de la República Argentina*, 25 de junio de 1920, 622.

[49] Hipólito Yrigoyen, *Pueblo y gobierno,* vol. IV (Buenos Aires: Editorial Raigal, 1956), 204.

[50] Alexandr Sizonenko, *Statovlenye otnoshenii SSSR so stranami Latinskoii Ameriki (1917-1941 gg.)* (Moscow: Nauka, 1981), 21.

[51] *La Prensa*, 15 de mayo de 1920, 10. Brasil had thanked Ruiz de los Llanos and sent a telegram to Yrigoyen on May 3 (letter to Aharonian, May 3, 1920, in ARA, Folder 400).

[52] *La Época*, 15 de mayo de 1920, 1.

Jane van Der Karr has brought forward an interesting question. Argentinean businessmen were decidedly in favor of the country joining the League of Nations, with "ideals" as the main motivation. "However," she wrote, "that circle forged its conviction of supporting the popular movement in favor of joining when the probability of Argentina to become mandatory of Armenia, Constantinople, or another area of the Near East appeared during the assemblies of the Society."[53]

Article 22 of the Covenant of the League of Nations established that "certain communities formerly belonging to the Turkish Empire" could be provisionally recognized as independent nations if they accepted the advisory role of a mandatory state until "such time as they are able to stand alone."[54] However, Argentina had accessed the League on July 12, 1919, which just entailed the acceptance of its general principles, without becoming a member.[55] General Secretary Sir Eric Drummond reported six days later that the League was not yet legally created.[56]

According to van Der Karr, who has given no source for these statements, "While 1919 came to its end, the rejection of Argentina to accept Armenia as mandatory of the League of Nations was a question with equally grave political consequences on the international front. Since Armenia did not have natural wealth, its maintenance would be a noticeable load for almost all mandatory nations to which it could be entrusted."[57] Armando Alonso Piñeiro added that "personally, we believe that the question was more complex," and that the Argentinean government "did not want international complications, which could not be prevented in this case."[58]

In a letter to *The Times*, British former MP Sir Robert Perks (1849-1934) discussed the obstacles before the League of Nations to protect and rebuild Armenia, including the issue of the mandate. He asked, in consideration of the apparent reluctance of the United States to take the

---

[53] Jane Van Der Karr, *La Primera Guerra Mundial y la política económica argentina* (Buenos Aires: Troquel, 1974), 183.
[54] *The Treaty of Peace and the Covenant of the League of Nations* (Philadelphia: The John C. Winston Co., 1920), 55.
[55] María Monserrat Llairó and Raimundo Siepe, *Argentina en Europa. Yrigoyen y la Sociedad de las Naciones (1918-1920)* (Buenos Aires: Ediciones Macchi, 1997), 62-66.
[56] Moreno Quintana, *La diplomacia de Yrigoyen,* 242.
[57] Van Der Karr, *La Primera Guerra Mundial,* 184.
[58] Armando Alonso Piñeiro, *La historia argentina que muchos argentinos no conocen* (Buenos Aires: Depalma, 1976), 319.

mandate, whether there was any hope that "one of the wealthy and progressive Republics of South America, aided by British administrative experience, may attempt and to her lasting honour successfully achieve (...) this Christian and humane task."[59] An editorial of *La Prensa*, "The United States and the Mandate over Armenia," analyzed the question of the United States mandate and mentioned Perks' proposal.[60] In June, Etienne Brasil wrote to Ruiz de los Llanos, still in vacation in Buenos Aires, about Argentinean potential help to Armenia. In his letter, he noted that, regarding the possibility of an Argentinean mandate, "it seems to me, personally, that this idea would not be admitted by the powers of Europe." The letter also included a draft of a bilateral agreement between Argentina and Armenia.[61]

The de facto recognition of January 1920 and the forthcoming signature of the peace treaty with Turkey had created a wave of optimism, despite the cumulating clouds. The second anniversary of Armenia's independence was marked with great enthusiasm worldwide in May 1920. There were also celebrations in South America, with events in Rio de Janeiro, initiated by Etienne Brasil,[62] and São Paulo.[63] The small community of Montevideo collected the amount of 2,460 francs at its event, which was sent to Aharonian and earmarked as a present to Armenian soldiers.[64]

However, the leadership of the community had suffered a division in Buenos Aires, which was the cause for separate celebrations. The Armenian National Union collected 8,095 pesos (around 29,000 francs) in the event of May 28, from which 4,500 were sent to Mihran Damadian for the self-defense of Cilicia. According to Israel Arslan, the Union's secretary, the amount did not reach its destiny due to a misunderstanding

---

[59] *The Times,* May 10, 1920, 8. Etienne Brasil referred to this proposal in a letter to Aharonian a few days later (Etienne Brasil to Avetis Aharonian, May 16, 1920, in ARA, Folder 400, Representation in South America).

[60] *La Prensa,* 30 de mayo de 1920, 10.

[61] Letter of Etienne Brasil to Mario Ruiz de los Llanos, June 22, 1920, copy in ARA, Folder 400, Representation in South America. See also Brasil's letter to Aharonian, June 23, 1920, in the same folder.

[62] Mkhitarian, *Prazilahay*, 14-15.

[63] Hovannisian, *The Republic,* 432.

[64] *Koch'nak Hayastani*, July 24, 1920, 958.

and was returned. Consequently, the entire amount was sent to Yerevan to be allocated to the Armenian army.[65]

The two major parties active in the Argentinean capital, the Social-Democrat Hunchakian Party and the Armenian Revolutionary Federation, which had abandoned the Armenian National Union at the beginning of 1920, held an event on the same day.[66] They cabled Etienne Brasil that they had collected around 30,000 francs, to which the latter responded that he had made a report to the Armenian government.[67]

On June 8, he suggested to the Inter-Party Body that a delegation should pay a visit to Ruiz de los Llanos, who had returned to Buenos Aires for vacation on May 31,[68] "to thank him for the efforts that he made upon his government in favor of the Armenian cause," and noted that he had also promised to do his best to procure a loan for Armenia.[69] In the end, a delegation of the National Union visited the Argentinean diplomat.[70]

Brasil had outlined the political and economic aspects of his work in his abovementioned letter to *La Nación.* The daily reported that as soon as Armenia was recognized by South American countries, it would designate consuls for the most important ones. Later, a special delegation would arrive to study ways to establish commercial exchange between South America and Armenia and other areas of the Near East. Brasil was available to whoever wanted to learn about the possibilities for Argentinean export and import that Armenian offered.[71]

Financial issues were relevant for Brasil, who wrote to the Inter-Party Body of Buenos Aires in May 1920 that he needed to present his official paperwork to the government of Argentina and others as "plenipotentiary minister" of the Republic to be able to designate consular employees and to sign agreements, but "unfortunately, our government has countless internal needs, and cannot satisfy external expenses; bearing all this in

---

[65] *La Razón,* 27 de mayo de 1920, 5; *Hay Kedron,* February 1942, 56. Cf. Ashot Artsruni, *Tarets 'oyts' Har. Amerikahayots'* [South American Armenians Yearbook] (Buenos Aires: Ararat, 1943), 21.

[66] *La Prensa,* 28 de mayo de 1920, 13; *La Razón,* 28 de mayo de 1920, 6.

[67] Binayan Carmona, *Entre el pasado,* 97. See *Armenia* (Buenos Aires), January 18, 1955, 2.

[68] *La Prensa,* 1 de junio de 1920, 11.

[69] *Armenia* (Buenos Aires), January 18, 1955, 2, where the date of the letter is July 8. It appears to be a misprint for June 8, since it would have been illogical to make such a suggestion 45 days after de los Llanos' departure, dated May 24 in the letter.

[70] *Hay Kedron,* April 1942, 56. Cf. Artsruni, *Tarets 'oyts',* 21.

[71] *La Nación,* 27 de abril de 1920, 4.

consideration, I leave it to you to think about these issues in a patriotic way."[72] He wrote on July 30 that he had requested the Argentinean government to recognize his credentials and asked his compatriots whether it was possible "to create local means to create a general consulate."[73] Eight days later, he added that "all means are being considered to be executed in order to have general consulates in the capitals, with Armenian commercial chambers attached."[74] Argentina accepted his credentials in October,[75] and the following month he suggested the name of Yervant Khachikian (1881-1933), an influential and well-connected community member in Buenos Aires, as consul.[76]

Recognition by Chile and Brazil

In his letter to Aharonian of January 4, 1920, Etienne Brasil had written that the day before he had maintained a long conversation with Alfredo Irarrazával Zañartu (1867-1934), Chilean minister to Brazil, who promised him his support to obtain the recognition of his country.[77]

According to a press report published in May 1920, "the consuls of Uruguay and Chile asked Mr. Etienne to make official applications to their governments in order to create commercial instruments with the Armenian republic, which would ease the recognition of Armenian independence."[78]

Chile recognized the independence of Armenia on August 7.[79] The recognition was celebrated in the meridional town of Llay-Llay – which appears to have been the main center of the small Armenian community – in the following month. The roofs were decorated with flags, an open-air

---

[72] *Armenia* (Buenos Aires), January, 17, 1955, 2.

[73] *Armenia* (Buenos Aires), January 18, 1955, 2.

[74] *Armenia* (Buenos Aires), January 19, 1955, 2.

[75] *Armenia*, November 17, 1920, 2.

[76] Hovannisian, *The Republic,* 433. He had previously suggested the name of Harutiun Takhtadjian (Tagtachian, 1888-1934), an A.R.F. member who owned a shoe factory, was well-educated, and was well-regarded by the community (letter of Brasil to Aharonian, May 3, 1920, in ARA, folder 400).

[77] ARA, Folder 400, Representation in South America. Brasil had been the tutor of Irarrazával Zañartu's two sons.

[78] *Hayrenik'*, May 5, 1920, 2.

[79] *La Nación*, 8 de agosto de 1920, 3. The date August 15 (Hovannisian, *The Republic,* 433) is inaccurate. The American embassy in Santiago de Chile gave the date November 4 (idem).

mass was celebrated, and a big dinner and fireworks were held in the evening.[80]

One of the organizers of this celebration was Alexander Manukian, whom Etienne Brasil suggested to Aharonian as potential consul in November 1920.[81] He had played the role of representative of the Armenian community and was recognized "semi-officially as consul" by the Chilean government.[82] For instance, when in late 1920, a group of Chaldeans, led by an individual self-styled as "Supreme Patriarch of the Armenian Church," extorted a substantial amount of money under the pretext of benefitting Armenian orphans, "Alexander Manukian, an Armenian who was zealous to protect national honor," had reported the incident to Etienne Brasil. The latter had contact Miguel Cruchaga, Chilean ambassador in Brazil, and the swindlers had been arrested.[83]

The archives of the Republic of Armenia in Boston contain a letter by Arturo Alessandri, incoming President of Chile, that he addressed "to the President of the Republic of Armenia" on December 23, 1920, to communicate the beginning of his first mandate that day: "While I make Your Excellency aware of this fact, I am pleased to declare to him that, in the execution of my functions, I will make an special effort to strengthen the ties of sincere friendship that happily unite our respective countries."[84]

Etienne Brasil's contacts also included the representatives of Uruguay, Paraguay, Bolivia, Peru, Ecuador, Colombia, and Venezuela in Brazil.[85]

However, his main and logical target was his adopted country, Brazil, as one of the belligerent parties in World War and member of the Council of the League of Nations. In his view, Brazil and Argentina could provide weapons, ammunitions, military advisors, and instructors to Armenia, as well as credits, in exchange for the status of privileged nation.[86]

---

[80] *Armenia*, November 17, 1920, 2.

[81] Hovannisian, *The Republic,* 433-434. The claim that Manukian was the Armenian "official representative" in Chile remains unsubstantiated (Artsruni, *Tarets'oyts'*, 345).

[82] *Armenia,* March 2, 1921, 3.

[83] *Armenia,* February 23, 1921, 3.

[84] ARA, Folder 400, Representation in South America. Alessandri was President for three terms (1920-1924, 1925, and 1932-1938). Indeed, the Republic did not have a presidential system of government, and the communication was issued exactly three weeks after the transfer of power to the Bolsheviks.

[85] See his letters to Avetis Aharonian of April 11 (Venezuela), April 21 (Colombia and Peru),

[86] Hovannisian, *The Republic,* 432.

On January 6, 1920, Brazilian Foreign Minister José Manuel de Azevedo Marques submitted to Pessoa the demand of recognition made by Etienne Brasil on behalf of the Republic of Armenia.[87] However, the question would remain in suspense for ten months, despite the Armenian diplomat's efforts and well-honed contacts at the upper level of the government. The reason was that Brazil, unlike Argentina, had certain engagements with France and Great Britain inherited from the previous government. However, as Undersecretary of State Rodrigo Octavio explained to Etienne Brasil on April 26, the recognition by the United States on April 23 was a breakthrough in the issue.[88]

In May, after a meeting between Brasil and Pessoa, the Brazilian Foreign Minister was ordered to go ahead with the recognition.[89] However, the question remained in suspense. On October 6, the indefatigable Brasil wrote to Naccache, president of the Armenian Benevolent Union in São Paulo:

> (…) Yesterday I was officially invited to the government palace. They officially informed me there that Brazil definitely recognized the Armenian Republic; they asked me the address of the Republic of Armenia to which the Brazilian government will immediately and officially communicate the news. The government decree will be published after the Armenian government is officially informed, and they will officially inform me again before the publication of the decree.
>
> (…) They also informed me that they admit me as representative of the Republic of Armenia; only official formalities are missing for me to become diplomatic representative.
>
> (…) It is necessary to start a fundraiser, half of it for the poor in Armenia and the other half to assist to the furnishing of the Armenian consulate, which will be established in Rio de Janeiro, on Avenida do Sul. The entire Armenian community must bring its help.[90]

---

[87] Letter of Etienne Brasil to Avetis Aharonian, January 15, 1920, in ARA, Folder 400, Representation in South America.

[88] Letter of Etienne Brasil to Avetis Aharonian, April 28, 1920, in ARA, Folder 400, Representation in South America.

[89] *Hayrenik'*, May 5, 1920, 1. See Etienne Brasil's letter to Aharonian, May 23, 1920, in ARA, Folder 400, Representation in South America.

[90] Vartanian, *Prazilioy*, 67. Cf. *Armenia,* November 17, 1920, 1.

On the same day, he wrote to Aharonian that the assistant to the Foreign Minister had called to show him Pessoa's personal orders. They had asked that the Armenian government turned him into either chargé d'affairs or plenipotentiary ambassador. Otherwise, he could not be officially recognized. A telegram from Aharonian would temporarily suffice.[91] Although the response was delayed, the decree of recognition appeared on November 7 in the *Diario Official*:

> The president of the Republic of the United States of Brazil declares that the Republic of Armenia and its current government are recognized, accepting all the consequences of that recognition.
> Rio de Janeiro, November 3, 1920
> 99th year of the Independence and 32nd year of the Republic of Brazil.[92]

Parliament member F. A. Carneiro da Cunha and Assistant Secretary of Foreign Affairs Rodrigo Octavio had contributed to the recognition.[93] The news was reported by *La Prensa* and *La Nación* in Buenos Aires on November 6.[94] Etienne Brasil suggested to Aharonian that Elian Naccache became consul in San Paulo. Nubar Ohanian would be consul in Rio, Dikran Astour, secretary of the embassy, and Hagop Ajemian, translator.[95]

The Question of Uruguay's Recognition

Ashot Artzruni had claimed in 1965 that, after the recognition de facto in January 1920, "36 states communicated the official recognition of the independence of Armenia, including Argentina, Uruguay, and Peru."[96]

---

[91] Hovannisian, *The Republic,* 433.

[92] See the Armenian translation in *Armenia,* March 2, 1921, 2.

[93] *Armenia,* November 17, 1920, 2.

[94] *La Prensa,* 6 de noviembre de 1920, 10; *La Nación,* 6 de noviembre de 1920, 3. Hovannisian dated the recognition November 5, noting that the British embassy in Rio de Janeiro communicated the date November 3 (Hovannisian, *The Republic*, 433).

[95] Hovannisian, *The Republic,* 433.

[96] Ashot Artzruni, *Historia del pueblo armenio*, translated by Ruben Artzruní, second edition (Buenos Aires: Fundación Ararat, 1971), 408 (reprint of the first edition of 1965). The names of the three South American countries have been eliminated in the posthumous and thoroughly revised edition of 2010. See idem, *Historia del pueblo armenio,* fourth edition (Barcelona: Sirar Ediciones, 2010),

Hovannisian has stated that only Argentina, Brazil, and Chile recognized the independence, with recognition by Peru and Paraguay apparently in the works.[97]

Etienne Brasil doggedly pursued Uruguay's recognition. On February 9, 1920, following the recognition de facto by the Peace Conference, he wrote to Bernárdez that, "therefore, the Republic of Uruguay, member of the Conference, has implicitly recognized the independence the fact of the Armenian people. I come to ask a special declaration of your government in this regard." Besides official relations and diplomatic presence, he promised a productive trade exchange, compromising to do everything "to introduce fine animals and other agricultural contributions to the Republic of Uruguay," and declared his readiness to sign a commercial agreement.[98]

In a letter to acting Minister of Foreign Affairs Rufino Domínguez on February 11, Bernárdez attached the copy of Brasil's Portuguese letter, observing that "these credentials are only for the government of Brazil, but Mr. Etienne Brasil told me that he expected the same credentials for the entire South America and that, in the meantime, he wants to start and go ahead with his tasks."

On May 6 Bernárdez cabled to new Foreign Minister Juan Antonio Buero that the Armenian representative had requested Uruguay's recognition of Armenia in a letter addressed to his embassy. He promised to send copies of his credentials. "In another letter," he added, "he asked me to let Your Excellency know that the Argentinean [and] Brazilian governments have just recognized the Armenian Republic.[99]

In early June, Minister Buero answered with the following ciphered telegram:

> (...) The government considers superfluous the explicit recognition of the Republic of Armenia, judging that it is enough the implicit recognition that was done by the Peace Conference, in which Uruguay participated as an associate state. The admission of Mr. Brasil's credentials would

---

394. It had been previously noted that Uruguayan official publications made no mention of the recognition. See Alberto Douredjian and Daniel Karamanoukian, *La inmigración armenia en el Uruguay,* vol. I (Montevideo: [n. p.] 1993), 55.

[97] Hovannisian, *The Republic,* 433.

[98] AGN, Caja 168, Carpeta 416. About this communication, see Etienne Brasil's letter to Aharonian, February 12, 1920, in ARA, Folder 400, Representation in South America.

[99] AGN, Caja, 168, Carpeta 416. Buero made a note "to take into consideration" on May 29.

consecrate that recognition, but I must tell to Your Excellency that the Armenian government has not asked yet for common credentials for the abovementioned gentleman; therefore, it is adequate to have that formality fulfilled, as it has always been the case with all other foreign diplomats. May Your Excellency have the kindness to tell us what the diplomatic post of Mr. Brasil is, because he has not declared yet whether his credentials are for head of state or Minister of Foreign Affairs.[100]

Brasil addressed a French letter to the president of the country on June 26, writing that "the recognition of our republic by Uruguay would be particularly pleasing to us, for (…) we direct our eyes with great sympathy towards the South American nationalities, filled with the ideal of Law and Justice." He added that "the Armenians, who rule over the entire commerce of the Orient (from Egypt to Greece), will not delay to enter into relationship with your beautiful country.[101]

On August 12 Etienne Brazil communicated to Bernardez the signature of the Treaty of Sevres and reported that the Parliament of Armenia had confirmed his nomination and entrusted him with the mission of organizing the diplomatic and consular representation in South America. He also noted that the government had denied, through an official cable, the claims of a Soviet invasion of Armenia, stating that "Armenia is not Soviet and will never be; the Russians, at their turn, have respected our borders to this day." He repeated that, "given the irreversible international situation of Armenia," Uruguayan recognition would not be delayed, "which I expect as a great honor for our nation."[102]

In November 1920 Etienne Brasil suggested the name of Hunchakian activist Nazaret Khulmunian as consul in Montevideo.[103] On November 10

---

[100] See AGN, Caja 168, Carpeta 416.

[101] Idem. Four months later (October 31), Bernárdez wrote in a note that, when he was in Montevideo, Brasil had delivered the abovementioned letter to the Uruguayan embassy, asking to be sent to the ministry. He added that, "Since our government has not recognized the Republic of Armenia yet, the consideration of that letter make it opportune (…)." Bernárdez had finished his service in Brazil and it is not unlikely that this was the reason of the delay to send the letter to the ministry (Daniel Karamanoukian, personal communication, March 2002).

[102] AGN, Caja 168, Carpeta 416. On September 11 Buero wrote under Bernardez's August 28 letter attached to Brasil's: "To say that what it is decided on this point will be communicated at an appropriate moment."

[103] Hovannisian, The Republic, 433. A history of the Hunchakian Party has claimed that Khulmunian, a party member, was "the representative of the Republic

Bernardez cabled to Montevideo that Brazil had recognized Armenia, "whose diplomatic representative asks me in writing to repeat the request of recognition to the government."[104] After his replacement by Dionisio Ramos Monteros, the Uruguayan Ministry of Foreign Affairs informed on December 2 to the new ambassador in Brazil that "in response, I have to tell His Excellency that we will communicate in due time what it is decided in that matter."[105] The due time, indeed, would never arrive.

The First Assembly of the League of Nations

Following the signature of the Treaty of Sevres, an editorial of *La Prensa* had made a penetrating and well-informed analysis:

> The signature of the Treaty of Sevres is, without doubt, an important step towards the pacification of the world, but its impact would have been much more efficient if the document had not been signed by representatives of the government of Constantinople, which are under the reach of the ships anchored in the Straits, but the representatives of Mustafa Kemal and other heads leading the Turkish nationalist movement, because even the nationalities that have come out of the Turkish rule are unhappy with their fate. Revolts in Mesopotamia and Syria continue, and the borders of Armenia have not been determined yet. If we add the uncertain situation of the newly-created states of the Caucasus, the republics of Georgia and Azerbaijan, on the border of Turkey, where the influence of either Turk nationalists or Russian Bolsheviks is sensed, it is evident that the signature of the Treaty of Sevres, even though a historical act of first magnitude, does not suffice to put peace on solid ground.[106]

Following the Treaty, the Armeno-Turkish war had ended catastrophically for the fledging Republic, with the Kemalist forces again

---

of Armenia in 1918" in Uruguay. See Arsen Gidur, *Patmut'iwn S. D. Hnch'akean Kusakts'ut'ean (1887-1963)* [History of the S. D. Hunchakian Party, 1887-1963], vol. 2 (Beirut: Shirak, 1963), 249.

[104] AGN, Caja 168, Carpeta 416.

[105] Ministerio de Relaciones Exteriores de la República Oriental del Uruguay, Fondo de Legaciones y Embajadas, Legación de la ROU en Río de Janeiro (MRE), Caja 1, Carpeta D, Legajo 1, "República de Armenia (su reconocimiento por parte del gobierno de Uruguay)."

[106] *La Prensa*, 11 de agosto de 1920, 11.

knocking at the doors of Yerevan. Etienne Brasil kept his optimistic and patriotic stance until the bitter end. On November 18, when Armenia was practically defeated after the fall of Kars and Alexandropol, the Foreign Ministry received an undated handwritten message in Armenian entitled "To the honorable gentlemen of the Parliament of Armenia" and bearing Brasil's signature in Armenian. Under the writing, there was an English-language map of Armenia from sea-to-sea with the caption "Armenian Republic":

> The Armenian communities of South America send their heartfelt salutation.
> They hail you as the first members of the first parliament, who defend the Freedom of Armenia.
> Hail, Honor and gratitude to our valiant soldiers.
> Hail, Honor, and gratitude to our diplomats and officials, who created and put our government on solid grounds.
> Hail to the people of United Armenia.
> We cry on our knees before the tomb of all martyrs.
>
> Dr. Etienne Brasil
> Representative of the Armenian Republic in South America.[107]

In this context, the first assembly of the League of Nations started on November 15. Brasil had ensured to Aharonian that the delegations of Argentina and Brazil had a pro-Armenian position.[108] On November 22, the Council of the League made a request to its members, as well as the United States, to intervene as mediators.[109] On the same day, Wilson made public his arbitral award of the boundaries between Armenia and Turkey.

After the tumultuous sessions of November 20-22, when Belgian representative Henri La Fontaine declared that "a million Armenians are being killed within the reach of the Allied warships,"[110] Antonio Huneus, head of the Chilean delegation and vice-president of the Assembly, noted that it was not practical to send "South American troops to European territories, both to supervise the areas of the referendum [of Lithuania] and Armenia. The best and most positive assistance of South America would

---

[107] ANA, fund 200, catalog 1, file 507.

[108] Hovannisian, *The Republic*, 433.

[109] *La Prensa*, 23 de noviembre de 1920, 7. The request was cabled on November 25 (see the entire text in AGN, Caja 176, Carpeta 1598, "Armenia. Acción internacional para socorrerla [Sociedad de las Naciones])."

[110] *La Prensa*, 21 de noviembre de 1920, 10.

be the provision of credits and, probably, the cooperation of its fleets."[111] Following La Fontaine's proposal on November 20, a committee was formed under his chairmanship to deal with the Armenian issue. Among its members was Foreign Minister Pueyrredón,[112] who, according to Daniel Antokoletz, member of the Argentinean delegation, "accepted that position taking into account the permanent sympathy of the Argentinean people towards Armenia."[113] However, Pueyrredón did not participate in the committee, since on December 2 he presented the Argentinean demands to amend the pact of the League, which were against Great Powers' policies and were considered pro-German for that reason. After the rejection of the proposals by 40 votes to 2 (Argentina and Paraguay), Argentina abandoned the assembly on December 4.[114]

Meanwhile, Wilson (in his personal capacity), Spain, and Brazil had accepted the petition to intervene in Armenia on December 1. The interest of both countries was probably part of their calculations to try to obtain a permanent seat at the Council of the League of Nations. Azevedo Marques, Foreign Minister of Brazil, cabled that "the government of Brazil is ready to participate, alone or jointly with other states, to put an end to the situation of suffering Armenia."[115] Lord Balfour declared: "If five years ago someone had suggested the cooperation of three big countries like the United States, Brazil, and Spain, on behalf of three continents, in favor of the Armenian people in a dark corner of the shore of the Black Sea, he would not have not only been declared as a dreamer, but he would have been a dreamer."[116]

The Council of the League thanked Brazil on December 3. It was also reported that Peru had suggested cooperating in the intervention in Armenia.[117] On December 4 Bolivia and Venezuela lamented the impossibility to participate and considered preferable that "just one strong nation acted."[118] The Minister of Foreign Affairs of Uruguay cabled on the same

---

[111] *La Prensa*, 26 de noviembre de 1920, 7.

[112] *La Prensa*, 24 de noviembre de 1920, 8.

[113] Daniel Antokoletz, *La Liga de las Naciones y la primera Asamblea de Ginebra* (Buenos Aires: Ministerio de Relaciones Exteriores y Culto, 1921), 158.

[114] Llairó and Siepe, *Argentina en Europa*, 78, 87, 120-123, 132-134.

[115] *La Prensa*, 2 de diciembre de 1920, 10; Antokoletz, *La Liga de las Naciones*, 158.

[116] *La Prensa*, 3 de diciembre de 1920, 10. Cf. George Scott, *The Rise and Fall of the League of Nations* (London: Macmillan, 1974), 71.

[117] *La Prensa*, 4 de diciembre de 1920, 7.

[118] *La Prensa*, 5 de diciembre de 1920, 8. On Venezuela, see also *La Prensa*, 7 de diciembre de 1920, 9.

day: "The government of Uruguay is happy to learn about the response of the United States, Spain, and Brazil for a joint moral activity in order to put an end to the critical situation of Armenia. It declares it wishes for total success to the intervention to restore peace."[119] Two days before, on December 2, independent Armenia had already fallen.

According to Antokoletz, "the admission of new members was examined in Geneva with greatest arbitrariness, overlooking the basic principles of courtesy. The running of representatives of certain free states from one delegation to the other was worth to see, as if they went from Herodes to Pilatos to ask for leniency. It was unimaginable, on the other side, the pretention of certain politicians to judge the right to live of this or that people."[120] The question of membership was decided by the fifth commission (presided by Huneus, with Uruguayan representative Juan Carlos Blanco as vice-president), which designated a sub-commission to study the cases of Lithuania, Estonia, Latvia, Georgia, and Armenia.[121] On December 7 it was proposed that only membership to technical organizations was allowed, and two days later the commission accepted this proposal in the cases of Armenia and Georgia.[122]

The admission of Armenia was rejected on December 16 by 21 votes to 6 (Peru, Uruguay, and Venezuela from Latin America), as well as the admission to technical organizations (21 votes to 8, which included the abovementioned three countries and El Salvador from Latin America). The only fruit bore by these diplomatic entreaties was a platonic motion by Canadian representative Rowell, which was unanimously passed: "All members of the League hope that, with the support of President Wilson, Brazil, Spain, and the Council of the League of Nations, soon the required steps will be taken to determine the borders of Armenia, establish a government, and save the remnants of the population, in order to allow its immediate admission to the League of Nations."[123]

Etienne Brasil maintained a staunch anti-Bolshevik position after the fall of the Republic. On January 8, 1921, it was reported from Rio de Janeiro that Sargis Kasian, president of the Revkom (Revolutionary Committee), the executive authority of Soviet Armenia, had cabled "inviting him to resign from his position." After informing the Brazilian government, Brasil had cabled Lenin: "I am waiting for the representative

---

[119] AGN, Caja 176, Carpeta 1598.
[120] Antokoletz, *La Liga de las Naciones,* 116.
[121] *La Prensa,* 6 de diciembre de 1920, 7.
[122] *La Prensa,* 10 de diciembre de 1920, 9.
[123] *La Prensa,* 17 de diciembre de 1920, 7.

of the intruder Soviet government, who will be summoned before the Criminal Court after solemnly delivering his credentials to the police."[124] In response to the interpellation by MP Carneiro da Cunha, President Pessoa declared that "the Brazilian government maintains its sympathy for Armenia in its entirety."[125] As a matter of fact, Brazil did not recognize the Soviet Union until 1945 and kept a hostile position towards it. In 1921 the correspondent to *Armenia* wrote that "it is even said that if an Armenian happens to come here as representative of the Soviet government, he would be arrested and jailed; the Soviet name already sounds bad here."[126]

In 1921 Brasil worked to assist the Armenian emigration from the Ottoman Empire to South America.[127] On June 25, in response to an inquiry by the Immigration Commission of Constantinople, the general commissariat of the state of São Paulo in Brussels responded: "About an emigration to Brazil, it is preferable that you address the representative of the Armenian Republic in Rio (capital of Brazil), who will be able to deal more easily with this issue, since this commissariat does not deal with that."[128] It means that Brasil kept his diplomatic functions for a while, which definitely ended after he lost his well-oiled contacts inside the government when Pessoa finished his presidential mandate in 1922. He would disappear from Armenian life until his death in March 1955.[129]

He had been completely forgotten by then. Two months before his death, his five letters to the Inter-Party Body of Buenos Aires were published in the Armenian-Argentinean press. As an irony of destiny, Terzian wrote that "the letters were signed in Armenian by a man of French origin called Dr. Etienne Brasil."[130]

---

[124] *Armenia*, February 23, 1921, 2.

[125] *Armenia*, March 2, 1921, 3.

[126] *Armenia*, February 23, 1921, 3.

[127] Brasil and Carneiro da Cunha conceived the idea of establishing an Armenian-Brazilian bank (*Armenia*, March 2, 1921, 3), which did not go further.

[128] *Verjin Lur*, May 23, 1922.

[129] Binayan Carmona, *Entre el pasado y el futuro*, 135. For an extensive analysis of Etienne Brasil's activities within the context of Brazilian foreign policy, see Loureiro's dissertation, "Pragmatismo e humanitarismo," 115-182.

[130] *Armenia* (Buenos Aires), January 17, 1955, 2.

Fig. 1 – Etienne Brasil
Photo: *Veratsnund*, Paris, January 1921

The Visit of Rev. Antoine Delpuch
to the South Caucasus in 1919:
An Attempt to Establish Diplomatic Relations
Between the Holy See and Yerevan?[1]

Jakub Osiecki[2]

This article deals with the visit of Rev. Antoine Delpuch from the Vatican to the First Independent Republic of Armenia in 1919. The relations between the Armenian and the Roman Catholic Church go back to the 11th century. Despite the fact that there were episodes in history when the relations between the Holy See and the Armenian Kingdom of Cilicia or Etchmiadzin were more than cordial, there were other periods in which Armenian Catholics were persecuted by their co-religionists. In the 19th century, when Armenian lands were conquered by tsarist Russia (1828-1918), Armenian Catholics found themselves in a new political and legal reality. After presenting a brief historical background, the article will discuss the motivations and engagement of the Holy See in the religious and political situation in the South Caucasus on the eve of World War I, the October Revolution, and the emergence of the Republic of Armenia. The final part of the article will address the activity of the Holy See in the region and the visit of Rev. Antoine Delpuch in 1919 to Georgia and Armenia.[3]

---

[1] This issue was researched by Mario Carola, *Vatican Diplomacy and the Armenian Question: the Holy See's Response to the Republic of Armenia, 1918-1922* (London: Gomidas Institute, 2010), 24-29; M. Carola, *La Santa Sede e la Questione Armena (1918-1922)* (Milano: Mimesis 2006), 137-153; and V. Poggi, "Antoine Delpuch Visitatore in Trancaucasia," *Studi sull Oriente Christiano* 5/2001, 93-130.

[2] This research was supported by Narodowe Centrum Nauki (Kraków, Poland) 2016/21/D/HS3/02770.

[3] Antoine Delpuch was born on May 4, 1868 in Villeneuve-sur-Lot in France. He graduated from the Catholic school in Saint Laurent (Rodez) and in 1888 joined the congregation of "padri bianchi" (White Fathers) – Seminary of St. Eugene in

Historical Background

Although relations between the Armenian and Roman Catholic Churches date back to the 11th century,[4] a new phase began in 1622 with the establishment of the Congregation for the Propagation of the Faith (*Sacra Congregatio de Propaganda Fide*). In its activities within Europe and the Middle East, the *Propaganda Fide* targeted such groups as the Slavs, Greeks, Syrians Armenians, Georgians, and Copts among others.

The Congregation policy also became visible among Armenian clergy of the Middle East in the 18th century. In 1701 Mkhitar of Sebastia established a new congregation. Soon after, he escaped from the Ottoman Empire and established a monastery for Armenian Catholics on the island of San Lazzaro, in Venice, in 1717. Thanks to the political support of the

---

Maison Carrée (Algieria). He became subdeacon in 1893 and the following year commenced his study of theology in Rome. In 1894, he was ordained a priest and sent to Jerusalem. In the seminary of St. Anna in Jerusalem he worked as a lecturer of moral theology until 1907. In 1912, he was elected vice-director of the congregation of *padri bianchi*. In 1914, he was appointed apostolic *visitator* to Istanbul (Constantinople) to the Institute of Georgian Catholics. From May–October 1917 by decision of Pope Benedict XV he was designated the first director of the Pontificio Instituto Orientale. In the same year he became the consultant within the papal policy toward Oriental Churches. Delpuch prepared a project of papal policy toward Eastern (Oriental) Churches, which was presented to the Pope by Mons. Giuseppe M. Croce. By comparing the religious situation in Eastern Europe and the Middle East, Delpuch tried to underline the diversity and religious pluralism typical to Oriental Christianity and different from the situation in Poland or Russia. His report was published in Rome in December 1917. In 1919, he was sent to the South Caucasus, to Tiflis, as the official apostolic visitator. See V. Poggi, *Benedetto XV, profeta di pace in un mundo di crisi* (Bologna: Minerva, 2008), 142-145.

[4] On Armenian and Roman Catholic relations see Nina G. Garsoïan, *L'Église arménienne et le Grand Schisme d'Orient* (Louvain: Peeters, 1999); Raymond-Joseph Loenertz, *La Société des frères péregrinant: étude sur l'Orient dominicain* (Rome: Institutum Historicum FF. Praedicatorum, 1937); S. Peter Cowe, "The Role of Correspondence in Elucidating the Intensification of Latin-Armenian Ecclesiastical Interchange in the First Quarter of the Fourteenth Century," *Journal of the Society for Armenian Studies 13* (2003, 2004), 47-68; Sergio La Porta, "Armeno-Latin intellectual exchange in the fourteenth century: Scholarly traditions in conversation and competition," *Medieval Encounters* 21 (2015), 269-94; Boghos Levon Zekiyan, "La rupture entre l'Église géorgienne et arménienne au début du VIIe siècle," *Revue des Études Arméniennes* 1982 (16): 155-174.

Roman Curia, the center of the new Armenian Church was established in the Middle East – the Catholic Church of the Armenian Rite in Aleppo. The leader of this group, the former Armenian Orthodox priest Abraham Artsivian from Aintab, later became Armenian Catholic Patriarch Abraham Petros I Artsivian.[5] In 1883 Pope Leo XI established the Pontificio Collegio Armeno in Rome.[6]

In the South Caucasus, structures of Armenian Catholics of the Latin rite were also established.[7] In the mid-18th century smaller communities of converts existed in Tschinvali (today's capital of the quasi-state Southern Osetia), Vale, Ude, and Arali.[8] After the Russo-Turkish War (1827-29) larger groups of Catholic Armenians (both Latin and Armenian rite) reached the South Caucasus. They moved from the Ottoman Empire to the region of Akhalkalaki[9] and Akhaltsikhe.[10] The Armenians who came from

---

[5] Ch. Frazee, *Catholics and Sultans: The Church and the Ottoman Empire 1453-1923* (London-New York, 2006), 186-187.

[6] G. Petrowicz, *La Chiesa Armena in Polonia e nei paesi limitrofi* (Roma: Pontificio Istituto di studi ecclesiastici, 1988), 361.

[7] As mentioned above, the Catholic denomination was spread among Armenians in two versions: Latin-Roman rite and Armenian rite. Union of the Armenian and Catholic Churches in Cilicia was declared in 1316 but was never implemented. It had more political than religious meaning. However, even before the collapse of the Cilician Kingdom, Dominicans and Franciscans resumed their activity among Mongols and Armenians. During that period (14th century), the Roman rite (celebrated in Classical Armenian and implemented by Dominicans) became popular within the Armenian Catholic community. The Armenian Roman rite was present in almost all Catholic dioceses in the Middle East (Persia, Nakhichevan, and Tiflis) and even in remote Beijing. From the 17th century, the active Catholic mission to the Caucasus was growing. Jesuits, Capuchins, Augustians, and Carmelites all had outposts in Georgia. Gradually, and also thanks to the Mkhitarist Congregation, the Armenian-Catholic rite was created. See Jakub Osiecki; Konrad Siekierski; Krzysztof Stopka, *Ormianie katolicy w Armenii i Gruzji* (Kraków: Uniwersytet Papieski Jana Pawła II w Krakowie, 2018), 16-18.

[8] Tymon Chmielewski, *Gruziński katolicyzm w XIX i na początku XX wieku w świetle archiwów watykańskich* (Toruń: Uniwersytet Mikołaja Kopernika, 1998), 292-310 at 300.

[9] Today these areas belong to Georgia. However, in the 19th century, the percentage of Orthodox Georgians in these areas was small. The majority were Muslims: Turks, Kurds or those who formerly were Christians and converted to Islam a century earlier.

[10] The Akhaltsikhe fortress was mostly demolished in 1828. About 15,000 former Turkish inhabitants died or had to flee the city. A total of 10,000 soldiers died on both sides during two battles between 21 and 28 August 1828. N. A. Shefov, *Bitvy*

the Ottoman Empire frequently settled in the lands and villages from which Muslims left. The total number of Armenian Catholics who came from the Ottoman Empire to Russia in the 1830s reached 20,000.[11]

On the basis of the tsarist correspondence with the Pope[12] as well as the *commercium epistolarum* between the Viceroy of the Caucasus and Tsar Nicholas I, one may clearly perceive the pro-Armenian sentiment of the tsar in the 20's and 30's of the 19th century. In the years 1826-1829, 32 Catholic churches were built or rebuilt in Akhaltsikhe (the first Armenian Catholic church in this city was built in 1836), Tori, Alastan, Varevan, Turtskh, Khulgumo, Bavra, Kartikash, Khizabavra, Udokmana, Emti, Abatchev, Cchaltbila, Vale, Neohreb, Sukhlis, Ude, Arali, Alexandropol, Tapadolak, Karaklisa, Palutli, Kaftarli, Hazanchi, Muslukhli, Shishtapa, Jiteli – Jitnkov, Shahnazar, Sarchapet, Karaklisa, Shiszhtapa, Siachat – Ararat).[13] According to the aforementioned concordat, all Armenian clergy and laymen were subordinated to the Latin Bishop of Tiraspol (with seat in Saratow).

According to an 1897 census, the number of Armenian Catholics had already reached 36,114.[14] Armenian Catholics started to apply to the tsar for acceptance of the Armenian bishop in Artvin (est. in 1850)

Rossii (Moskva 2002), 34 and H. Marutyan, "Gorod Akhaltsckha. Voprosi etnicheskoi istorii i traditsionogo zhilishchiia," *Vestnik Obshchestvennich Nauk* 6 (1990): 20.

[11] Tymon Tytus Chmielewski, *Gruziński katolicyzm w XIX i na początku XX wieku w świetle archiwów watykańskich* (Toruń: Uniwersytet Mikołaja Kopernika, 1998), 292-310.

[12] Emperor Nicholas I's letter (written in Bazardgik) to Pope Leo XII (Rome), June 2, 1828. Periodo I, Russia e Polonia, Volume IV, Archivio della Segreteria di Stato / Congregazione degli Affari Ecclesiastici Straordinari, Città del Vaticano [hereafter: AA EE SS], 74-75.

[13] This refers most likely to the houses of prayer organized in private apartments, for there is no other document which would confirm the existence of so many Armenian Catholic churches in this region in the 18th century or at the beginning of the 19th century. Therefore, these buildings had to be new churches constructed by Catholic Armenians who fled from the Ottoman Empire. On the sacred buildings in the South Caucasus coordinated by the order of Capuchins, see Chmielewski, *Gruziński katolicyzm w XIX i na początku XX wieku w świetle archiwów watykańskich*, 112-118.

[14] http://demoscope.ru/weekly/ssp/rus_rel_97.php?reg=3 (Accessed April 12, 2015).

incorporated into Russia after 1878.[15] However, Nicholas II did not agree to a new bishopric seat in Russia. In 1909 Sarkis Ter-Abrahamian became the Apostolic Administrator for the Armenian Catholics of Russia and the entire Caucasus. Prior to the October Revolution of 1917, there were already seven efficiently functioning deaneries with over 150 parishes and 172 churches and around 50,000 believers in the South Caucasus.

Diplomacy of the Roman Curia and the October Revolution

At the beginning of the 20th century, the Catholic Church was managed by two ruling structures: The General Secretary (*Sezione Segretaria di stato*) and the Secretary responsible for relations with states (*Sezione per i rapporti con gli stati*). Of course, the Church was able to maintain, for the most part, cordial relations with Christian or, more precisely, with Catholic countries.

We have to bear in mind that the Republic of Armenia was established on the territory of the formerly tsarist Russia, where the Catholic Church was allowed to operate but with some limitations, mostly based on the abovementioned concordate (1847). Despite pressure from Rome in 1910, tsarist Russia refused to create a separate diocese in the South Caucasus for Armenian Catholics. However, it agreed on creating an Apostolic Administration for the Armenian Catholics. The spiritual leader of this Church, Sarkis Ter Abrahamian, was now based in Tiflis.[16]

After the abdication of Tsar Nicholas II in March 1917, Prime Minister Alexander Kerensky announced that he was interested in launching a new dialogue with the Holy See.[17] It would not be an exaggeration to say that in some circles of Catholic clergy, the idea of the conversion of all of

---

[15] On the bishopric seat in Artvin after 1878, see Stopka, Osiecki, and Siekierski, *Ormianie katolicy w Armenii i Gruzji*, 215.

[16] The Apostolic Administration of Catholics of the Armenian Rite had its headquarters in Akhaltsikhe and later in Tiflis, but not in Artvin as Ch. Zugger mentioned, in Christopher Lawrence Zugger, *The Forgotten: Catholics of the Soviet Empire from Lenin through Stalin* (Syracuse, N.Y.: Syracuse University Press, 2001), 59. According to *Ōrats'uyts' Hay Kat'olik Ekeghets'u* [Calendar of the Armenian Catholic Church], published in Tiflis in 1920, the administrator and members of the board were H. Dionesios Kalataznan, Ter Anton Gaboyan, Ter Hakop Kirakosian, Franciskos Aghajanian, Ter Stanisław Kaczkaczow, who were inhabitants of Tiflis.

[17] Hansjakob Stehle, *Tajna dyplomacja Watykanu: papiestwo wobec komunizmu (1917-1991)* (Warszawa: Real Press, 1993), 17.

Russia to the Catholic faith revived at that time. Kerensky's gesture was met with great expectations in Rome. Lvov's archbishop of the Greek-Catholic Church, Count Rev. Andrzej Szeptycki, sent representatives of this idea to St. Petersburg with "special privileges and tasks." The second envoy was Archbishop Edward von Ropp, who received the mission to establish a new catholic hierarchy in post-tsarist Russia. The government of Kerensky was not against the activity of the Catholic Church or even the Russian Orthodox Church. Kerensky took part in the Synod meeting of the Russian Orthodox Church in Moscow in summer 1917, and also agreed to establish new Catholic dioceses within Russian territory (Mohylev, Minsk, Kamienets, Zhitomir, and Tiraspol)[18] and even to invite Jesuits to Russia. The October Revolution did not lead to a breakdown of relations, at least not in the beginning. We find confirmation of this fact in one of the interviews with Catholic clergy:

> The attitude of Bolsheviks toward Catholics at that time (1917) was more than tolerant, if I may say so; they even gave Catholics some privileges. We cannot say the same about the Russian Orthodox Church, which was persecuted... Bolsheviks treated Catholics as the victims of the former Czarist reign.[19]

One of the first legal documents of the Bolsheviks on this matter was a decree on the separation of the Church and Soviet state. The document was issued by the Executive Committee of the All-Union Communist Party (Bolsheviks), which invoked the decree by the Council of People's Commissars of the RSFSR of 23rd January 1918. The decree was adopted in full by the Central Executive Committee of Armenia on November 26, 1922. In Georgia, it was adopted on April 15, 1921. According to this decree, religion was each citizen's private matter. Any citizen might profess any religion or profess none. Religious faith did not entitle one to any privileges or benefits. The Church should be separate from the state. Freedom to observe religious rites was guaranteed as long as they did not disturb the social order or infringe the rights of other citizens. Whenever this condition was not met, local authorities had the right to use any means necessary to protect the social order and public safety. It was not permitted to teach religious subjects in any kind of state schools or social or private universities where general subjects were also taught. All property in the

---

[18] There were around 600 Catholic priests and 600 churches in Russia in 1917.

[19] An interview with Rev. prof. Stanislaw Trzeciak published in *Czas* (Polish journal): 336/1921.

territory of the republic that belonged to the Church or religious communities henceforth became the property of the nation. Buildings and artefacts that served strictly religious purposes were handed over for use to religious communities by the legal or central authorities pursuant to separate agreements.[20]

In this harsh political and legal situation, both Orthodox and Catholics had to find a modus vivendi with the Soviet regime. The newly elected Patriarch of the Russian Orthodox Church chose the path of confrontation, but the Catholic Patriarch decided to lead negotiations with the atheist government. From February 1919, Vladimir Lenin and Georgy Chicherin on behalf of the Soviets, and Cardinal Pietro Gaspari on behalf of the Holy See, commenced secret negotiations. Lenin was critical toward the Orthodox Church, which was in his opinion one of the elements of the former tsarist reality. However, he treated relations with the Catholic Church pragmatically. Under these circumstances, the Secretary of the State of the Holy See revitalized the idea of an evangelical mission to Russia. The plan was drawn up by the Congregatio Pro Ecclesia Orientali (Congregation of the Eastern Church). The plan entailed the establishment of strong Church structures within the Ukrainian Catholic Church, headed by the above-mentioned Andrzej Szeptycki (Catholic-Greek rite), Catholics of the Armenian rite, and the Georgian Catholic Church (Georgian-Greek rite), supposedly to be led by cardinal Angelo Maria Dolci.[21] It is important to note that Georgian Catholics became known in Rome at the end of the nineteenth century thanks to the activities of Rev. Michael Tamarati (Tamarashvili), Georgian Catholic bishop and author of the book, *L'église géorgienne des origines jusqu'à nos jours*, published in 1910.[22]

---

[20] HAG f. 607-60s/o. 2/d. 3736, p. 6. HAG f. 607-60s/o. 2/d. 21, p. 1, HAG f. 281/o. 1/d. 202 - Decrees of the Revolutionary Committee of the Soviet Socialist Republics of Georgia, Armenia, and Azerbaijan, 54-55. *Sobranie Uzakonieniy i razporyazenii rabochie-krestianskovo pravitelstva*. No. 18, 1918, p. 263 and HAG f. 281/o. 1/d. 202, 54-55, Decrees by the Revkom nos. 1-100.

[21] Stehle, *Tajna dyplomacja Watykanu*, 334-336.

[22] Since the nineteenth century, Georgian Catholics wanted to establish a monastic congregation and were asking for confirmation of the Greek-Georgian (Byzantine) order from Rome, especially for their monastery of the Servants of the Mary Immaculate in Constantinople. The Roman Curia and Department Pro Russia agreed to establish a new monastic congregation in 1930 when Georgia was already a Soviet country. See Chmielewski, *Gruziński katolicyzm w XIX i na początku XX wieku w świetle archiwów watykańskich*, 341.

Rev. A. Delpuch in the South Caucasus

After the end of the World War I, there were dozens of newly established or renewed states on the international arena with whom the Holy See, especially Pope Benedict XV, was willing to launch dialogue. However, this required great effort from the papal administration. In May 1918, the Pope sent his envoy, Achille Ratti, the future Pius XI, to Poland.[23] Although Ratti was not able to enter Bolshevik Russia, he maintained contact with the Russian government via telegraphic connection from Warsaw. The Pope sent Mgr. Couturier with the Apostolic Visitation to Egypt and Rev. Angelo Genocchi to Ukraine. The Roman Curia also had his representatives in Germany, Latvia, Romania, and many other countries.

What about Armenia and Georgia? It has to be emphasized that high ranking Roman Catholic clergy were not frequent guests in the South Caucasus. The last episcopal visit took place at the beginning of the 20th century. In fact, from 1828-1918 Edward von Ropp was the only Catholic bishop who visited the Russian Caucasus in 1902.[24] Therefore, it would be untrue to say that Armenia in the South Caucasus was significant for the Catholic Church in terms of political relations, evangelization or conversion. The greatest hope of the Roman Curia as mentioned above was linked with the Russian Orthodox Church.[25] On the other hand, Popes never renounced the idea of the union of all Christian Churches. The abdication of Tsar Nicholas II seemed to be a great opportunity in this regard.

Before describing the visit of Delpuch to Armenia, we have to explain the context of his trip to the South Caucasus. After the abdication of Tsar Nicholas II, it became obvious that the political vacuum also had its religious aspect. The position of the Russian Orthodox Church weakened, which meant that formerly independent Churches, such as the Georgian Church, might re-establish themselves under the supervision of exarchs. On September 17, 1917, the new Georgian Catholicos was elected by clergymen and laymen. Eight days later, Georgian Catholicos Kirion II sent a letter to Pope Benedict XV in which he mentioned that September

---

[23] For more on the political and religious activity of Ratti in Poland and Bolshevik Russia, see Stehle, *Tajna dyplomacja Watykanu,* 17-22.

[24] Concerning the only bishopric visit in the South Caucasus, see J. Kessler, *Geschichte der Tiraspoler Diozese*, 140.

[25] Richard Pipes, *Rosja Bolszewików* (Warszawa, Studia Podlaskie, 2005), 362-364.

17 was the day of restoration and happiness for the Georgian Church. Furthermore, he noted that he was willing to continue dialogue with the Roman Catholic Church. Kirion reminded Benedict XV that in the territory of Georgia there was a significant community of Georgian Catholics and it seemed important to improve their religious conditions and re-establish a bishopric seat in Tiflis.

The Holy See transmitted Kirion's letter to the Apostolic delegate in Istanbul, Angelo Maria Dolci. In August 1918, a delegation of the Georgian Government met with Archbishop Dolci in Constantinople and officially invited him to Tiflis. The Georgians also asked Dolci for the support of the Holy Father to consolidate the "nascent Republic."

A month prior, in July 1918, Archbishop Dolci had cordially received an Armenian delegation, which had come to sign a peace agreement with the Turks. [26] In his report, he mentioned the very friendly atmosphere and indicated the sympathy of the Holy See with the Armenian position. The Armenian Prime Minister explicitly desired to establish official diplomatic relations with the Holy See. However, Cardinal Angelo Dolci, who was supposed to visit Georgia and Armenia, for some reason did not go, but sent his secretary Antoine Delpuch.

Apostolic visitor Antoine Delpuch came to Armenia in the autumn of 1919. The country had been independent for a year, but its status in the international arena continued to be vague. Armenia was only nominally an independent country– the Allied countries continued to be reluctant to recognize it as a sovereign entity. Moreover, the voice of Armenian politicians still could not be heard in the most important peace conference which concluded World War I, the Paris Peace Conference of 1919. [27]

Armenia also faced the problem of executing the decisions of the Armistice of Mudros. [28] Even though Armenia had every right to assume

---

[26] Mon. Angelo Dolci was sensitive to the Armenian question, for on June 15, 1915, he was one of the first bishops to raise his voice about the Armenian Genocide. In an encrypted telegram to Rome, he wrote to the Pope about the hundreds of Armenian victims and the instances of persecution perpetrated by the Turks. See Jacques Kornberg, *The Pope's Dilemma: Pius XII Faces Atrocities and Genocide in the Second World War* (Toronto: University of Toronto Press, 2015), 198.

[27] R. G. Hovannisian, *Republic of Armenia: From Versailles to London, 1919-1920*, vol. 2 (Berkeley; London: University of California Press, 1982), 2.

[28] The Mudros Armistice was signed on October 30, 1918 in a small port village on the Greek island of Mudros. Under the terms of the armistice, the Allies were to occupy the Straits of Dardanelles and the Bosporus, Batum, and the Taurus

control over some parts of western Armenia and thus to annex the lands which until recently were Ottoman and tsarist lands (the Kars Oblast', Ardahan, Olti). However, due to the internal weakness of Armenia, Armenian-Georgian territorial disputes, and above all, the lack of open military support on the part of the Allies, these regulations were left unfulfilled to a certain extent.[29]

A. Delpuch in Etchmiadzin (first from left).
Photo A. Poidebard. Copyright Bibliothèque Orientale-
Université Saint-Joseph, Beyrouth

It is worthwhile emphasizing that Armenia as country was isolated by its neighbours Georgia and Azerbaijan, which resulted in difficulties in the transportation of commodities and energy resources. Armenia was struggling with famine and hunger. The dramatic situation of the Republic was also shared by the Armenian Church, but the position of the Church as an

---

tunnel system. In addition, the Ottomans surrendered their remaining garrisons in Hejaz, Yemen, Syria, Mesopotamia, Tripolitania, and Cyrenaica. As to the six Armenian provinces, the Allies won the right to occupy them "in case of disorder" and to seize "any strategic points." See Jan Reychman, *Historia Turcji* (Wrocław: Ossolineum, 1973), 288-290.

[29] George Bournoutian, *A Concise History of the Armenian People* (Costa Mesa, Calif.: Mazda Publishers, 2012), 301.

organization was conditioned by other factors. One can trace the roots of the economic and political crisis in the Armenian Church as early as the beginning of the 20th century.

It is a myth that the Dashnaktsut'iwn (the Armenian Revolutionary Federation) and later on the Republic of Armenia and the Armenian Church shared warm and cordial relations. It was already Archbishop Maghakia Ormanian who considered the social-nationalists and liberals the "initiators of anticlerical movement."[30] Catholicos Mkrtich Khrimian legitimately emphasized that the lack of people who felt the calling to join the seminary in Etchmiadzin was a result of the anticlerical and secularization ideology of the Dashnaks, who in their political program considered the conservative clergy one of the enemies of revolutionary changes.[31]

The Armenian Church was deprived of its estate in two stages. First, in 1903, still during the period of tsarist Russia and the rule of Viceroy Grigory Golitsyn, and then in 1914. By the decision of Catholicos Gevork V and in agreement with the Patriarch of All Russia, the most precious objects which belonged to the Armenian Church were moved to Russia. Gevork V decided to hand over to the Russian Orthodox Church, as a deposit, the most valuable materials, documents, and relics of the Armenian Church. When the October revolution broke out (1917) and the Revkom (revolutionary committee) proclaimed the nationalization of all Church estates in Bolshevik Russia, it was almost a foregone conclusion that the Armenian Church would never reclaim its estate.

The Armenian Church also lost its leading role in primary education in the Republic of Armenia (1918-1920). When the socialist Dashnaktsut'iwn took over power in Yerevan, one of the first decisions made was the complete separation of Church from state. The role of the Church after Armenia regained independence was supposed to be marginalized, especially in the field of education.[32] Dashnaks were aware of the fact that for years education – especially at the elementary level – was managed by

---

[30] Maghakia Ormanian, *Kościół Ormiański* (Kraków: Ormiańskie Towarzystwo Kulturalne, 2004), 150.

[31] At the beginning of the 20th century in Etchmiadzin, the majority of the pupils did not intend to enter the clergy. Only a small minority of students had taken orders. See H. F. B. Lynch, *Armenia: Travels and Studies* (London: Tauris, 1901), 220-22; K. S. Papazian, *Patriotism perverted* (Boston: Baikar Press, 1934), 33; M. K. *The Impact of Soviet Policies in Armenia* (Leiden: Brill, 1962), 21-22.

[32] J. Osiecki, *Apostolski Kościół Ormiański w Armenii sowieckiej 1920-1932* (Kraków: Księgarnia Akademicka, 2016), 65-74.

the clergy, hence it was impossible to replace the entire pedagogical staff in schools. General secularization of education was one of the demands of the Zhoghovrdakan party.[33] Eventually, it was decided that clergymen could continue teaching at schools until lay teaching staff could be introduced, but all real estate owned by the Church and used for teaching was to become the property of the state. We must recognize that the nationalization of the Church lands had not been directly dictated by a pattern of persecution (as the Bolsheviks did later on), but was only the consequence of the agrarian reform and secularisation policy of the state.[34] In his first letter, Delpuch characterized such a situation by describing it as a process of "complete laicization" of the nations of the South Caucasus.[35] Moreover, the economic maintenance of Church structures (refurbishment) required resources which the Armenian Church did not have, and therefore the decision to nationalize parish schools was not received with outrage but rather with relief. Secularization of Armenian primary schools in the frame of a concordate was signed on September 19, 1919, by Arch. Khoren Muradbekian and Ministry of Culture Sirakan Tigranian.[36] In this social, political, and religious situation, in the middle of September 1919, Antoine Delpuch came as the apostolic visitor to Transcaucasia and to Armenia.

Rev. Antoine Delpuch (M. Afr.) was the first rector of the Pontifical Oriental Institute from 1917-1919.[37] He was familiar with Eastern

---

[33] The Armenian Populist Party (Arm. *Hay Zhoghovrdakan*) was a liberal party founded on April 11, 1917 in Tiflis (Tbilisi). Initially, it was only a branch of the Russian Democratic-Constitutional (Kadet) Party, but in September 1917 became an independent party. M. Babajanian was the first leader of this party. Their official press was *Mshak* (issued in Tiflis) and *Zhoghovurd* (issued in Yerevan). They were the second political power in Russian (Eastern) Armenia. In the elections to the National Armenian Congress, they received 43 of 204 seats. After the elections of August 1, 1918, they received 6 seats in the Parliament. See Hovanissian, *The Republic of Armenia: The First Year 1918-19,* 42.

[34] S. Merlo, *Russia e Georgia: Ortodossia, dinamiche imperiali e identità nazionale (1801-1991)* (Milano: Guerini, 2010), 143.

[35] Ibid.

[36] ANA f.48/ts.1/p.967, s. 26-28, Khoren Muradbekian, written correspondence with the Ministry of Education and Culture, 19/6 September 1919, and Mary Kilbourne Matossian, *The Impact of Soviet Policies in Armenia*, (Leiden: Brill, 1962), 79-82.

[37] The Pontifical Oriental Institute (PIO) was founded on October 15, 1917 by Benedict XV. It was entrusted to an assorted group of religious and lay people under the direction of the White Father – Antoine Delpuch. Then it was run by

Christianity (in particular with the Catholics of the Armenian Rite and Georgian Orthodox Church) and had good relations with Pope Benedict XV and of course Angelo Dolci, prefect of Eastern Churches. He went first to Batumi by ferry from Constantinople and then by train to Tiflis. After a few days of rest in the Georgian capital, he came to the province of Javakheti, where the number of Catholics was greatest (Catholics of the Armenian rite, who, as reported by Delpuch, greeted him "with manifestations of extreme joy)."[38] He met with manifestations of absolute deference to the Pope. In one of the villages, he was even supposed to have heard the following: "Tell the Pope that we are his devoted children and that we are ready to give everything we have to the Pope."[39]

In his first letter to his superior, Mon. Angelo Dolci, on September 19, 1919, he wrote that in Tiflis he had met his fellow countryman, a Frenchman named Antoine Poidebard SJ, a Jesuit and captain in the French Army.[40] Poidebard became Delpuch's companion during the entire course of his visit to Armenia.[41] "Soon I will be off to Yerevan in the company of Poidebard," Delpuch wrote. "He has great influence over the

---

the Benedictine Abbot of St. Paul Outside the Walls, Rev. Ildefonse Schuster, OSB. On September 14, 1922, Pius XI assigned the PIO to the Society of Jesus. See Robert F. Taft (ed.) *The Christian East: Its Institutions and its Thoughts: A Critical Reflection* (Roma: Pontificio istituto orientale, 1996), 217-244.

[38] AAEESS Pos. 25 scatola, Fasc. 163 Orientali in Russia, 10, letter of A. Delpuch to Mons. A. Dolci, September 19, 1919.

[39] Ibid.

[40] AAEESS, Pos. 25 scatola, Fasc 163 Orientali in Russia.

[41] Antoine Poidebard was born in 1878. He entered the Spiritual Seminary in Lyon at the age of nineteen. He was ordained as a priest in 1910 and the following year was sent to the Ottoman Empire to serve the Armenian communities in Tokat, Marsovan, and Sivas, where he learned Armenian and Turkish. In 1914, he joined the French Army and the French Military Mission to the South Caucasus. Between 1917 and 1921, he was the representative of the French Army in the Republic of Armenia. After the sovietization of Armenia he moved to Batumi and when the Bolsheviks captured the city he escaped to Persia and then to Beirut. The archive of Rev. Antoine Poidebard is now located in the Oriental Library of the St. Joseph University in Beirut. For more information on A. Poidebard's activities in the Middle East and the South Caucasus, see Levon J. Nordiguian, F. Salles, *Aux Origines de l'Archéologie aérienne: A. Poidebard (1878-1955)* (Beirut: Université Saint-Joseph, 2000); Levon Nordiguian, F. Denise, *Une aventure archéologique: Antoine Poidebard, photographe et aviateur* (Beirut: Université Saint-Joseph Press, 2004); A. Poidebard, *Au Carrefour des routes de Perse,* (Paris: G. Crès, 1923), 3-44.

Armenian government and over the Catholicos of Etchmiadzin. He will be of great service to me."

Delpuch's visit did not happen in a vacuum but was the result of the exchange of correspondence in the period from October 22 to November 13, 1919, between Delpuch and Prime Minister Alexander Khatisian.[42] He came to Yerevan by train from Baku. He met Khatisian (Delpuch referred to him as *Khatisov*) and the speaker of the Armenian parliament.

The preliminary conditions of the agreement were determined during the first meeting. Khatisian pointed out that Armenia was a liberal country and that freedom of religion was a priority in Armenia, and each religion could be practiced freely. He assured Delpuch that he would do everything he could to ensure support to the future apostolic nuncio in Armenia. Delpuch was asked to convey gratitude to the Pope for his intercession and his activities to advance the cause of the Armenians in the tragic period after 1915. It seems that the classified letter sent by Benedict XV (via Angelo Maria Dolci) to Sultan Mehmet V on 10 September 1915 was familiar to Khatisian.[43]

Delpuch writes that Khatisian allegedly expressed an impassioned request that the Pope would "also take an appropriate stand in the most critical moment when the Armenian case would be decided in Europe." Eventually Khatisian handed over to Delpuch a written declaration of support for the establishment of the activities of an apostolic nunciature in Armenia and the development of the structures of the Catholic Church in Armenia.

Delpuch himself – as he writes – made the situation quite clear, indicating that for the time being the founding of a separate apostolic delegation for Armenia would be pointless. The most logical solution

---

[42] What is significant is that in a letter, Khatisian addresses Delpuch as the minister of the Holy See in Armenia. He wrote, *inter alia*, "I have the honor to confirm that I received the letter dated October 22, 1919, from the Apostolic Minister of the Holy See in Armenia" AAEESS, Pos. 25sc, fasc. 163, p. 15. Orientali in Russia, *Letter to rev. A. Delpuch from Ministry of Foreign Affairs of Armenia*, November 13, 1919.

[43] Pope Benedict XV (1914-22) condemned the Armenian Genocide in public to the College of Cardinals at the Consistory meeting on December 6, 1915 and sent the official letter to Mehmed V via his Apostolic Delegate in Constantinople, Archbishop Angelo Maria Dolci. See *Acta Apostolicae Sedis* 1915/7, 510-511. http://www.vatican.va/archive/aas/documents/AAS-07-1915-ocr.pdf.
AAEESS, Pos. 25sc, fasc. 163, Orientali in Russia, Letter send by rev. A. Delpuch to A. M. Dolci, November 21, 1919.

would be to establish a Yerevan office for the apostolic administrator from Tiflis (Tbilisi) or a joint nunciature for both countries with a seat in Tiflis.

Delpuch also visited Gen. Nazarbekian and inspected his army. At a certain point Gen. Nazarabekian had been the commander of the Caucasian front in the Imperial Army, and at that time he commanded the Armenian units which consisted, above all, of people from Urmia, Van, and Bitlis. The commanding officer defended his country with extreme zest and commitment. During a dinner organized on the initiative of the Prime Minister of Armenia, a toast was raised for the Holy See.[44]

Before Delpuch left Yerevan, he was also received by the Catholicos of All Armenians who was in the city. As Delpuch emphasized, Catholicos Gevork V did not know how to express his veneration for the Holy Father for his inexhaustible beneficence. The archbishop of Yerevan, Khoren Muradbekian, remarked that, if circumstances permitted it, the Catholicos intended to dispatch a delegation to Rome in order to thank His Holiness personally. In Etchmiadzin, the secretary of the Catholicos, Bishop Tirayr (Ter Hovhannisian), and the venerable Mesrop (Ter Movsisian), the former Archbishop of Tiflis, gave Delpuch a tour of this ancient site of the Armenian nation and, as he observed, exhibited a great deal of respect to him at every turn.

In the correspondence to Mon. Dolci, Delpuch makes a passing remark that "for the sake of clarity I will leave aside all things that are associated with the Catholic Armenians and Gregorian Armenians. The consideration of this question would render my argumentation [unnecessarily] complex. The Armenians are a group which is too important and particular, and I will make this group the subject of a separate report." Indeed, Delpuch did return to Armenian religious concerns.

After the meeting with Catholicos Gevork V and the visit in Etchmiadzin, the Government of Armenia had a train provided for Delpuch's exclusive use so that he could visit the region of Kars. The regional commander of Kars put an officer at Delpuch's disposal to show him the entire region.

After he returned to Tiflis, Delpuch related his observations to Mon. Angelo Dolci in Constantinople. These observations were associated with Armenian statehood, the position of the Church, and, what is particularly interesting, the possibility of a union. Delpuch mentions the following:

---

[44] AAEESS, Pos. 25 scatola, Fasc 163 Orientali in Russia, Letter of A. Delpuch to Mon. A. Dolci, November 21, 1919.

> In all of its acts, the government and the parliament of the
> Republic of Armenia is inspired above all by broad liberalism,
> without, however, embracing complete secularisation of the
> estate of the Armenian Gregorian Church. All officials
> belonged to the 'Dashnaktsutyun' revolutionary party with a
> tendency toward significant socialism, although they rather
> pursued political goals. Many representatives of the Armenian
> Gregorian clergy at all levels of the hierarchy offered their name
> and were active in the party.[45]

Delpuch also wrote the following:

> Unfortunately, in Armenia itself a considerable number of
> fractions operate, which are quite opposed to each other and
> who are not completely aware about what the future of this
> unhappy people should be. This does not ensure stability.
> However, everyone is united in the feeling of profound hate
> toward their close neighbours, the Muslim Turks and Tatar
> people, who remain in their opinion enemies for generations.
> For years these were the hated oppressors of the Armenian
> people.[46]

We do not know whether Dolci relayed to the Pope Delpuch's
activities in Transcaucasia but the question of the independence of
Armenia was an object of interest in Rome, especially in the Secretary of
the State, to the extent that a separate collection of acts/documents was
named *Armenia Indepedenza* (Independent Armenia).

Conclusion

As this article has demonstrated, besides support for the young
government of the Republic of Armenia, the Holy See was also interested
in the question of union with the Armenian Church. The Roman Curia
maintained contacts with the Cilician Catholicosate but there were still
instances of contact with Echmiadzin. The relations between these
Churches (Rome and Echmiadzin) had been frozen for a long period of
time, and especially after the First Vatican Council, which brought about
a schism in the Catholic Church and which resulted in open division into
heretics and orthodox ("Reversurus" encyclical). It was at that time that

---

[45] Ibid.
[46] Ibid.

Patriarch Maghakia Ormanian converted from the Armenian Catholic Church to the Apostolic Church.[47]

Delpuch stressed that the question of union in that particular moment was impossible "without an appropriate mission." At this point Delpuch criticized a "Prof. Novarese" from Rome, who allegedly campaigned *apud* the Pope in favour of an Armenian-Catholic Union and considered himself an Armenian envoy *apud* the Pope. According to Delpuch, during a conversation with the Catholicos, the word "union" was mentioned recurrently, although it seemed that the Catholicos was completely unaware of the true sense of this term. Delpuch wrote the following:

> A union lies not in the nature of the faithful. It is only the hierarchs who whisper about a union. In general, the people of the Caucasus, both Georgians and the Armenians (mainly due to the persecution by the Czar), never had the possibility to gain a comprehensive account of what Catholicism was about and what the Catholic faith was about. There are two rites in the Caucasus – the Latin rite and the Armenian rite – the latter has exclusively the married clergymen. For years, it was disallowed for Armenian Catholics to have a bishop of their own. As a rule, one almost never saw even a Latin bishop here.[48]

"Today, Catholicism is a thing of the elite, something which attracts elites, the intelligentsia; there is no Catholic unity and coherence of the whole society," Delpuch confessed. By making reference to a conversation with an anonymous Armenian, Delpuch wrote that he shares the impression that the "Armenian Church is internally dead...This Church did little, it even completely neglected the spiritual life of the faithful, the religious life. The thing which now satisfies the aspirations of the Armenian people has to do with national ideas." Delpuch concluded his reflections saying: "I generally consider this journey to be very important, although it failed to produce any results."[49]

After the trip to Armenia, Delpuch went back to Europe and Rome where he presented his full report to Pope Benedict XV: "Rapporto sulla situazione politica e religiosa del Caucaso e sui provvedimenti richiesti dagli interessi Della religione cattolica in quella regione" (Report on the

---

[47] J. Osiecki, "The Catholics of the Armenian Rite in Armenia and Georgia (1828-1909)," *Internationale Kirchliche Zeitschrift* 4/2016, 316-317.

[48] AAEESS, Pos. 25 scatola, Fasc 163 Orientali in Russia, Letter of A. Delpuch to Mon. A. Dolci, November 21, 1919.

[49] Ibid.

political and religious situation in the Caucasus and the means which provide the interest of the Catholic religion in this region"). In March 1920, the *English Tablet* wrote that Father Delpuch was planning to go back to Armenia and the Caucasus in 1920, but he never did.[50] The political and religious situation in the South Caucasus was observed by Bishop Adrian Smets, Vatican Delegate to Persia, who received monthly reports from Tiflis and Batumi.[51]

The sovietization of Armenia and the entire South Caucasus halted the process of gradual rapprochement between the Armenian Church and the Holy See for many years. Direct contact between the Armenian and Catholic churches during the existence of the USSR was not possible. Catholics of the Armenian rite from Georgia and Armenia were persecuted, the majority of the clergy were arrested and sent to prisons and labour camps such as in the Solovietskie Islands or to the Republic of Komi.[52]

Father Delpuch's visit also had political goals. It might have had great importance for the Armenian international position, but the Holy See was excluded from the Peace Conferences under pressure from France and Great Britain, so the Armenian request to the Pope to "take an appropriate stand in the most critical moment when the Armenian case would be decided in Europe" was not fulfilled.

To fully understand the potential political importance of Delpuch's mission to Armenia we have to compare it to similar activities of the Roman Curia in Eastern Europe, such as the mission of Achille Ratti to Poland.[53] This papal representative played a significant role in Poland after 1918. Historians underline that despite the unstable political situation of Poland and the threat of Bolshevik invasion, he was able to visit most of the cities and regions recognized as Polish by the Polish government. Moreover, Ratti was able to combine two posts – religious representative of the Pope and spiritual supervisor of Catholics in Poland – but also act as a political player. Of course, his first mission was to look after all the

---

[50] *Tablet,* weekly newspaper and review from March 6, 1920, 2.

[51] AA EE SS, Pos. 25 scatola, Fasc 157, Orientali in Russia, Letter of 12 January 1924 (On the "Administratio apostolica Tephelicensis") from A. Smets to cardinal Tucchi, 53-54.

[52] For more on the persecutions toward Armenian Catholics, see Stopka, Osiecki, and Siekierski, *Ormianie katolicy w Armenii i Gruzji,* 272-283.

[53] S. Wilk, *Nuncjusz Achilles Ratti i jego rola w procesie kształtowania się państwa polskiego,* Powrót Polski na mapę Europy, ed. Cz. Bloch (Lublin, [n.p.] 1995), 331–333.

Catholics in Poland and to mediate in religious disputes, but soon after he became a crucial ally in Polish internal and foreign policy, especially toward Bolshevik Russia. He was appointed Apostolic Nuncio (July 1919) according to official diplomatic protocol and treated as an ambassador of the Holy See. Moreover, on October 23, he was consecrated a Polish bishop by the Archbishop of Warsaw, Aleksander Kakowski. As he wrote in his memoirs: "I was consecrated on Polish soil, by the Poles, and from that time on I will feel and act as a Pole."[54] It is that kind of nuncio that Armenia was probably hoping to acquire. However, Antoine Delpuch, who also had a desire to support the nascent Armenian Republic, did not have the opportunity to continue and complete his mission in Armenia. Poland was able to protect its independence and defeat the Red Army, but Armenia, without allies and left alone, was forced to sign a treaty with Moscow's Bolsheviks. In December 1920, the Red Army entered Yerevan. The envisioned Apostolic Nunciature for Armenia and Georgia, promoted by Khatisian in 1919, was established only in 1992 by decision of Pope John Paul II after the collapse of the Soviet Union.

---

[54] Cited by J. Gnatowski, *Z Polski do Rzymu, Papież Pius XI* (Warszawa [n.p.], 1920), 45.

Domestic Politics in the Republic of Armenia, 1918-1920: A Flip or a Flop?

Garabet K. Moumdjian

The first Republic of Armenia lasted barely two and a half years (May 1918 to November 1920). Some might argue that such a historical event may not seem conducive for exhaustive research due to the short time span of its existence, since such processes need time to develop and mature. Nevertheless, it can be stated that it was the culmination of Armenian political parties' efforts for statehood since the collapse of the Cilician Kingdom in 1375. Political disagreements among Armenian factions which reached its peak on the eve of World War I were put aside for a higher goal: salvaging whatever had remained from the Armenian populated territories. As one historian of the period argues:

> Regardless of all its shortcomings, one thing is exceptionally clear. In the period 1918-1920, Armenia was threatened by foreign powers, which intended to perhaps demolish it and its people. It was in such instances that all internal bickering was put aside, and the political parties united in the face of this existential threat.[1]

There were important reasons as to why Armenia had to declare its independence during a tumultuous and critical time, as was the case on May 30, 1918.[2] Had the Tbilisi-based Armenian National Council (see

---

[1] Ararat Hakobyan, *Hayastani Khorhrdaranĕ yew k'aghak'akan kusakts'ut'yunnerĕ, 1918-1920 t't'* [The Parliament of Armenia and the Political Parties, 1918-1920] (Yerevan: Hratarakch'ut'yun H. H. Dashnakts'ut'yan, 2005), 83. It must also be stated that Prof. Richard Hovannisian devoted five hefty volumes to the study of the two and one half years of the existence of the Republic. See Richard G. Hovannisian, *The Republic of Armenia*, 4 vols. (Berkeley: University of California Press, 1971–1996).

[2] Even though Armenian Independence Day is celebrated on May 28, the decision of the National Council was taken on May 30, 1918, retroactive to May 28. It must be underlined that the decision of the National Council was not a declaration of

below) not announced itself as the supreme power of Eastern Armenian districts – an area that was not more than 12,000 square kilometers – then those districts would have been absorbed by Turkey, Azeri-Tatars, and Georgia. This becomes clear if one considers the announcements of Turkey and Germany, the de facto masters of Transcaucasia in those days.

To provide even the general reader with a short essay that simplifies the intricate web of domestic politics characterizing inter-party relations in the Republic of Armenia between 1918 and 1920 is not an easy task. The limitations of a short essay makes an in-depth analysis of the topic under discussion unfeasible.

In an attempt to approach the issue from another perspective, I will first present brief sketches of the major participant political organizations. Then, I will identify and explain some of the important issues relating to inter-party relations during the period under discussion. Finally, I will try to draw some conclusions, which might bear educational value for current Armenian endeavors toward democracy and national unity.

Moreover, the reason for such a declaration of independence was not an act of desperation taken under duress due to Turkish coercion as some authors, such as Aramayis Yerzngyan and others, have tried to persuade the public. In reality, events imply that Turkey would have probably not only prevented Armenia from declaring independence, but also not have wanted any Armenians left in Transcaucasia, which would have solved its Armenian issue once and for all. This means that even a feeble declaration of Armenian independence was a necessity and the Armenian National Council had no other alternative.[3]

The declaration of Armenian independence was also a statement against Russia. In the words of one famous Soviet-era historian:

> Armenian nationalist and non-nationalist political parties had every reason to despair from [Soviet] Russia. The main reason for this hopelessness was that Communist Russia not only allowed Turkey to occupy those Western Armenian territories that were liberated at the expense of sacrifices and

---

independence, but rather a declaration that it was assuming power since the dissolution of the Transcaucasian Federation had created a vacuum.

[3] Aramayis Yerzngyan, *Ashkhataworut'yan dataranin (ējer dashnakts'akanneri gortserits')* [To the Tribunal of the Workers: Pages of the Dashnakts'akans' Activities] (Tbilisi, 1927), 37; Rupen Tarpinian, *Bolshevizmĕ yev hayastanĕ* [Armenia and Bolshevism] (Izmir: Keshishian Publishing, 1922), 35; M. Seropian, *Hayastani ankakhut'ean aṛitov* [On the Occasion of Armenia's Independence] (Cairo: [n.p.], 1950), 9-10.

loss of lives during 1914-1917, but it further allowed Turkey to annex the province of Kars up to the Akhurian River. This meant, if anything, that Soviet Russia agreed to hand over territories that were won during the Russian campaign of 1877-1878 against the Ottoman Empire.[4]

The Republic of Armenia was a fledgling country trying to build permanent democratic institutions. The Western orientation of the government had profound effect on the internal political atmosphere. Moreover, this course of action created keen rivalry among the political organizations and groups in the Republic since leftist parties and, to some extent, the only rightist party in the Republic, were adamantly against such a Western direction. Simply put, nothing could have prevented the bickering between the various political organizations, given their contradicting ideologies and political agendas.

The effort to emulate the West – with its traditions of democracy and the rule of law – by the leadership of the Republic was part of its desire to be considered a worthy ally. The ruling Armenian political organization, the Armenian Revolutionary Federation (Hay Heghapokhakan Dashnakts'ut'iwn in Armenian, ARF hereafter), itself of socialist ideology, was committed to practical and realistic republican principles, which, had it not been for the abrupt absorption of the Republic within the Soviet sphere, would have undoubtedly paved the way for the realization of democratic governmental institutions based on a multi-party, parliamentarian political system.

At the core of the disagreements were some fundamental socio-political beliefs related to the shaping of the future democratic state. Add to this the strong atmosphere of mistrust and uncertainty that existed between the various political actors, who had not yet worked within a single governmental entity. This distrust among the political forces produced a perfect example of a political quagmire.[5]

The political-ideological spectrum in the Republic extended from the right to the extreme left. The bourgeoisie, represented by the Eastern Armenian Populists, or Popular Democrats (Zhoghovrdakan), and the Western Armenian Constitutional Democrats (Ṛamkavar) occupied the

---

[4] Lendrush Khurshudyan, *Haykakan harts'ĕ* [The Armenian Question] (Yerevan: Hamazgayin Hay Krt'akan yew Mshakut'ayin Miut'yun, 1995), 52-53.

[5] As it will be seen below, the ideological spectrum was almost full, from extreme leftists to rightists. Add to this the envy that existed between parties, each of whom wanted to grab power, and the above mentioned quagmire becomes self-evident.

right spectrum,[6] while the socialists, ranging from Marxist Social Democrat (SD's, Bolsheviks), the Social Revolutionaries (SR's, or Cadets, Mensheviks), to their splinter groups dotted the left spectrum. The ruling party, the ARF, still adhering to a socialist ideology, pragmatically assumed a centrist position.[7]

The Right Spectrum
a- The Constitutional Democrats (Sahmanadir Ṛamkavar)

The Armenian Genocide, perpetrated by the government of the Young Turks in the Ottoman Empire, incapacitated the mainly urban, Western Armenian Constitutional Democrats. The party was formed in the wake of the Ittihadist (Young Turk) coup d'état of 1908 that resuscitated the Ottoman Constitution of 1876. The restoration of the Constitution gave impetus to the party's platform of free enterprise and the pursuing of Armenian reforms through non-violent, legal means. It should be noted, however, that the absorption of the more militant Armenakans[8] and a faction of the Reformed Hnchakians (Verakazmial)[9] into its ranks made the party more susceptible to notions of nationalism and of defensive armed struggle.

With its strength in the Republic diminished by its Eastern Populist counterpart,[10] the Populists (see below), the Ṛamkavars tried to

---

[6] Note that the Ṛamkavars never took part in any governmental institution in the Republic of Armenia.

[7] Hakobyan, *Hayastani Khorhrdaraně*, 61.

[8] The Armenakan Organization was formed in 1885, in Van. Megerdich Portukalian, a teacher who was exiled from Van, settled in Marseilles (France) even before the party was formed by several of his most revolutionary students. Portukalian followed events in Van from his exile and wrote about them in his newspaper, *Armenia* (thus the name of the organization). However, the Armenakan party remained a localized one and did not spread to other Western Armenian locales. In 1908, most of its members were absorbed by the newly formed Sahmanadir Ṛamkavar party.

[9] The Hnchakian part, formed in 1887, was divided into two factions by 1897 since its Western Armenian leaders were at odds with the workings of the Eastern Armenian ones. The division happened after the first Armenian rebellion in Sasun in 1894-95. The mostly nationalist Western Armenian Hnchakians left the party and formed the Reformed (Verakazmial) Hnchakian organization.

[10] This was due to the fact that this party was solely a Western Armenian one and its nexus of operations was confined to Constantinople and its environs. Thus, in this new Eastern Armenian milieu there was a local party that advocated the same

overshadow the ruling party, the ARF, by extending their activities among diasporan Armenian communities. Leaders such as writers Vahan Tekeyan and Arshag Chobanian, worked closely with Boghos Nubar Pasha and his National Delegation in Paris, in an effort to strengthen the position of the latter within Allied circles vis-à-vis the government of the Republic of Armenia.[11]

In the day-to-day affairs of the Republic, however, the Ramkavars managed to keep only a bare semblance of party organization. Their presence was due to some Western Armenian refugees from Van (mainly former Armenagans). Although they published the semi-weekly *Hayastani Dzayn* (Voice of Armenia) in Yerevan, and in mid-1919 reached as far as negotiating with the ruling party for participation in the government (about which more is to be said later), their active political role in the Republic was negligible.[12]

The Ramkavars were diametrically opposed to Communist Russia. They were considered a right-wing political party and, as such, had a very close affinity to their Eastern counterparty, the Armenian Populist Party, and by September 1919 they had even negotiated to coalesce into a single entity. This amalgamation did not occur and the two parties decided to postpone until a final solution was found for the Armenian Question.[13]

---

principles. The Sahmanadir Ramkavar Party's only grassroots force was the members who had settled in Eastern Armenia after being uprooted from Western Armenia.

[11] Before WWI had started, Boghos Nubar Pasha, the scion of an Egyptian Armenian aristocratic family and the founder of the Armenian General Benevolent Union (AGBU, 1906), was asked by Gevork V, Catholicos of All Armenians, to travel to Paris and head the Armenian National Delegation in order to pursue the Armenian case. Armenians were regarded by the Allied powers as an ally in their war effort. Even the representative of the Armenian Republic, writer Avedis Aharonian, initially joined Nubar's delegation in Paris. The final schism came about in May 1919 when the government of the Republic pronounced the act of unified Armenia and proclaimed itself as the sole representative of all Armenians.

[12] Ararat Hakobyan, *Hayastani Khorhrdaraně*, 82-86. See also Armenian National Archive (ANA hereafter), Fund 4045, List 1, Document 3, 35-36. [Called Hayastani azgayin arkhiw].

[13] Ardag Tarpinian, *Hay azatagrakan sharzhman ōrerēn: husher 1890ēn 1940* [From the Days of the Armenian Liberation Struggle] (Paris: Hrat. "Hay Azgayin Himnadram," 1947), 393, 395-396.

b- The Populist Democrats (Zhoghovrdakan Kusakts'ut'iwn)

The ruling party in Armenia, the ARF, entered into a coalition government from November 1918 to June 1919 with the Eastern Armenian Populist Party (Hay Zhoghovrdakan Kusakts'ut'iwn). The dictates of its Western orientation and the set aim of attracting Armenian and other capitalist circles to the newly established Republic, rather than its social ideology, had persuaded the ARF into willingly entering this uneasy partnership with the antirevolutionary bourgeoisie.[14]

The Populist Party was a newcomer into Armenian political life. Tsarist imperial-colonial policies did not provide fertile grounds for the creation of liberal democratic parties. Only after the demise of the Russian imperial regime in 1917 did Armenian commercial and professional circles in Tbilisi, Baku, and Elisabethpol (today known as Ganja, in Azerbaijan; Gandzak in Armenian) provided the grassroots support for such a party to materialize.[15] The main catalysts in this formation were Armenian members of the Russian Constitutional Democrat (Cadet) party, who were advocates of cultural autonomy within a Russian democratic, liberal federation.[16] The geographical distribution of its grassroots support suggests that the party was more influential in all parts of Transcaucasia except in the predominantly agrarian Armenian Republic.[17]

It was during the second Populist party congress in September, 1919, in Yerevan,[18] that the representatives of the Eastern Armenian bourgeoisie displayed, for the first time, "an emphatic Western orientation by expressing deep admiration for the Allied Powers."[19] It was during this congress too that the party's delegates put aside their previous advocacy of cultural autonomy and endorsed national independence. The party congress also characterized the condition of the country as desperate and the workings of the ARF-led government as worrying.[20] It thus called upon all

---

[14] Hakobyan, *Hayastani Khorhrdaranĕ*, 66-68.

[15] The town was in the historic Armenian province of Utik.

[16] ANA, Fund 292, List 1, Document 5; Y[eghishe] Charents Museum of Literature and Art Archives Collection, Unnamed Fund, Document 78, 1. See also A. Hakobyan, *Hayastani Khorhrdaranĕ*, 63-64.

[17] Hakobyan, *Hayastani Khorhrdaranĕ*, 67.

[18] This was in the wake of the collapse of the coalition government and the Populist Part's boycotting of 1919 parliamentary elections during the preceding months.

[19] *Zhoghovurd*, September 24, 1919.

[20] ANA, Fund 404, List 1, Document 39. See also *Hayasdani Dzayn*, October 3, 1919.

anti-socialist elements to unite to oust the ARF and form a new government based on the principles of free, capitalistic enterprise.[21]

2. – The Left Spectrum
a- The Eastern Social Revolutionaries

The adherents of the Russian Social Revolutionary Movement also had a nominal presence in the Republic. Like the populists, their support was based on student and intellectual circles in Tbilisi and Baku. Many of its members were former ARF members who had abandoned the party in 1907 because of its absorption of and adherence to the movement to liberate "Turkish-Armenia," which led the party to assume a somewhat indifferent position towards the Russian leftist opposition movement of the day.[22]

A decade later, in 1917, Armenian SR's joined the Georgian Mensheviks and fought hard to exclude the ARF from the Transcaucasian revolutionary councils, which were shaped as a result of the political vacuum created by the toppling of the tsarist regime.[23]

Despite their lack of a strong support group within the Republic, and in spite of their feeble membership, Armenian SR's campaigned vigorously in parliamentary elections. Although they attained meager results, they continued to advocate a single Transcaucasian entity within an all-Russian federative democracy.[24] Their failure was a direct result of their disbelief in the concept of national independence. Even when the majority of its delegates, perhaps out of expediency, voted in favor of working within separate Transcaucasian republics during the party's conference held in Tbilisi in August of 1919, the party could not formulate a working strategy out of their demand. Its organ, *Sots'yal Hegha-*

---

[21] *Tsragir Hay Zhoghovrdakan Kusakts'ut'ean* [Program of the Armenian Populist Party] (Yerevan: Luys, 1919), 5.

[22] ANA, Fund 4047, List 1, Folder 237, Document 53.

[23] The problem was that the number of factory workers in Armenia was negligible. Moreover, the workers leaned towards the ARF. In fact, the SR's were abhorred by the other parties as being anti-national. Hnchakian leader Stepan Sabahgulian went as far as denouncing them as "people who were against Armenia's independence" (*Yeritasard Hayastan*, September 15, 1920). *Yeritasard Hayastan* was the central organ of the Hnchakian Party abroad.

[24] The SR's occupied four seats in the 1919 parliament. Their meager success was due to the votes of Russians living in Armenia. Noteworthy is the fact that their organ, *Sots'yal Heghap'okhakanĕ* (The Socialist Revolutionary), was printed in Russian and their delegates spoke only Russian during sessions of the parliament.

p'okhakanĕ (The Socialist Revolutionary), continued publishing contradictory views about issues related to self determination and national independence, thus broadening the gap between the party and the general populace.[25]

b- The Eastern Social Democrats

The collapse of the empire, the partition of Transcaucasia, the end of the Baku Commune, disagreement over tactics, and the final schism between Bolshevik and Menshevik factions had weakened the Social Democrats and reduced them into three rival groups:

> 1.   The Armenian Section of the Georgian SD (Menshevik) Party that had a negligible role in the Republic.
> 2.   Adherents of the International Russian SD (Menshevik) Party.
> 3.   Adherents of the Russian SD (Bolshevik) Party, who were advocates of Transcaucasian Soviet republics and national Communist parties as affiliates of the Russian Communist Party. There was some resistance from Armenian and Georgian Bolshevik circles to this separatist agenda, but it was finally agreed upon by all Bolsheviks in the region, especially when Lenin and the Central Committee in Moscow advocated it.[26]

The Bolsheviks had lots of disagreement over tactics. Some, like Arshavir Melikian, advocated educating the public through legal means rather than revolutionary agitation because the Republic was in shambles. Young extremists opposed this view. The Bolshevik boycott of parliamentary elections in the summer of 1919 suggests that extremists were in control of the party.[27]

In the summer of 1919 there were no more than 500 Bolsheviks in Armenia. This was due mainly to the "repatriation" of several hundred people who had arrived from Georgia and Azerbaijan due to the repressive measures in both countries against Communists and especially non-native ones. The addition of a number of agitators and propagandists that the Soviet government sent to Armenia and the initially blasé stance of the

---

[25] ANA, Fund 201, List 1, Folder 43, Document 85.
[26] ANA, Fund 4047, List 1, Folder 237, Document 53.
[27] ANA, Fund 4012, List 1, Folder 32, Document 1.

ARF-led government regarding the Bolsheviks may explain why the Republic became a center of gravity for them.[28]

In fact, many ARF leaders and bodies did inform the government of this increasing Bolshevik menace. However, Minister of Interior Abraham Giulkhandanian seemed to be unimpressed with such calls for vigilance, since his answer was that "since he himself is a revolutionary he cannot prosecute other revolutionaries."[29]

In September 1919 the first Bolshevik underground party conference was held in Yerevan. Only twelve delegates were present. There was a conflict between Melikian's mild views and Kriakom (Bolshevik Transcaucasian Committee) members Askanaz Mravian and Sargis Kasian. The conference decided to start subversive actions against the existing government.[30]

This decision was carried out in April 1919 by the creation of the Spartak Communist Youth Organization under the leadership of Ghukas Ghukasian.[31] Armenkom (Bolshevik Central Committee of Armenia) was created in January 1920.[32] Nevertheless, the party remained in the underground.

The government started taking severe measures only after the Bolshevik-led uprising in May 1920.[33] The ARF's benign stance toward the Armenian Bolsheviks could have been the result of its adherence to a socialist ideology. Moreover, the ARF leadership may have thought that not harassing Bolsheviks in Armenia would create better relations with the fledgling Soviet Russia. Needless to say that this belated action of the government would be characterized as futile at best.

c- The Eastern Social Democratic Specificists

The Social Democratic Specificists were intellectuals who adhered to the principle that Armenians had the right to choose their own approach to socialism. They advocated for the existence of distinct national Marxist parties. Their political outlook may be summarized as follows:

---

[28] ANA, Fund 4012, List 1, Folder 32, Document 3; ANA, Fund 4056, List 1, Folder 65, Document 7.

[29] Rupen Ter Minassian, *Hay heghap'okhakani mě hishataknerě* [Memoirs of an Armenian Revolutionary], Vol. 7 (Los Angeles: Horizon, 1952), 223.

[30] ANA, Fund 4012 List 1, Folder 32, Document 1.

[31] Ibid.

[32] ANA, Fund 1022, List 3, Folder 257, Document 1.

[33] ANA, Fund 4020, List 1, Document 16, 14-15.

Those were former ARF members who had left the party after 1907 due to the party's advocacy and reinstatement of a national liberation struggle for the emancipation of Western Armenia from Ottoman oppression. As a democratic political party vying to represent the workers of Armenia, the Specificists were for the independence of the Republic. It was also a West-oriented party, specifically in relation to the United States of America. Their ideologue, Bakhshi Ishkhanyan, stated in his writings that the new Armenian Republic should be backed by the following forces in order of appreciation: 1) The United States of America, 2) Great Britain, and, if need be, 3) Russia.[34]

It is interesting to note what famous Bolshevik leader Sargis Kasian had to say about the Specificists:

It is a misnomer to consider the Specificists a full-fledged leftist party. In fact, one can easily say that they represented a right orientation within the socialist-Marxist ideology; the Specificists were more of a nationalist bourgeois organi-zation...[35]

After the formation of the Republic, Armenian SD Specificists such as Davit Ananun (Ter Danielyan), Bakhshi Ishkhanian, and Stepan Zorian (Arakelian) moved to Yerevan to work within governmental institutions and legal structures. In January 1920, they founded the Social Democratic Labor Party of Armenia as a legal organization. They hailed the restoration of national independence and proclaimed that they would participate in the process of state building. They ridiculed the Ramkavars' assertion that Western Armenia should be the nucleus around which the Armenian state was to be formed. They also criticized other SD factions for their subversive and intrusive agitation and thus they attracted animosity from Marxists and the bourgeoisie alike.[36]

---

[34] ANA, Fund 1022, List 7, Document 44, 3-11; Document 96, 29.
[35] Sargis Kasian, *Spetsifiknerĕ yew spetsifizmĕ* [Specificists and Specificism] (Tbilisi, 1928), 5.
[36] ANA, Fund 404, List 1, Folder 5, Document 1.

d- The Social Democratic Hnchakian Party

Finally, mention should be made of the Social Democratic Hnchakian Party, the oldest established Armenian SD group and the only one with Eastern and Western Armenian members. The party reached its peak in 1894-96 during the emancipation movement in Western Armenia, which was followed by a period of fragmentation. The party had traditional strongholds in Cilicia and the Balkans. In 1919 many Hnchakians (see below) left the party to join either the Mensheviks or the Bolsheviks. The party's organ, *Proletar*, was published in Tbilisi, through which they:

    1. Criticized the ARF for its pseudo socialism, its honeymoon with bourgeoisie, and its usurpation of power for assuming the leadership position in the Republic.

    2. Criticized all parties that boycotted parliamentary elections.

    3. Criticized Populists for opportunism, as they first worked with the ARF and then came out of the coalition government.

    4. Criticized intellectuals, especially the Eastern Social Democrats, because they could not differentiate between state and government. They insisted that while the former was permanent, the latter was transitory. So, if the government was now held by incompetents (with special reference to the ARF) that should not mean abandoning the state or undermining it, but rather it meant aiding it by providing a new leadership as an alternative.

    5. Opposed the presence of two delegations in Paris because that was contrary to the notion of one nation, one struggle.[37]

    6. Regardless of their ideological differences with the ARF and unlike the Eastern Leftist organizations' anti-independence position, the Western Armenian Hnchakians put their lot with the rest of the nationalist forces in defending the newly created Armenian Republic.

---

[37] The reference is to the delegation of the Republic of Armenia headed by Avetis Aharonian. The Hnchakians maintained that since Western Armenians were already represented in Paris through the Armenian National Delegation headed by Boghos Nubar Pasha, the Armenian government should send representatives to be part of that delegation rather than producing one of its own, a decision that showed Armenians as divided in the eyes of the Allies.

Arsen Gidur, a Hnchakian leader active at the time, emphasized more than four decades later that:

> ...in 1918, the Hnchakian party abroad showed strong support for the independent Republic, even though it had many issues with the ruling party, the ARF, whom it considered a power that had usurped the government...[38]

At the time, Stepan Sabah-Gulian, another Hnchakist leader, opined:

> ...We now have a state, it is ours and it is in our blood and we will defend it with our life if needed. It is our baby son and we have to nurture it and protect it from all enemies...[39]

Sabah-Gulian also opined:

> ...if there are parties in Armenia that do not adhere to the notion of Armenian independence, they are the leftists (i.e. SR and SD). Thus, such a left has no place within Armenia, where parties adhere to the basic notion of Armenian independence...[40]

3. – The Center
The ARF

Although crippled by the Armenian Genocide, which shattered its network in the Ottoman Empire, and the Russian civil war, which battered its organizational machine in the former tsarist empire, the Armenian Revolutionary Federation was, in 1918, still considered to be the dominant Armenian political organization upon whose shoulders rested the task of providing leadership for the fledgling Republic. A cursory look at some archival material reveals that the ARF strength in Transcaucasia was not negligible:

> If one wants to form a more or less complete opinion regarding the ARF influence in the Republic...it must be stated that even in 1907 the ARF was instrumental in the formation of

---

[38] Arsen Gidur, *Patmut'iwn S.D. Hnch'akean Kusakts'ut'ean, 1887-1962* [History of the S.D. Hnchakian Party], Vol. 1 (Beirut: Hratarakut'iwn S.D. Hnch'akean Kus. Kedr. Handznakhumbi, 1962-1963), 11.

[39] *Yeritasard Hayastan*, September 15, 1920.

[40] Ibid.

some 110 trade unions in Transcaucasia alone. During the same year, the ARF had 23,300 workers in its ranks in Transcaucasia. The ARF's impact was even larger among villagers in rural areas. It is not a coincidence then that the famous Bolshevik intellectual, Stepan Shahumyan had written in 1916 that the ARF was cherished by all villagers. The ARF policy regarding the communalization of land – which was adopted from the Social Revolutionaries' political platform, gave it impetus within the rural circles in Eastern Armenia. Thus, the ARF boasted some 67,000 rural members within its ranks in 1907. If one also considers the fact that almost 90 percent of the Eastern Armenian population was comprised of villagers, it becomes clear what popularity the ARF enjoyed in Eastern Armenia.[41]

A report presented to the Socialist International Congress held in Stuttgart in 1907 mentions that the worldwide rank and file of the ARF consisted of some 165,000 active members.[42]

For the three decades since its formation, the ARF had acted as a medium through which conservative Western and progressive Eastern Armenian ideological fermentations and political aspirations could be funneled into a cohesive working agenda for the realization of self-governance for Armenians within the confines of the Ottoman state. It was only in 1919 that this goal was changed to "Free, Independent, and United Armenia." Now that the nucleus of that state had been achieved in Eastern Armenia, the old party program with its revolutionary zeal was inadequate to meet the challenges of a newly formed governmental apparatus. If we add the popular discontent towards the ruling party of a newly established state, the internal differences within its rank and file, it becomes obvious that the ARF had to undergo some radical changes in order to meet the challenges of the new situation.

As Levon Sarkissyan, who lived during those tumultuous times, writes:

> Although the ARF was a socialist organization since 1907, and as such was considered a leftist political party, in matters of governance it adopted a very centrist position. It also must be stated, that regardless of the party's ideology, the ARF had

---

[41] ANA, Fund 4047, List No. 1, Document 237, 53-58; Stepan Shahumyan, *Yerkeri liakatar zhoghovatsu* [Complete Collection of Works], Vol. 3 (Yerevan: Hayastan, 1978), 50.

[42] ANA, Fund 4047, List 1, Folder 237, Document 55. The above number includes 23,000 worker members and 67,000 peasant members.

its internal divisions. The party's rank and file did not represent a cohesive unison. The majority of the party's Eastern Armenian members adhered to leftist, socialist ideology regarding social and economic policies (communal lands, government owned manufacturing, etc.), while the Western Armenian members – and some Eastern members for that matter – advocated for a more nationalistic approach that supported private ownership of land and means of production. The membership represented the whole spectrum of ideological schools from workers and villagers all the way to petty bourgeois entrepreneurs.[43]

There were three distinct groupings within the party: At the one side were the Western Armenian members, who advocated an evolutionary social reform program; on the other extreme stood the internationalist socialist intellectuals, mostly Eastern Armenian, who pushed for radical social and political change; in the middle stood the old leadership, the members of the party's highest executive body, the ARF Bureau which, out of pragmatic considerations, put aside its revolutionary character, and tilted towards moderation, thus weakening the position of the party's left. The adoption of a moderate stance by the party's leadership was also evident in the articles appearing in the ARF organ, *Haṟaj* – under the direct control of the Bureau – which stressed gradualism instead of radical social and political reform, thus almost alienating the party's Eastern Armenian left.[44]

The clash between the first two groups was inevitable during the sessions of the party's 9th congress in October 1919. Issues ranging from the ideological framework of the party to the relationship between party and government were hotly debated under the watchful eyes of Allied intelligence services, who followed the sessions with keen interest.[45] After several weeks of deliberations, the Congress formulated its decisions. It upheld the principles of moderate, democratic government and instructed the newly elected Bureau to exert an indirect control of the government,

[43] Levon Sarkissyan, *Yerker* [Works], Vol. 1 (Yerevan, 1959), 48. Sarkisyan was a founding member of the ARF. He later severed his ties with the party and sharply criticized its leaders in the Tbilisi Armenian journal *Murj* (Hammer), where he served as editor in chief. Regardless, his arguments here about the ARF, its composition, and its future role, seem to be very balanced and to the point.
[44] ANA, Fund 4047, List 1, Folder 237, Document 53.
[45] Ter Minassian, *Hay heghap'okhakani mĕ hishataknerĕ*, 155.

avoiding intereference in its affairs, but rather staying in its shadow and extending supportive hand to it.[46]

Later events, however, such as the Bolshevik agitation that led to the uprisings in May 1920, brought to an end this notion of indirect control of government. At that juncture, the ARF Bureau came out of the shadows and assumed the government itself. These were, it seems, dire days that necessitated a policy of direct intervention by the highest body of the ruling party in the affairs of its own government for the sake of rescuing the state from imminent danger.

4. – The Parliaments

It is true that democracy in a state is first and foremost assessed through the workings of its parliament, and the quality of laws passed within this institution. Regardless of their bickering against each other in the media of the day, the political institutions in the Republic of Armenia learned how to respect and work with one another. In the words of one author:

> ...It was in the National Assembly of the Republic of Armenia that Armenian political organizations were able to start to learn how to work with each other. This coexistence turned out to be a valuable achievement for the future...[47]

This seemed to be a promisory beginning, since the first Armenian National Council was appointed in Tbilisi in 1917 following this line of thinking. It was composed as following:

- ARF   6
- Populist   2
- SD   2
- SR   2
- No party affiliation   3
- Total   15[48]

---

[46] Ibid.

[47] Simon Vratsian, *Hayastani hanrapetut'iwn* [The Republic of Armenia], second edition (Beirut: Tparan Mshak, 1958), 47.

[48] *Banber Hayastani Arkhivneri*, 1992, No. 1-2, 102-103. The absence of Western Armenians was explained through the fact that they would join a parliament after their status was decided by the Allied Powers in Paris. Needless to say, this Eastern Armenian way of thinking was considered problematic by Ṛamkavars and Hnchakians alike.

When the Council relocated itself to Armenia after the declaration of Armenia's independence on May 30, 1918, its members established a new legislative body by taking the membership of the first Council and multiplying it by a factor of three. Thus, this Council, which worked from August to November 1918, was composed of:

- ARF   18
- Populist   6
- SD   6
- SR   6
- No party affiliation   2
- Tatars   6
- Russian   1
- Yezidi   1
- Total   46[49]

It must be noted that all parties were in agreement with such a step. Arsham Khondkarian elaborated more on this issue saying:

> The number of deputies allotted to each political party seemed to be reached after due diligence and meticulous negotiations. The ARF could have easily been represented by a two-thirds majority (and even more) in the chamber, since it had the highest rating within the population. However, it accepted fifty percent representation so that the parliament could have a really diverse representation.[50]

Regarding the leftist members in the Council, he added:

> The leftist political parties in the newly appointed Armenian National Council, namely the Social Revolutionaries and the Social Democrats (Mensheviks and especially the Bolsheviks), were in fact against the notion of Armenian independence. Even if they sometimes showed affinity to the idea of independence, that was only a ruse, since secretly they were trying to weaken the very fabric of independence. As to the Armenian Populist Party, considered to be the only rightist

---

[49] ANA, Fund 282, List 1, Document 2, December, 1918, 2. Here, too, there were no Western Armenians appointed to the Council.

[50] *Vem*, 5, 1934, Paris, 47. It must also be stressed that this appointed body included three women. It is important to note that Arsham Khondkarian was a former SR representative in the Parliament.

political organization in the Council, it was the only rival to the ARF and competed with the latter for assuming the leadership position in the Republic. However, unlike the leftist parties, the Populists were for Armenian independence, but had a distinct anti-ARF stance.[51]

The only popular elections in the Republic of Armenia took place in June 1919 and yielded a parliament composed as follows:

- ARF: 72[52]
- SR: 4
- Tatars: 2
- Yezidi: 1
- No affiliation: 1
- Total: 80[53]

The minorities in the parliament(s) of the Republic also had their own political attitude towards an independent Armenian state. The Tatar (later known as Azeri) representatives mostly conveyed a non-partisan stance during parliamentary sessions and votings. It must also be stated that the Russian minority's stance within the parliament was not pro-Armenian. "The Russians living in the Republic," writes a non-partisan Eastern Armenian, "never wanted to consider themselves citizens of the Republic and never showed any devotion to it. They considered themselves a privileged class since tsarist times and they wanted to keep that auspicious status."[54]

On the other hand, the Kurdish Yezidis living in the Republic showed a strong pro-Armenian position:

> The only minority whose representative was pro-Armenian was the Yezidi one. They were the only minority that sided with Armenians at all times. They were weak and they needed Armenians in order to be protected. It so happened that the vote of the single Yezidi parliamentarian's vote was necessary for a certain legislative piece to pass. It was at this crucial juncture

---

[51] Ibid., 52.

[52] Twelve of these were Western Armenians, all ARF members.

[53] It must be noted that there were three female representatives in this elected parliament. Interesting to note also is that only the Eastern Social Revolutionaries participated in the elections, while all other political parties boycotted them.

[54] G. Chalkhushian, *Inch' ēr yew inch' piti lini mer ughin* [What Was and What Must Be Our Way?] (Vienna: Mekhitarists, 1923), 13-14.

that the single Yezidi representative, A. Patalyan, would vote
with the ARF faction.[55]

If one is to accurately assess the work of the Armenian legislature
some interesting facts come to view. In its two and a half years of
existence, the parliament(s) of the Republic of Armenia discussed some
1,000 law proposals and passed about 300 of them. Moreover, there were
very hot debates within the Parliament, especially against the government
and the ARF. It is evident that party organs were completely free to
criticize the government if one takes even a cursory look at the newspapers
of the time. Moreover, even the ARF party organ, *Haṛaj*, is full of news,
and op-eds. that were very critical of the government.[56]

There is an ongoing debate regarding the formation and workings of
the Armenian Parliaments of 1918-1920. Thus, while some consider it as
an exemplary institution that helped in advancing the democratic tradition,
others, like Khondkarian, criticized it for being an instrument of the ruling
party:

> The 1918 Armenian parliament and those that followed,
> regardless of them being elected or appointed, were straight
> forward legislative organization(s). They represented the
> supreme power of the Armenian state. The government, the
> executive body of the state, was under the control of the
> legislative council. The legislature not only elected the mem-
> bers of the cabinet, but had an important saying in the political
> and financial workings of the government through its
> representative, the state controller. Thus, the Republic was one
> where parliament was the supreme power.[57]

On the other hand, Hovhannes Kachaznuni, the first Prime Minister of
the Republic of Armenia, wrote in hindsight:

> There was no real parliament in Armenia. There was a
> legislative body that was a hollow form with no real substance

---

[55] Ibid, 14; Artashes Babalian, *Hayastani ankakhut'ean patmut'iwně yew ayl
hishatakner* [The History of the Armenian Independence and other Memories]
(Glendale, CA: "Navasart," 1997), 13.
[56] Vahan Navasardian, *H.H. Dashnakts'ut'ean anelik'ě* [What the Armenian
Revolutionary Federation Has to Do] (Cairo: Tparan "Husaber," 1924), 189;
ANA, Fund 198, List 1, Folder 57, Document 7; Ter Minassian, *Hay heghap'okhakani mě*, 233.
[57] *Vem*, No. 5, 1934, 47, 52.

to it. Issues were addressed in closed meetings of the ARF parliament faction. Decisions taken in closed chambers were then presented at parliament meetings, which only rubber-stamped them. In fact, I would go as far as stating that there was no ARF faction in the parliament, since that cluster was under the direct supervision of the ARF Bureau and had to bring that body's decisions to the parliament for ratification.[58]

5. – Partisan Politics

Perhaps one of the most important political processes in the Republic was that of the coalition government between the ruling party and the Populist Democrats, the Armenian Populist Party, which lasted from November 1918 to June 1919.

Headed first by Hovhannes Kachaznuni and then by Alexander Khatisian, the coalition was not a complete semblance of national unity, since the left-wing parties were against participation in a government where right-wing parties were represented. The coalition government provided the opportunity for the Eastern Armenian bourgeoisie to participate in the state-building process. Many of their Tbilisi-based cadres relocated themselves to Yerevan or alternated between the two cities in an effort to plan and implement projects in the spheres of economy, social welfare, education, the judiciary among others.[59]

As to the Western Armenian multitudes who had found refuge within the Republic of Armenia, it can be said with much certainty that:

> While there were Eastern Armenian circles that sided with the leftist Social Revolutionaries and Social Democrats, Western Armenians in the Republic, in general, remained loyal followers of the ARF... The Social Revolutionary party's mouthpiece, *Sots'ealist heghap'okhakaně*, stated in one of its issues that there are no leftists among Western Armenians....[60]

---

[58] Hovhannes Kachaznuni, *H.H. Dashnakts'ut'iwně anelik' ch'uni aylews* [The Armenian Revolutionary Federation Has Nothing to Do Anymore] (Vienna: Mikhit'arean Tparan, 1923), 45.

[59] *Zhoghovurd*, June 8, 1919, 3; Hakobyan, *Hayastani Khorhrdaraně yew k'aghak'akan kusakts'ut'yunneř, 1918-1920 t't'*, 65.

[60] *Sots'ealist heghap'okhakaně*, August 21, 1919.

The newspaper indicated that the intolerance of Western Armenians to socialist ideology was because of their adherence to the ARF and also to Ramkavars.

6. – The Act of Declaration of United Armenia

The coalition government, however, came to an abrupt end because of the Act of United Armenia in May 1919. The act itself should have been a culmination of the dreams of all Armenians, since it declared the unity of Eastern and Western Armenia. However, the problems arose due to the fact that the Eastern Armenian government made this proclamation unilaterally, without negotiating with Western Armenian leaders (i.e. Boghos Nubar Pasha and his Paris delegation, the Ramkavar and the Hnchakian parties). Even though all Populist ministers in the government had signed the act and participated in its official declaration, the Populist Central Committee in Tbilisi – at the time, it seems, in coordination with Boghos Nubar's camp in Paris, which insisted that such an act was the prerogative of a constitutional congress where both segments of Armenians (i.e. Eastern and Western) were represented – protested the act and called upon its ministers to withdraw from the government. Furthermore, it boycotted the forthcoming parliamentary elections to be held in the coming weeks. The Populist Central Committee declared that:

> The government's action (i.e. singlehanded declaration of the Act of United Armenia) is not only a coup d'état and a strong blow against the unity of the Armenian nation, but it is even something that is beyond the powers of parliament. In lieu of this brutal disregard to law, the Populist Party does not recognize the parliament and the government as legitimate entities. We thus relinquish our positions in parliament and government and declare that we will boycott any upcoming elections...[61]

---

[61] *Zhoghovurd*, August 29, 1919 Issue. The Populists, in general, and the Tbilisi faction in particular, were not happy with the Russian orientation the ARF started putting forth. They made it clear that if the Armenian people were to benefit from a change in such orientation – in other words, if it was necessary to adopt a Western orientation for the benefit of the people – the party would not hesitate to make such a change.

It was at this juncture that the Populists altered their course. Instead of banding together with the ARF as they had done in the past eight months, they took a sharp retreat from their previous position:

> The Eastern Populists adamantly demanded that the ARF leave the political arena altogether, since they were the reason for all the disasters that Armenians encountered during the war (WWI). The Populists further ascertained that dealing with Turkey demands that a totally new political organization (meaning the Populists themselves) should be given the right to take the initiative in future negotiations.[62]

The Populist Center's unexplainable position spread confusion within the party's rank and file. Many cadres questioned the validity of the center's decision.

Moreover, things were not calm within the Populist Party's different factions. For example, there were strong differences between the party's Tbilisi Central Committee – which considered itself the supreme power of the party – and its Yerevan counterpart – which considered itself the central hub of the organization due to its localization within the state. Populist leaders in Yerevan tried to be more observant and prudent towards the ARF than what the Tbilisi faction recommended. This internal tension within the Populist Party was made public in the pages of *Mshak*, the organ of the Tbilisi Populist faction, and *Zhoghovurd*, the mouthpiece of the Populists' Yerevan group.[63]

Although the Populist center's decisions were rectified during the party conference held several months later, the collapse of the coalition just before the general parliamentary elections did damage efforts for a new coalition government between the two most influential political segments in the Republic. The coalition experiment was never repeated and this was to the detriment of the Republic.[64]

In explaining the Populist center's stance of bringing to a complete halt all ties with the ARF, one should take into consideration the negotiations conducted at the time between the Zhoghovrdakans (Populists) and their Western Armenian counterparts, the Ṛamkavars, regarding their merger. It might be inferred that the Zhoghovrdakan

---

[62] Vratsian, *Hayastani hanrapetut'iwn*, 178.

[63] Ibid., 180-182.

[64] ANA, Fund 1022, List 2, Folder 8, Documents 1-3; ANA, Fund 393, List 2, Folder 118, Documents 1; *Zhoghovurd*, July 6, 1919.

center's position regarding the Act of United Armenia was partially a result of Ramkavar influence on its Tbilisi leadership.

The Act of United and Independent Armenia also created confusion within circles adhering to the newly established Hay Azgayin Azatakan Miut'iwn (Armenian National Liberal Union) which was under formation by the joint forces of the Populists, Ramkavars, and some Reformed Hnchakian Party as a counterbalance to the ARF. The latter were worried by the prospect that the Act of United Armenia might lead to the dissolution of the Boghos Nubar Pasha-led National Delegation. In fact, it was now the Republic of Armenia that was to negotiate directly with the Allies in Paris, thus bypassing Boghos Nubar's delegation altogether. Consequently, such an action would rally Armenians worldwide around the "Ararat Republic" – a term Ramkavars and some Hnchakian circles used to undermine and mock the existing Armenian Republic and its ruling party – to the detriment of the independence of the Western Armenian provinces and Cilicia, which Nubar had been adamantly demanding from the Allies. Hence, worried that the recognition of this Eastern Armenian state by the Allies, delegates from the above mentioned Hay Azgayin Azatakan Miyut'iwn, poet Vahan Tekeyan and Dr. Nshan Der Stepanian traveled first to Tbilisi. There they were joined by Populist Central Committee chairman Samson Harutiunian, and from there they headed to Yerevan to negotiate the Union's participation in the government. The plenary sessions of the negotiations coincided with the convening of the 9th ARF Congress. Simon Vratsian represented the ruling party, the ARF. Proposals and counter-proposals led to compromises on both sides, but the end result was that the negotiations created more confusion than the mutual understanding that both sides envisioned and were dropped.[65]

On the other hand, the single event that required unanimous Armenian unity was the Armenia-Georgian border conflict that happened during the tenure of the coalition government. Armenian parties represented in the Azgayin Khorhurd (National Council; Parliament) unconditionally protested the Georgian militant stance and backed the government in its efforts to resist the aggressor.[66]

---

[65] US Archives, RG 256,184.01602/89, cited in Richard G. Hovannisian, *The Republic of Armenia, Vol. 1: The First Year, 1918-1919* (Los Angeles: University of California Press, 1971), 469.

[66] Ibid., 470-471.

7. – Conclusion

Burdened with numerous external and internal hardships, the Armenian Republic of 1918-1920 was a country in shambles. War, famine, and thousands upon thousands of bewildered refugees threatened the very fabric of Armenian existence and, in the words of Armenia's first Prime Minister, Hovhannes Kachaznuni, rendered the country into a "formless chaos" (*andzev kaos*). Despite these painful birth pangs, the Armenian quest for freedom and independence was on the march. In this chaotic situation internal partisan divisions were inevitable. Yet, the high politicization of the parties and the populace at large was not a promising factor for a future democracy. Armenian political organizations had differences of opinion on the principles and the broader issues, and not secondary or tertiary details. The Republic was not – and should not have been – the monopoly of a single party. Even though the ruling party influenced the shaping of government, an outspoken opposition did materialize and a multi-party pluralistic system was starting to work.

If one thing should be stressed here, it would be the fact that national interest was clearly defined and all of the major participant political organizations – the extreme leftist organizations aside – were in agreement regarding its elements. Governmental decisions were tailored according to national interest, rather than predicated by external influences and pressures.

It is said that history repeats itself. It is also said that learning from past mistakes is a virtue that only few could muster. Are Armenians bound to repeat the mistakes of the past if they do not learn from their past and present experiences? The period of the First Armenian Republic had plenty of mistakes and lots of efforts were made to rectify them. It was a new experiment and mistakes were most probably unavoidable.

The Unrealistic Territorial Demands of the Armenian Republic 1919-1920

George Bournoutian

This article is a theoretical argument on the unrealistic territorial expectations of the Armenian and non-Armenian political leaders between 1918 and 1920. It also examines some of the naïve political decisions that played a role in the final outcome.[1] My goal is to urge young historians and political scientists to re-examine previously accepted notions and to conduct further research on some of the points raised herein.

The first problem occurred prior to the formation of the First Republic. The leaders of the Armenian National Council in Tiflis were well aware of the eventual outcome of the Treaty of Brest-Litovsk, signed by the Bolsheviks on March 3, 1918. The treaty returned the territory of the Kars and Batum oblasts, that is the regions of Kars, Ardahan, and Batum, won by Russia in the 1877-1878 Russo-Turkish War, to Turkey. According to the treaty, these districts had to be immediately cleared of Russian troops. Russia promised not to interfere in the reorganization of the national and international relations of these districts, but leave it to their population to carry out this reorganization, in agreement with the neighboring states, especially with Turkey.

Although these districts were never part of the Russian Yerevan or Tiflis guberniias, the Armenian volunteers and troops in the Russian army, at the behest of their leaders, had remained in Kars after the withdrawal of the Russian army. Realizing their military weakness, the Armenian National Council in Tiflis would have been wise to inform the Turks that they would be satisfied with the original borders of the Yerevan Guberniia, which as I have demonstrated, was no longer the backwater envisioned earlier and which was the only region in the Caucasus with an Armenian

---

[1] The general political framework, as well as the dates and the names of the key players are gleaned from Richard G. Hovannisian, *The Republic of Armenia*, 4 vols. (Berkeley, Los Angeles and London: University of California Press, 1971-1996).

majority and a viable infrastructure.[2] The documents dealing with the decisions of Turkish military staff to determine if the Turkish generals discussed such a notion have to be examined by historians. Instead, the Armeno-Georgian leadership of the newly organized Transcaucasian commissariat in Tiflis, composed of Georgians, Armenians, and the reluctant Tatars (Azeris), rejected the treaty, hoping to wrestle some concessions from the Turks. The Armenian leadership seemed to have disregarded the still fresh Armeno-Tatar conflict of 1905-1907 and the fact that their National Council resided in the Georgian capital and that many Georgians resented the Armenian economic power in Tiflis.

When the delegates from Transcaucasia, headed by a Georgian Menshevik, arrived in Trebizond on March 14, 1918, the Turks demanded that Treaty of Brest-Litovsk should serve as the basis for all further proceedings. The Muslim (later Azeri) delegates, who sympathized with the Turks and whose territory was not affected by the provisions of the said treaty, agreed. It is possible that if the Armenian delegates had also agreed, they may have concluded a temporary peace, delayed the Turkish invasion, and would have had time to remove the much-needed stockpiles of arms from Kars to the Yerevan Guberniia. Instead, they placed their trust in the Georgian leaders, who stated that they, together with the Armenians, would oppose any Turkish claim to the 1877-78 territories. Using the Treaty of Brest-Litovsk and the absence of any legitimate states in the Caucasus as justification, the Turks moved to occupy the lands awarded to them by the new Russian government. After the Turks occupied Batum, the Georgian leaders were forced to choose realpolitik over principles. Within the lapse of two months, they abandoned the Armenians, declared their independence, raised the German flag, and saved most of the territory of their republic. Taking advantage of the military weakness and unpreparedness of the Yerevan Guberniia, the Turks, seeking to reach Baku, marched toward Yerevan. Their advance forced the Armenian National Council in Tiflis to declare an independent Armenia on half of the territory of the Yerevan Guberniia on May 28, 1918.

The fledgling Armenian Republic managed to survive the prior terrible days to its inception and the first six months following thanks to the efforts of the local Armenian troops and the administrative structure of the tsarist period. The Mudros Armistice signed on October 30, 1918, brought great joy to Armenians everywhere, especially to the leaders of

---

[2] See George Bournoutian, *Armenia and Imperial Decline: The Yerevan Province, 1900-1914* (London: Routledge, 2018).

the Armenian Republic, who witnessed the restoration of half of its territory and all of its rail lines, which had been handed to the Turks by the Batum treaty on June 4, 1918. The numerous Allied statements on behalf of the Armenians also promised a path for the rebirth of a viable Armenian state.

It has to be noted that until the end of World War I, despite the many plans and dreams of Armenian political parties for a revival of an Armenian state, the question of the "exact" borders of such a state was not envisioned by anyone, including those non-Armenians who sympathized with the plight of Armenians within the Ottoman Empire. Therefore, the Armenian Parliament (*Khorhrdaran*), after some discussions, decided to send a delegation to the Paris Peace Conference. Despite the objection of some Dashnaks, who considered him a romantic of mediocre ability, they named Avetis Aharonian to head the delegation.[3] The fact is, that compared to their Turkish counterparts, who had a centuries-long tradition of service in embassies and were experienced diplomats, the Armenian delegates were novices.

On December 8, 1918, the Armenian delegation led by Aharonian left Yerevan and, after many obstacles, arrived in Paris on February 4, 1919. Aharonian was instructed to claim the six Armenian *vilayets* plus a corridor to the Black Sea.

A second Armenian delegation, representing all Turkish Armenians, headed by Boghos Nubar, was already active in Paris. The Armenian National Delegation had been created by Catholicos of All Armenians Gevorg V in 1913 at the time of the reopening of the Armenian Question, and Nubar was appointed as his representative.[4] The latter demanded the creation of an Armenia from the Caucasus to Cilicia. He even went as far as to ask that the Armenian Republic (which he, along with many others, called the Araratian Republic) dissolve itself and merge into this new Armenia. The two sides could not be any more different. The government in Yerevan was dominated by the ARF, while Boghos Nubar did not trust revolutionaries or socialists.

It is inconceivable that neither Aharonian nor Boghos Nubar were unaware of the secret Sykes-Picot agreement of 1916. After all, the Bolsheviks had published the contents of the agreement in *Izvestia* and

---

[3] Hovannisian, *The Republic of Armenia*, vol. I, 251-252.

[4] See the letter of Catholicos Gevorg V to Boghos Nubar, December 4, 1918 (*Boghos Nubar's Papers and the Armenian Question 1915-1918: Documents*, edited and translated by Vatche Ghazarian, Waltham, MA, 1996), 444-445.

Pravda on November 23, 1917, right after the October Revolution, and, on November 26, the *Manchester Guardian* had informed the world of its existence.

Let us recall the terms of that agreement. According to this document, Britain received the control of areas roughly comprising the coastal strip between the Mediterranean Sea, the river Jordan, southern Iraq and an additional small area that included the ports of Haifa and Acre. France received control of southeastern Turkey, northern Iraq, Lebanon and Syria, which included Cilicia. Russia was going to get Istanbul, the Straits, and most of historic Western Armenia.[5]

Although it is true that the Bolsheviks had renounced the agreement, the Russian nationalists and monarchists in their civil war against the Reds wished to restore the borders of the former empire. In fact, had the anti-revolutionary forces succeeded in taking Moscow in the summer of 1919, the allies would have probably accepted the borders of the former Russian Empire and handed them the areas promised in Sykes-Picot.

Despite such realities, the inexperienced Aharonian yielded to Boghos Nubar, a man "who moved with confidence in continental diplomatic circles, who as acknowledged as a reputable Armenian spokesman by Allied officials, and who presumably was best qualified to judge the disposition of the victorious powers."[6] Thus, the united Armenian delegation submitted the Armenian claims proposed by Boghos Nubar to the peace conference. They included the six Armenian *vilayets* plus the *vilayet* of Trebizond, the 4 *sanjaks* of Cilicia (Marash, Sis, Jebel-Bereket and Adana, with the port of Alexandretta; the Lori and Akhalkalak (Javakhk) districts from Georgia; Mountainous Karabagh and Zangezur from Azerbaijan, as well as the Kars province, which the Armenians annexed soon after. Since Cilicia and southeastern Turkey were already awarded to France by the Sykes-Picot agreement, Armenian claims to that region were logically dead on arrival and, as we shall see, were not taken into consideration at the time of the Treaty of Sèvres.

The writing was on the wall when the Armenian delegation was excluded from the sessions of the Peace Conference. Armenians were thus not privy to any discussions or deals made by the Allies and had to rely on

---

[5] For details, see David Fromkin, *A Peace to End All Peace: The Fall of the Ottoman Empire and the Creation of the Modern Middle East* (New York: H. Holt, 1989), 286-288, and J. C. Hurewitz, *The Middle East and North Africa in World Politics: A Documentary Record. British-French Supremacy, 1914-1945* (New Haven: Yale University Press, 1979), 16-21.

[6] Hovannisian, *The Republic of Armenia*, vol. I, 260.

rumors and hearsay. It is true that the Armenians were the only small national group that received a hearing, but this fact, in my opinion, deluded the Armenians even more.

The Allied promises resulted in a number of other miscalculations. In my view, the Armenian annexation of Kars in 1919, when the Republic lacked the military power to hold it and was engaged in border disputes with Azerbaijan and Georgia, was a serious mistake. The Bolsheviks still controlled Moscow and St. Petersburg, and the annexation would later hamper future Armeno-Soviet negotiations. The Armenians also relied on the statements issued by the British, French, and Americans during a time when the question of the fate of the Ottoman Empire was not yet decided and the large Turkish army remained intact.

Although Hovannisian makes an excellent argument as to why the Armenians had to continue to have faith in the Allied promises,[7] the Armenians may have been wiser to make serious efforts to come to terms with the Bolsheviks. It is possible that they might have received some concessions. The Levon Shant mission, which arrived in Moscow on May 20, 1920, that is, after Denikin's forces had retreated to the Crimea, continued to insist on the unification of Russian and Turkish Armenia. Since the Bolsheviks planned to negotiate with the Turks, they advised Armenia to abandon its illusionary hopes based on Western promises. Armenian delegates argued that the Allied Powers had already sanctioned a united Armenia with an outlet to the Black Sea. Chicherin, the Commissar for Foreign Affairs, countered that the Armenians had often been deceived by European imperialists and were, once again, beguiled – his words proved prophetic. The Shant mission ended in failure.

Obviously, any deal with the Bolsheviks which did not include at least some of the western Armenian provinces was anathema to the Armenian government.[8] After all the entire *raison d'être* of the Armenian political revival had to do with the resurrection of original homeland. They would be branded traitors by their party and future generations. The ARF leaders ended up being blamed in any case by the Soviet Armenian leadership for losing Mt. Ararat and Nakhichevan.[9]

---

[7] Ibid., 250-257.

[8] For more details, see Hovannisian, *The Republic of Armenia*, vol. IV, (Berkeley, University of California Press, 1996), 46-62.

[9] For details, see A. G. Hovhannisyan, et. al. eds. *Hay Zhoghovrdi Patmut'iwn*, VII (Yerevan: Haykakan SSH Gitut'yunneri Akademiayi Hratarakch'ut'yun, 1967), 95-112.

Meanwhile, the Azerbaijani leaders had not only made contact with the Bolsheviks, but also convinced them that they favored their cause and demanded the inclusion of Karabagh, Sharur-Daralagiaz, Nakhichevan, and Zangezur in a future Soviet Azerbaijan. In fact, in May 1919, Mikoyan, who was in Baku, wrote to Lenin that the Armenian Dashnaks had no socialist spirit, were relying on Denikin and the West, and that the Armenians of Karabagh and other border regions wished to be part of Azerbaijan.[10]

Although the government in Yerevan could not know that in October 1919, Wilson had suffered a stroke, they did know that on June 1, 1920, the US Senate had rejected an American mandate of Armenia by a vote of 53 to 23. Yet, Armenia continued to rely on the United States and rejected Moscow's unacceptable proposals regarding Nakhichevan, Karabagh, and Zangezur.[11]

The final disappointment came soon after. The Sèvres treaty signed in August 1920 promised an Armenia based on Wilson's map, but had no teeth or provisions to enforce it. Greece refused to ratify the treaty, the United States was not a signatory and the Ottoman signatories were minor ex-officials. Once Britain and France received their territories outlined in Sykes-Picot, Armenia was left to its fate. I agree with the late historian, Vahakn Dadrian, that the Sèvres treaty served mainly to compound the misfortunes of the Armenians.[12] In fact, the treaty prompted the already mobilized Turks and the Turkish Grand National Assembly, led by Mustafa Kemal (Atatürk) in Ankara, to prevent the breakup of Turkey. Since the Allied promises lacked credibility, both the Turks and Bolsheviks knew well that no one would come to Armenia's aid.

In the end, the Republic could not withstand the combined invasions by both the Turkish and Red armies, and, on December 2, 1920, it accepted Soviet rule. The Turks and the Bolsheviks then proceeded to redraw the borders of the former Yerevan Guberniia and the Armenian Republic. The Armenian uprising of February 1921 against the Bolsheviks, that is, after Sovietization and during the critical border negotiations in Moscow, did not help Armenian claims. The Treaty of Moscow signed on March 16, 1921 between RSFSR and Turkey awarded the Surmalu district (with Mt.

---

[10] Mikoyan's letter to Lenin, dated May 22, 1919, in *Tsentralnyi Partiinyi Arkhiv: Institut Marksizma-Leninizma*, Fond 461, no. 45252.

[11] See Boris Legran's mission in Hovannisian, *The Republic of Armenia*, vol. IV, 72-77; see page 74 in particular.

[12] Vahakn N. Dadrian, *The History of the Armenian Genocide* (Providence, RI: Berghahn Books, 1995), 359.

Ararat), as well as the Kars region (minus Batum) to Turkey and the former Nakhichevan, Sharur, as well as the western part of the Daralagiaz districts to Soviet Azerbaijan. Moreover, the Armenian-populated districts of Javakh and Shushi were left outside the territory of Soviet Armenia— the first in Soviet Georgia and the second as an autonomous Armenian enclave within Soviet Azerbaijan. On October 13 of that same year, representatives of Soviet Armenia, Georgia, and Azerbaijan, as well as the RSFSR and Turkey signed the Kars Treaty, which formalized the Moscow agreement and set the current borders between present-day Turkey, Armenia and Georgia.[13]

I recall Richard Hovannisian's understandably bitter statement during one of our courses at UCLA: "Turkey was the only defeated nation which ended up with additional territory in the Trans-Caucasus after the war." Armenians, like all people, desire a large and powerful national state. After all, following the Genocide they had and continue to have the "moral" right to demand this. However, as a historian who believes in the notion of *realpolitik*, that is, a system of politics or principles based on practical rather than moral or ideological considerations, I, together with most objective political scientists, as well as social and economic historians, have a hard time understanding and accepting the impractical territorial expectations of that time.

We have to remember that in 1918 there had been no Armenian state for centuries. The only Armenian province, that is, the Yerevan Province, had been part of the Russian Empire. Furthermore, three of the seven districts of this province (Surmalu, Sharur-Daralagiaz, and Nakhichevan) had a Muslim majority prior to World War I. In 1914, the Armenian population of the province totaled just over 600,000. The rest of the Armenians in the Trans-Caucasus lived within what would become the Georgian and Azerbaijani republics.

Thus, unlike Poland, which had ceased to exist in 1795, that is, only 123 years prior to its resurrection in 1918, and 90 per cent of whose population had remained intact,[14] the Armenians had been killed or forced to leave their homeland over the course of centuries. They had been scat-

---

[13] It is important to note that despite the abovementioned territorial losses, Soviet Armenia ended up being 233.6 square miles larger than the former Yerevan Guberniia. This came as a result of the addition of the Zangezur district from the former Elisavetpol Guberniia and the Lori district from the former Tiflis Guberniia to Soviet Armenia; Bournoutian, *Armenia and Imperial Decline*, 96.

[14] M. MacMillan, "Poland Reborn," *Paris 1919: Six Months That Changed the World* (New York: Random House, 2007)

tered all over Eastern Europe and the Middle East. As we know, most of the two million Armenians in Turkey were killed or deported during the Genocide. War, famine, and epidemics had also decreased the population of the Armenian Republic.

Economists agree that a large land mass (unless it contains gold, diamonds, or oil) has little value without people. Every major global power had and has a large population, industry, raw materials, or colonies to sustain their economy and military forces.

Therefore, even if an Armenian state was formed on the more than 110,000 square-mile territory envisioned in 1919, or the 60,000 square-mile land mass drawn by President Wilson, it is doubtful that a small number of Armenians in Transcaucasia, together with the survivors of the deportations, could defend such a huge landmass without the presence of large numbers of European or American troops? Europe, exhausted after the Great War, was in no mood or condition to commit arms, troops and, provisions to a faraway region, especially since the outcome of the Russian civil war remained unresolved. Unfortunately, the United States Senate quashed the idea of an American mandate over Armenia.[15]

Another question has to be addressed. What would happen to the Muslim population that formed a majority of the remaining inhabitants in the proposed territory? Would they be cordoned off behind walls (like the Palestinians in Israel) or subjected to apartheid? Although it is true that some of that region was depopulated, large clusters of Kurds, Turks, Greeks and Assyrians remained. The chances of formal population exchanges, like those that occurred between Poland and Germany and Czechoslovakia and Germany and Poland and the USSR after World War II, is debatable.[16] Would such large clusters of non-Armenians give a future Turkish state the excuse to intervene on behalf of its ethnic people and demand the return of those regions after the departure of the foreign

---

[15] At the height of the Vietnam War, during a lecture in a course on modern Armenia, Richard Hovannisian lamented that the United States had no problems sending over 500,000 troops to faraway Vietnam, when 20,000 American soldiers could have made Wilsonian Armenia a reality.

[16] It has to be noted that although following the Treaty of Lausanne, Greece and Turkey, in 1923-1924, agreed to such an exchange, Greece had been an independent nation since the early 19th century, most of the Greek population had already left Turkey prior to the formal exchange, see Y. Katz, "Transfer of Population as a Solution to International Disputes: Population Exchanges between Greece and Turkey as a Model for Plans to Solve the Jewish-Arab Dispute in Palestine during the 1930s," *Political Geography*, 11/1 (1992), 57.

troops, something very similar to the 1938 and 1939 German demands over Sudetenland and Danzig?

Some of my Armenian colleagues always bring out Israel's success in creating a state after two millennia and a holocaust. First: Israel was originally created on a territory less than 7,000 sq. miles (this, even compared to the more than 11,000 square miles of present-day Armenia, is small). Second: The Jews had prepared the road by many years of gradual immigration and by slowly purchasing contiguous strips of lands in main population centers. Third: The Soviets, who viewed a socialist Israel with communal farms as a base against British power in the Middle East, were in favor of such a state. As a young man, I witnessed trainloads of Polish and Russian Jews on their way to the newly-established state of Israel. Fourth: The United States Congress gave its full support and continues to provide tremendous financial and military aid. Fifth: The Jewish demands for additional land came gradually and after military victories attained by their own people. One has to note, however, that despite having a superb military and nuclear weapons, Israel, even after seventy years, continues to face many problems.

In conclusion, I believe that regardless of our personal feelings, it is time that we reassess this crucial period in our history. Otherwise, we will continue to retread old ground and, instead of learning from the past, repeat it.

Armenia, according to the terms of a Memorandum officially presented by the Armenian National Delegation to the Peace Conference in Paris, 1919. From *America as Mandatary for Armenia*, New York, 1919.

Contributors

Richard G. Hovannisian is Professor Emeritus of Modern Armenian History at the University of California, Los Angeles and Presidential Fellow at Chapman University. He is the author or editor of more than 30 volumes, including five on the first Republic of Armenia, five on the Armenian Genocide, and 14 in the series "Historic Armenian Cities." A Guggenheim Fellow, he has received numerous awards and commendations from scholarly and civic organizations, the heads of the Armenian Church, the governments of Armenia and Artsakh, and became the first social scientist living abroad to be elected the Armenian Academy of Sciences in the waning years of the Soviet Union.

Houri Berberian is Professor of History, Meghrouni Family Presidential Chair in Armenian Studies, and Director of the Armenian Studies Program at the University of California, Irvine. Her research interests include revolutionary movements, women and gender, and identity and diaspora. She is the author of a number of articles and two books, *Armenians and the Iranian Constitutional Revolution of 1905-1911: The Love for Freedom Has No Fatherland* (2001) and, most recently, the award-winning *Roving Revolutionaries: Armenians and Connected Revolutions in the Russian, Iranian, and Ottoman Worlds* (2019), as well as the co-editor of *Reflections of Armenian Identity in History and Historiography* (2018).

Ari Şekeryan received his Ph.D. from the University of Oxford in 2018, with a dissertation titled "The Armenians in the Ottoman Empire after the First World War (1918-1923)." He edited *The Adana Massacre 1909: Three Reports* and *An Anthology of Armenian Literature 1913*. His latest articles appeared in the *British Journal of Middle Eastern Studies*, *Turkish Studies*, *the Journal of the Ottoman and Turkish Studies Association* and *War in History*. Şekeryan is the Kazan Visiting Professor in Armenian Studies at California State University, Fresno for Spring 2020.

Seda D. Ohanian (Ph.D., History) is a researcher in the National Academy of Sciences, Institute of History, Department of Armenian Communities and Diasporan Studies, Yerevan. Her research interests include the history of Armenian communities in the Middle East, in particular the Iraqi community. She is the author of a number of articles and one book, *The Armenian Community in Iraq in the 20th Century* (2016). Her second forthcoming book is titled *The Armenian Community in Mesopotamia (Iraq) from Antiquity to the 20th Century.*

Rubina Peroomian, Ph.D., is an independent scholar, formerly lecturer of Armenian Studies, and has authored several research articles, chapters in books, and monographs on the Armenian Question and the Genocide. She teaches on the Genocide, Armenian Genocide literature, Bolsheviks and the First Republic, and women's issues. She has lectured widely and participated in international symposia. She is the author of textbooks on the *Armenian Question* (Hay Dat), for grades 10-12 in Western Armenian and *The History of the Armenian Question* (Haykakan harts'i patmut'iwně) for schools in Armenia. Her guidebook for teaching the Armenian Genocide in grades K-12 is available in print and electronic versions. She has been recognized and awarded for her academic and educational endeavors.

Vartan Matiossian is the Executive Director of the Eastern Prelacy of the Armenian Apostolic Church (New York). A historian and literary scholar, he has a Ph.D. in History from the Institute of History, National Academy of Sciences of the Republic of Armenia, and lives in New Jersey. He has published scores of articles, translations, book reviews, and essays, mostly in Armenian, Spanish, and English. He has authored seven books in Armenian, Spanish, and English, edited several others, and translated twenty volumes into Spanish and English.

Jakub Osiecki graduated in 2008 with a degree in Russian Studies from the Jagiellonian University in Kraków. In January 2014, he was awarded a Ph.D. in history with his thesis titled "The Armenian Apostolic Church in Soviet Armenia 1920–1932" (published in Polish in 2019). He is also the author of publications on the Catholics of the Armenian rite in Armenia and Georgia. Osiecki works at the Research Centre for Armenian Culture at the Polish Academy of Arts and Sciences. He is a member of the Association Internationale des Etudes Arméniennes (AIEA) and the Society for Armenian Studies (SAS).

Garabet K. Moumdjian holds a Ph.D. in History from UCLA. He is an archival historian and an Ottomanist who has conducted research in the

Ottoman Archives. Moumdjian has held several academic positions. He has written a multi-volume Armenian history textbook for grades 4-9, titled *Our History* (Mer Patmutʻiwnĕ). He is the author of two monographs, ten chapters in academic volumes, as well as scores of articles in academic journals and newspapers.

George Bournoutian is a retired professor of East European and Middle Eastern History at Iona College. He has been a visiting professor of Armenian History at Columbia University, Tufts University, the University of Connecticut, Rutgers University and California State University, Fresno. He is the author of *A Concise History of the Armenian People* (six editions), which has been translated into Spanish, Arabic, Turkish, Armenian, Russian, Persian, and Japanese. He translated and edited numerous Armenian primary sources into English. He is the author of *The 1820 Russian Survey of the Khanate of Shirvan* (Gibb Memorial Series, Cambridge, 2016) and *Armenia in Imperial Decline: The Yerevan Guberniia 1900-1914* (London, Routledge 2018).

Note on Transliteration

Transliteration of Armenian titles of books, newspaper, and journals, follow the Library of Congress Transliteration format for Armenian. Last names of Western Armenian authors end with *ian* and names of Eastern Armenian authors with *yan*.

Armenian

Vernacular	Romanization	Vernacular	Romanization
Upper case letters		*Lower case letters*	
Ա	A	ա	a
Բ	B [P] (see Note 1)	բ	b [p] (see Note 1)
Գ	G [K] (see Note 1)	գ	g [k] (see Note 1)
Դ	D [T] (see Note 1)	դ	d [t] (see Note 1)
Ե {	E / Y (see Note 2)	ե {	e / y (see Note 2)
Զ	Z	զ	z
Է	Ē	է	ē
Ը	Ě	ը	ě
Թ	T'	թ	t'
Ժ	Zh (see Note 3)	ժ	zh (see Note 3)
Ի	I	ի	i
Լ	L	լ	l
Խ	Kh	խ	kh
Ծ	Ts [Dz] (see Notes 1, 3)	ծ	ts [dz] (see Notes 1, 3)
Կ	K [G] (see Note 1)	կ	k [g] (see Note 1)
Հ	H	հ	h
Ձ	Dz [Ts] (see Notes 1, 3)	ձ	dz [ts] (see Notes 1, 3)
Ղ	Gh (see Note 3)	ղ	gh (see Note 3)
Ճ	Ch [J] (see Note 1)	ճ	ch [j] (see Note 1)
Մ	M	մ	m
Յ {	Y / H (see Note 4)	յ {	y / h (see Note 4)
Ն	N	ն	n
Շ	Sh (see Note 3)	շ	sh (see Note 3)
Ո	O	ո	o
Չ	Ch'	չ	ch'
Պ	P [B] (see Note 1)	պ	p [b] (see Note 1)
Ջ	J [Ch] (see Note 1)	ջ	j [ch] (see Note 1)

Ռ	R	ռ	ṙ
Ս	S	ս	s
Վ	V	վ	v
Տ	T [D] (see Note 1)	տ	t [d] (see Note 1)
Ր	R	ր	r
Ց	Ts'	ց	ts'
Ւ	W	ւ	w
Ու	U	ու	u
Փ	P'	փ	p'
Ք	K'	ք	k'
Եւ	Ew (see Note 5)	եւ	ew (see Note 5)
Եվ	Ev (see Note 6)	եվ	ev (see Note 6)
Օ	Ō	օ	ō
Ֆ	F	ֆ	f

Notes

1. The table is based on the phonetic values of Classical and East Armenian. The variant phonetic values of West Armenian are included in brackets but are intended solely for use in preparing references from West Armenian forms of name when this may be desirable.
2. This value is used only when the letter is in initial position of a name and followed by a vowel, in Classical orthography.
3. The soft sign (prime) is placed between the two letters representing two different sounds when the combination might otherwise be read as a digraph (e.g., Դզնունի D'znuni).
4. This value is used only when the letter is in initial position of a word or of a stem in a compound, in Classical orthography.
5. Romanization for letters in Classical orthography, sometimes appears as ẇ.
6. Romanization for letters in Reformed orthography, sometimes appears as ẇ.